# Filters and Freedom 2.0

## Free Speech Perspectives on Internet Content Control

Electronic Privacy Information Center
Washington, DC

## *About the Electronic Privacy Information Center*

The Electronic Privacy Information Center (EPIC) is a public interest research center in Washington, D.C. It was established in 1994 to focus public attention on emerging civil liberties issues and to protect privacy, the First Amendment, and constitutional values. EPIC works in association with Privacy International, an international human rights group based in London, UK and is also a member of the Global Internet Liberty Campaign, the Internet Free Expression Alliance and the Internet Privacy Coalition.

The EPIC Bookstore provides a comprehensive selection of books and reports on computer security, cryptography, the First Amendment and free speech, open government, and privacy. Visit the EPIC Bookstore at www.epic.org/bookstore/.

**EPIC Staff**

Marc Rotenberg, Executive Director
David L. Sobel, General Counsel
Andrew Shen, Senior Policy Analyst
Sarah Andrews, Research Director
Chris Hoofnagle, Staff Counsel
Mikal Condon, Staff Counsel
David Banisar, Senior Fellow
Wayne Madsen, Senior Fellow

**Acknowledgments**

The Electronic Privacy Information Center gratefully acknowledges the many individuals and organizations, particularly the members of the Internet Free Expression Alliance (IFEA) and the Global Internet Liberty Campaign (GILC), who have drawn attention to the problems associated with content controls and the need to ensure that freedom of expression is preserved in the online world. We also appreciate the work of the following foundations that are supporting efforts to protect free speech: the EPIC Trust, the Ford Foundation, the Fund for Constitutional Government, the HKH Foundation, the List Foundation, the Norman Foundation, the Open Society Institute, the Rockefeller Family Fund and the Scherman Foundation.

# Preface

Since the first publication of *Filters & Freedom* in 1999, the controversy over Internet content controls has intensified. While filtering and rating proposals have been debated at the local, national and international levels, no clear consensus has yet emerged. In the United States, the Children's Internet Protection Act was enacted in 2000, requiring schools and libraries receiving certain federal subsidies to install filtering systems on their Internet-connected computers. That federal mandate recently has been challenged in the courts on constitutional free expression grounds. At the same time, numerous local communities have debated the issue and elected not to employ blocking technologies. While much rhetoric has surrounded the issue of Internet filtering, there has been a concerted effort on the part of free expression advocates to produce reports and analyses detailing the real-world impact of content control systems.

The international human rights and free expression communities have been in the forefront of the debate, fostering more deliberate consideration of technological approaches to Internet content control. The Global Internet Liberty Campaign (www.gilc.org) has monitored the development of filtering proposals around the world. In the United States, the Internet Free Expression Alliance (www.ifea.net) has been an important voice in the national debate on content regulation, identifying new threats to free expression and First Amendment values on the Internet, whether legal or technological. The members of these coalitions have produced many of the ground-breaking papers and reports that are contained in this collection.

Included in this revised edition are several important new contributions to the public debate. In "Filtering Fever," Marjorie Heins provides a detailed account of how the rush toward filtering and rating systems developed in the United States and internationally. Christopher Hunter puts the current situation in context with "A Brief History of Censorship." In its "Statement on Library Use of Filtering Software," the American Library Association (ALA) concludes that, "blocking Internet sites is antithetical to library missions because it requires the library to limit information access." Also included is an ALA statement to Congress opposing the mandatory installation of filters on library computers. The Electronic Privacy Information Center's "Statement Before the Commission on Online Child Protection" addresses the privacy implications of efforts to restrict online content to individuals of a particular age. The international aspects of Internet content rating are discussed in the Global Internet Liberty Campaign "Member Statement Submitted to the Internet Content Summit."

New research findings are presented in several reports. The Electronic Frontier Foundation's "Blacklisting Bytes," and Peacefire's "Amnesty Intercepted" and "Blind Ballots," detail the imprecision of filtering and blocking systems and the ways in which they effectively censor important information.

A number of seminal pieces from the first edition of this collection are also included here. In "Fahrenheit 451.2: Is Cyberspace Burning?," the American Civil Liberties Union warns that, "government and industry leaders alike are now inching toward the dangerous and incorrect position that the Internet is like television, and should be rated and censored accordingly." The principal technical standard for rating and filtering content – the Platform for Internet Content Selection – is critiqued by Irene Graham of Electronic Frontiers Australia in "Will PICS Torch Free Speech on the Internet?" A British perspective on Internet content controls is presented in "Who Watches the Watchmen: Internet Content Rating Systems, and Privatised Censorship," a report prepared by Cyber-Rights & Cyber-Liberties (UK).

The theoretical benefits of filtering systems have been undercut by hands-on testing that demonstrates the actual (and troubling) impact of these techniques. Two early studies are included here. The Electronic Privacy Information Center's "Faulty Filters: How Content Filters Block Access to Kid-Friendly Information on the Internet," was one of the first reports that documented the potential damage to free expression that can result from a ratings regime. The Censorware Project examined the real-world impact of a filtering system in "Censored Internet Access in Utah Public Schools and Libraries." These reports present important findings that filtering proponents must address. In an updated version of its "Filtering FAQ," Computer Professionals for Social Responsibility provides detailed answers to commonly asked question about software filters.

The global nature of the Internet requires multinational participation in the development of standards and policies that could irreparably alter the Internet's potential to facilitate freedom of expression. The Global Internet Liberty Campaign (GILC) has adopted as a founding principle that "on-line free expression not be restricted by indirect means such as excessively restrictive governmental or private controls over computer hardware or software, telecommunications infrastructure, or other essential components of the Internet." The GILC statement, "Impact of Self-Regulation and Filtering on Human Rights to Freedom of Expression," reflects the international concern over "voluntary" proposals to control on-line content.

As noted, libraries increasingly are becoming battlegrounds in the debate over Internet filtering. The American Civil Liberties Union's "Censorship in a Box: Why Blocking Software is Wrong for Public Libraries" demonstrates how all blocking software censors valuable speech and gives librarians, educators and parents a false sense of security when providing minors with Internet access.

Partly as a result of these writings, the headlong rush toward the development and acceptance of filtering and rating systems has slowed. From a free speech perspective, thoughtful consideration of these initiatives is clearly desirable. Although generally well-intentioned, proposals for "self-regulation" of Internet content carry with them a substantial risk of limiting free expression and damaging the medium in unintended ways. The views expressed in this updated collection must be considered carefully if we are to prevent such an outcome.

David L. Sobel
April 2001
Washington, DC

# Table of Contents

## Table of Contents

# Filtering Fever

Marjorie Heins

In June 1997, the Supreme Court ruled that the Communications Decency Act of 1996 (the CDA), which essentially banned all "indecent" speech in cyberspace, violated the First Amendment because it would unconstitutionally chill a wide range of online expression, on subjects ranging from "prison rape or safe sexual practices, artistic images that include nude subjects, and arguably the card catalogue of the Carnegie library." The Internet, explained Justice Stevens for the Court in *Reno v. ACLU,* was a great "new marketplace of ideas," with content "'as diverse as human thought.'"[1]

The Supreme Court's stirring words about the expressive potential of the Internet were exhilarating to First Amendment aficionados but did little to alter the politics of child protection. Just days after the Court struck down the Communications Decency Act, the White House began to float alternative proposals for controlling cyberspace. The new emphasis was on Internet rating and filtering - software programs of the type the Court had referenced in *Reno* to suggest that "less burdensome alternatives" to the CDA were available to protect minors. Within the month, the White House convened a "summit" meeting to promote filtering; the attendees ranged from online corporations to advocacy groups as disparate as the Enough is Enough antipornography campaign and the Center for Democracy and Technology (CDT), which had helped organize the plaintiff Citizens Internet Empowerment Coalition in *Reno.*

A measure of the new mood was a press release from SurfWatch congratulating itself on the Supreme Court decision, which it attributed "in large part to testimony concerning the effectiveness of Internet filtering," in particular its own software. The release described Surfwatch's "ability to offer daily updates" as giving parents "even more peace of mind" as hundreds of thousands of new pages are "added to the web each day."[2]

Even before the White House summit, the coalition that successfully litigated *Reno* had begun to fragment. While the CDT prepared an "Internet Family Empowerment White Paper" touting rating and filtering,[3] the American Library Association formalized its opposition to Internet filters. Emphasizing that the job of libraries is to provide free access to information, even for minors, the ALA'S resolution explained that rating/filtering programs rely either on mindless keyword-based blocking or on subjective, private corporate judgments about offensiveness, and offered examples of librarians' experiences: one program blocked the NASA Web site on exploring Mars because the address (marsexpl.htm) contained the letters SEX; indeed, . "any word with SEX as a root would be blocked: sextant, for math.... sextet .... sextillion, . . . sexton, . . . or sextuplet." Filtering based on "intolerance" restricted research on civil rights and religious cults. Information about drugs, contraceptives, HIV, alcohol, and secondhand smoke "were all off-limits as a result of filtering software."[4]

Despite the ALA's exertions, local libraries were often not able to resist profiltering pressures. The Boston Public Library was one of the first to succumb, announcing in early 1997 that it would install Cyber Patrol on all computers. After public protests, it eventually adopted a compromise: filters in children's rooms only. Of Cyber Patrol's twelve blocking categories (including "violence/profanity," "militant/extremist" and "satanic or cult"), Boston selected three: full nudity, partial nudity, and sex acts.[5] Other products - among them SurfWatch, Net Nanny, CYBERsitter, CyberSnoop, PlanetWeb, Net Shepherd, SafeSurf, Microsoft Plus for Kids, and X-Stop - were now competing as well for lucrative school and library markets. The big ISPs (Internet service providers) - America Online, Prodigy, CompuServe - also offered parental controls, usually relying in turn on SurfWatch or Cyber Patrol software. Microsoft Network simplified the process by making "controls on" the default setting for its browser.[6]

Each of the filtering programs used a combination of keywords and individual site blocking based on human judgment, however fleeting; and each had its own amusing and appalling instances of ideologically based, controversy-averse, or simply mindless overblocking. CYBERsitter, described by *Time* magazine as "the most aggressively conservative filtering program," blocked the National Organization for Women's Web site and virtually all gay and lesbian information. Cyber Patrol blocked the Queer Resources Directory; SurfWatch blocked Associated Press and Reuters articles about AIDS.[7] California's Log-On

Data Corporation marketed a "felony load" library version of X-Stop, claiming that it blocked only "illegal" child pornography and obscenity[8]- an impossibility, given that even hard-core pornography is not necessarily obscene until a court or jury decides that it offends "contemporary community standards", appeals to "prurient" interests, and lacks "serious value" under the Supreme Court's three-part *Miller v. California* obscenity test.

More worrisome - because built into computer browsers - was PICS (the Platform for Internet Content Selection). By the fall of 1997, this online technology offered three rating systems: RSACi, Net Shepherd, and SafeSurf. The Canada-based Net Shepherd claimed to have rated by far the greatest number of sites (its estimates ranged from 300,000 to 500,000), but its third-party classification system relied on subjective judgments by volunteers who were paid a few cents per site to judge the "quality" and "maturity level" of various Web pages. RSACi, initially developed by the Recreational Software Advisory Council for video games, relied on self-rating and perhaps for this reason was quickly becoming the industry favorite. For as one executive explained, with "60 million-plus pages on the Web" in 1997, "it takes about one minute per page to rate. To rate every existing Web page," therefore, "would take about 60 million minutes - or one million hours - or over 114 years. Using 114 people working 24 hours a day, the job would take a full year. But the bad news is that as soon as everything was rated, the process would have to start all over again, because within a year the Web would change drastically."[9] Self-rating was the only practical alternative to mindless keyword-based blocking.

RSACi's self-rating system had four categories of disfavored content - nudity, sex, language, and violence - and five settings within each category. Under this scheme, "rape or wanton, gratuitous violence" was rated at level four; sports-related violence at level zero (not blocked). "Frontal nudity (qualifying as provocative display)" ranked at level four; "revealing attire" or "mild expletives" at level one. By the end of 1997 RSACi claimed to have 50,000 self-rated sites (by 1999, it claimed 125,000); the rest of the Internet, including most major newspapers, it automatically blocked. Microsoft Explorer adopted RSACi ratings; and four of the major search engine firms - Lycos, Excite, Infoseek, and Yahoo! - said they would cooperate in "self-regulation" by excluding from their listings any Web sites that did not self-rate. Senator Patty Murray proposed legislation punishing those who "misrated," while her colleague John McCain introduced a bill requiring any public school or library receiving federal aid for Internet connections to install software that labels and blocks "inappropriate" sites. McCain's bill did not pass (he would re-introduce it in subsequent years), but a major step had been taken toward making voluntary filters not so voluntary after all.[10]

A larger "Online Summit" was now planned for December 1997. Christine Varney, a former FCC commissioner, was to chair this conference; a public relations representative for Cyber Patrol handled media registration. Although "parental empowerment" was the dominant theme of the promotional publicity, a careful reading made clear that voluntary filtering on home computers was not the only goal, Netparents.org, a Web site devoted to the Online Summit, explained the virtues of a "Family-Friendly Internet," complete with filtering for schools and libraries.[11] New profiltering groups such as Family Friendly Libraries weighed in with material pressuring libraries to install Cyber Patrol, X-Stop, or Bess (a stand-alone program featuring an adorable golden retriever as its icon) or risk poisoning "young people's minds" with pornography. Enough is Enough was equally unsubtle about countering ALA policy and pushing libraries to adopt filtering.[12] Another Web site promoting the conference, kidsonline.org, advertised what former *Reno I* plaintiff Declan McCullagh described as "a three-day love-fest for censorware applications like PICS and RSACi." McCullagh reported to his "fight censorship" e-mail list in November that Cyber Patrol had blocked the entire Yahoo! Web site, in addition to about 200 gigabytes of files at mit.edu.[13]

The ACLU and EPIC (the Electronic Privacy Information Center) now became more vocal about the problems with rating and filtering. EPIC's director, Marc Rotenberg, wrote in an open letter to "the Internet community" that "the fundamental purpose of a rating system" is "to allow one person to decide what information another person may receive." Although recognizing that "there is indeed some material on the Internet that is genuinely abhorrent," Rotenberg said, "we do not believe you can hide the world from your children.... Good parenting is not something found in a software filter."[14] A few weeks later, the ACLU released *Fahrenheit 451.2: Is Cyberspace Burning?* The "ashes of the CDA were barely smoldering," this pamphlet began, "when the White House called a summit meeting to encourage Internet users to self-rate their speech." Cyber-libertarians at this point became "genuinely alarmed" by the "unabashed enthusiasm for technological fixes" that would "make it easier to block or render invisible controversial speech."

> People who disseminate quirky and idiosyncratic speech, create individual
> home pages, or post to controversial news groups, will be among the first
> Internet users blocked by filters and made invisible by the search engines.
> Controversial speech will still exist, but will only be visible to those with

the tools and know-how to penetrate the dense smokescreen of industry "self-regulation."[15]

Explaining that keyword-based technology blocked such sites as www.middlesex.gov or www.SuperBowlXXX.com, while human judgment-based blocking tended to eliminate safer-sex or gay rights information, *Fahrenheit 451.2* tried to justify the ACLU's argument in *Reno I* that the software was nevertheless a "'less restrictive' means of addressing the government's asserted interest" in protecting youth. While user-based blocking does "present troubling free speech concerns," the pamphlet said, it is "far preferable to any statute that imposes criminal penalties on online speech."[16]

Law professor Lawrence Lessig was not so sure. Taking issue with the ACLU, he argued that *Reno I* "set us in a direction that we will later regret," pushing the "'problem' of kids and porn towards a 'solution' that will (from the perspective of the interest in free speech) be much worse. The 'less restrictive means' touted by free speech activists in *Reno* are, in my view, far more restrictive of free speech interests than a properly crafted CDA would be."[17] That is, Lessig said, blocking software is "opaque" (the lists of banned sites are secret), and it censors too much material. PICS is even worse. "'The MIT geniuses who thought it up realized it had broader potential than just blocking indecent speech.' . . . Taken together, filtering software and PICS lead to a hard-wired architecture of blocking that is antagonistic to the original free-wheeling and speech-enhancing values of the Internet."[18]

The December 1-3, 1997, Internet Online Summit was indeed the censorware love-fest that Declan McCullagh had predicted. Its meeting rooms, in a large Washington hotel, were littered with promotional materials and displays of blocking software. A press release from Cyber Patrol announced a new "white list of safe Internet chat and message boards." ("Whitelisting" was a polite term for mechanisms that eliminated the Internet from computers by blocking all of it, except for preselected "safe" sites.) The American Digital Network distributed booklets touting its ISP-based (rather than freestanding) Parent's Choice technology that allowed both control and monitoring of children's online activity. Click & Browse Jr., manufactured by NetWave, offered a whitelist of preselected sites that it was offering free to "America's 86,000 public schools." A press release and glossy brochure from Landmark Community Interests announced that "GuardiaNet the first server-based Internet filtering package," would include Web sites rated by RSACi, and promised to "make your PC like Fort Knox." Web Chaperone claimed to "scan ... every Web page as it is loaded, instantly rejecting inappropriate pages"; TwoDog.Net traded on endearing puppy pictures to promise a whitelist that "excludes literally all objectionable material"; CyberSnoop's colorful handout, also using a canine motif, promised to deliver Internet access with "a new leash on life"; while SurfWatch announced a new PICS - compatible version of its product. Like the other promotions, SurfWatch's materials used various terms interchangeably to describe the speech it blocked: "objectionable," "controversial," "inappropriate," "dangerous."[19]

Among the mass of literature were several items from Net Shepherd, which now had a new Family Search site that it said would bring "network television content standards to the Internet." Net Shepherd (whose graphics also featured a happy dog) candidly announced that it "chose to focus its filtering technology on a family-friendly search site simply because, as an advertising supported profit center, it offers the greatest potential for immediate sales revenue." Family Search filtered out sites "judged by an independent panel of demographically appropriate internet users to be superfluous and/or objectionable to the average family."[20]

Family Search, as it turned out, filtered most of the Internet. At a press conference on the opening day of the Online Summit, EPIC released a study showing that Family Search blocked 90 to 99 percent of responsive Web sites when "American Red Cross," "Museum of Modern Art," "National Zoo," or "Dr. Seuss" were typed in as the search terms. Family Search eliminated hundreds of thousands of sites relating to charities, cultural institutions, and basic research information. Net Shepherd responded by acknowledging that its "community of people" rating the Internet were being "very conservative," but that the system was designed "as both a screen for inappropriate content and a lens to find more relevant material."[21]

Vice President Al Gore was the administration's star attraction at the Online Summit the following day. His speech mixed formulaic genuflections to the First Amendment with calls for blocking minors' access to "offensive speech" that he analogized to various physical dangers - live electrical outlets in one metaphor; poisons in the medicine chest a moment later.[22] Such analogies were not, of course, original with Gore: the reductionist equation of disfavored ideas with physical risks, and the consequent failure to appreciate the indirect, multifaceted way in which expression is processed by different individuals had long been a mainstay of harm-to-minors rhetoric.

Just as those who had opposed the CDA broke ranks when it came to rating and filtering, those on the political right were not of one mind on the virtues of the Online Summit. While Enough is Enough had a major role (Donna Rice Hughes, speaking at one panel, complained that without filters "a 14-year-old boy with his raging hormones" could access adult entertainment), the Christian Coalition, the Family Research Council, and the American Family Association "derided the meeting as a 'love-in'" whose primary goal was damage control for the online industry.[23] *The New York Times,* reporting the controversy, noted that most journalistic Web sites had refused to self-rate under RSACi and that in any event the White House's enthusiasm for filtering had not deterred legislators such as Dan Coats from proposing new online censorship laws.[24] Coats's Child Online Protection Act (COPA), a trimmer version of the CDA, was in fact on its way to passage despite announcements at the industry love-in that "self-regulation" was the answer to online porn.

### State Laws, Loudoun County, and Reno II

Despite the Supreme Court's ruling in *Reno,* state legislatures were now passing their own Internet censorship laws. New York's, the first, criminalized communications to minors "which, in whole or part, depict actual or simulated nudity, sexual conduct or sadomasochistic abuse," if they are "harmful to minors" within the meaning of the three-part variable-obscenity test. (Variable obscenity is simply a variation on the three-part legal test for obscene, and therefore constitutionally unprotected, expression: it must be "patently offensive"; appeal to "prurient" rather than healthy, sexual appetites; and lack "serious literary, artistic, political, or scientific value.") The ACLU brought a constitutional challenge (with the American Library Association as lead plaintiff), and federal judge Loretta Preska invalidated the law on the ground that it violated the Commerce Clause (Article 1, section 8 of the Constitution). That is, the law burdened interstate commerce by imposing New York's censorship standards on "conduct that occurs wholly outside New York," and it intruded into a field that was so intrinsically national rather than local that only Congress could regulate it.[25] While New York did not appeal, New Mexico did – unsuccessfully - when its similar law was struck down in 1998. Georgia, Michigan, and Virginia also passed CDA variants; in all three states, the laws were invalidated, but legislators showed no signs of losing interest in Internet censorship laws.[26]

Just a few weeks after the Online Summit, a citizens group called Mainstream Loudoun filed the first legal challenge to Internet filtering in public libraries. The Loudoun County, Virginia, library board had voted to require that all library computers, "to the extent technically feasible," block both "obscene material" and "material deemed Harmful to Juveniles under applicable Virginia statutes and legal precedents."[27] Presumably because of its claims to block only illegal obscenity, the Log-On Data Corporation's X-Stop program was the chosen filtering product. Web sites blocked using X-Stop's "felony search," however, included the American Association of University Women, Glide Memorial Methodist Church, the Heritage Foundation, Zero Population Growth, and the Yale Graduate Biology Program.[28]

Mainstream Loudoun charged that the mandatory filters burdened its members' First Amendment right "to receive otherwise available speech and information via the Internet," and reduced adults "to even less than material suitable for children." Its federal court complaint described X-Stop's "foul word" function, which blocked any reference to "pussy" (as in "The Owl and the Pussycat") or "bastard" (as in a recent National Book Award finalist, Dorothy Allison's *Bastard Out of Carolina*). Two months later, a group of online publishers, including the Renaissance Transgender Association and the Safer Sex Web Page, intervened in the case, with representation from the ACLU.[29]

This was the first lawsuit challenging online library censorship, and it was carefully watched. Loudoun County's lawyers argued that nobody had any right to see or read anything in particular at a public library - the choices had always been made by library staff - so no First Amendment rights were infringed. The plaintiffs' and intervenors' lawyers responded that X-Stop involved not selection but removal of material already included in the Internet's worldwide library - and removal, moreover, by a private company with undisclosed cultural and moral criteria, which kept its protocols and lists confidential. Even in school libraries, as the Supreme Court had ruled sixteen years before, removal decisions are not immune from constitutional scrutiny and, under the First Amendment, cannot be ideologically motivated. As the ACLU pointed out, Loudoun County's argument meant that "no constitutional violation would be stated if, as a matter of policy, a public library decided that only Democrats had valid ideas and therefore only bought books by Democrats; or if the library purged all books by non-Christians because no religion other than Christianity is valid." Attorney Robert Corn-Revere's brief for Mainstream Loudoun noted that X-Stop added 300 new blocked sites to its list every day, and "could be pursuing an avowedly political or discriminatory agenda for deciding which sites to block, and Loudoun County librarians would never know the difference."[30]

Judge Leonie Brinkema eventually agreed. She ruled that the Supreme Court's 1982 school library decision surely applied to public libraries as well, and limited their ability to restrict access to literature and information within their collections. Nor were Loudoun's asserted interests in "minimizing access to illegal pornography and avoidance of a sexually hostile environment" furthered by reducing all Internet users to the "harm to minors" level or delegating censorship decisions to X-Stop. Among the "less burdensome alternatives" were filters installed on some computers just for minors.[31] Brinkema did not explain how blocking such items as "The Owl and the Pussycat" would advance the interest in protecting youth; but her minors only approach soon became the preferred option for many libraries.

As libraries continued to be beset by demands for Internet filtering,[32] frustrations and anomalies multiplied. At one library using filters, patrons received sex-toy Web sites in response to a search request for "toys," but were confronted with screens flashing yellow Cyber Patrol police badges when attempting to research the artists Georgia O'Keeffe and Vincent van Gogh. Federal judges discovered they could no longer access their travel agent online because filtering software blocked the agent's promise of "vacations to exotic locales." The American Family Association felt the sting of Internet filters when Cyber Patrol blocked its Web site on grounds of intolerance toward homosexuals. And the Censorware Project reported in 1999 that SmartFilter, used by Utah in all of its public schools and some of its libraries, blocked more than 500,000 sites, among them the Declaration of Independence, the Koran, Shakespeare's plays, and *The Adventures of Sherlock Holmes.*[33]

In Congress, meanwhile, the American Library Association testified against Senator McCain's bill mandating that school and library computers filter out "inappropriate" content as a condition of federal aid. It argued that the overzealousness of filtering deprives both children and adults of information "on subjects ranging from AIDS and breast cancer to religion and politics."[34] Al Gore argued in rebuttal that the McCain bill's vague standard of "inappropriateness" was actually an advantage, in that it would "empower schools to make decisions based on local values."[35] (McCain was to substitute "harmful to minors" for "inappropriate" in his 1999 version of the bill, but he left it up to local school and library districts to decide what the term meant. In late 2000, House and Senate leaders agreed on the filtering mandate and President Clinton signed the "Children's Internet Protection Act" into law.[36])

Even without a federal mandate, many public schools were signing up for filtering. In November 1998, the entire Tennessee school system adopted Bess, the filter featuring the cute golden retriever, which had thirty-four separate blocking categories, including tobacco, games, medical, alcohol, chat, gambling, "recreation/entertainment," "tasteless/gross," sports, stocks, and swimsuits.[37] A year later, parents and children complained that the New York City schools' computer software blocked "categories like news and sex education, including those of major news outlets, policy groups and scientific and medical organizations"; students were unable to research breast cancer, anorexia, child labor, or AIDS, or to read parts of Steinbeck's *The Grapes of Wrath.* Highlighting the by now recognized "digital divide" that disadvantages lower-income youth in gaining computer skills, *The New York Times* noted that some "prestigious schools" were able to circumvent the filters by accessing university Internet servers.[38]

Filtering euphoria did not, as some of its boosters hoped, forestall more coercive approaches to online speech. In 1998, Congress passed Senator Coats's Child Online Protection Act (COPA), which barred Web sites engaged in commercial activity from expression that violated the variable-obscenity standard first announced by the Supreme Court in *Ginsberg v. New York.*[39] The ACLU again represented a group of online speakers in challenging the law (the case would be known as *Reno II);* plaintiffs included Androgyny Books, OB/GYN.net, Condomania, Artnet, RiotGrrl, and Powell's Bookstore, a bibliophile's paradise in Portland, Oregon.[40] Although variable obscenity was obviously a tougher standard to challenge than indecency, the ACLU's arguments were basically the same as in *Reno I:* because of the economics and technology of the Internet, COPA had the unconstitutional effect of reducing adults to reading or publishing only what was fit for children; and children, moreover, anywhere from zero to 17 years of age.

Judge Lowell Reed, Jr., invalidated COPA in a February 1999 decision reflecting the same sort of ambivalence that had characterized the Supreme Court's decision in *Reno I.* On the one hand, he suggested, "perhaps we do the minors of this country harm if First Amendment protections, which they will with age inherit fully, are chipped away in the name of their protection." But on the other, he expressed "personal regret" at "delay[ing] once again the careful protection of our children."[41] On appeal, the Clinton Justice Department argued simultaneously that COPA should be narrowly interpreted to bar only material that would lack serious value for older minors, and that the law was necessary to socialize young ones lest pornography "distort their views of sexuality." Voluntary filtering was not an adequate substitute, the government said: whether "because of inertia or distraction" or "because of the technical complexity or cost of blocking software," parents may fail to use it, "thereby leaving their children (and other children that may use their computers) completely unprotected."[42]

There was no recognition here that parents are not all of one view on matters of sexuality and child rearing. Those who eschew Internet filters are not necessarily inert; they may simply disagree with the government's approach to socializing their children.

The Court of Appeals, in any event, agreed that COPA violated the First Amendment. In a striking decision that put into question the very viability of the legal test for obscenity, the court said that applying "contemporary community standards" in cyberspace would unconstitutionally force Internet speakers to comply with the most conservative communities' notions of what was corrupting or offensive.[43]

### The French Letter and Internet Watch

Filtering fever was also taking hold in Europe. Great Britain had long had more restrictive censorship laws than the European Continent, especially when the subject was sex. Given this tradition of sex censorship, Britain not surprisingly took the European lead in attempts to control the Internet when that revolutionary medium arrived on the scene. An early salvo, in August 1996, was a missive from Chief Inspector Stephen French of London's Metropolitan Police to the country's Internet service providers (ISPs), urging them to remove from their servers some 150 online sites that the police considered "pornographic" and "offensive." (Wags couldn't help dubbing this the "French Letter" - one of England's many euphemisms for a condom.) French warned that obscenity prosecutions could follow if the industry did not "move quickly toward the eradication of this type of Newsgroup from the Internet." His appended list of disapproved online sites began "cleverly," as one reporter observed, with "unpleasantly titled paedophile" groups; it "was only the persistent reader who would realise that the police also wanted to restrict access to newsgroups which clearly dealt with adult consensual sexual activities - many of them lesbian and gay interest groups."[44]

Although civil libertarians protested the French Letter's preemptive demand to purge "offensive" speech without any judicial finding of illegality, the major ISPs were conciliatory. Within a month of the letter, they had negotiated a "Safety-Net Agreement" with the Metropolitan Police, the Home Office, and the Department of Trade and Industry. The Agreement promised that ISPs would work not only to rid computers of Internet content they thought illegal but to develop methods of blocking legal but "offensive" speech by requiring all online speakers to "rate their own web pages" using the RSACi system that had been developed in the United States. ISPs would also "remove web pages hosted on their servers which are persistently and deliberately misrated," though it was not clear who would decide what the correct ratings should be.[45]

The Safety-Net Agreement prefigured the British online industry's formation of the Internet Watch Foundation, or IWF, whose two purposes were to police potentially illegal material (mostly child pornography) and to promote an international rating and blocking system for legal but "offensive" (alternately denoted "potentially harmful") speech. Eager to characterize blocking as benign, informational parental empowerment, fully consistent with free expression, the IWF set about assembling an Advisory Committee, and asked media lawyer Mark Stephens to be the nominee of Liberty, Britain's leading civil liberties group. Stephens called Liberty, whose chief legal staffer agreed to the appointment. The executive director, John Wadham, explained two years later that "no one, including me, on the staff was on top of the issue," but this did not mean "we had given our approval to the IWF, supported it's aims, or that we would be seen as being represented on its board."[46]

Mark Stephens chaired the IWF Advisory Committee and became one of the primary authors of its March 1998 report, *Rating and Filtering Internet Content: A United Kingdom Perspective.* The report was circulated months before its official publication date; indeed, its ideas were floated by David Kerr, IWF's director, as early as July 1997, when he told a meeting of European ministers in Bonn that global ratings must be more extensive and wide-ranging than U.S.-based programs. There is a "whole category of dangerous subjects" that demand ratings, Kerr said, including "discussions advocating suicide, information about dangerous sports like bungee-jumping, and more common areas of concern such as drugs, cigarette advertising, sex and violence." Moreover, he said, rating of profanity "needs internationalization: "The language and references are all American in current rating proposals."[47] Kerr did not explain how a global rating system would take account of all the potentially "harmful" or offensive words that might be found in scores of different languages and on millions of Internet sites.

All of these anomalies found their way into the IWF's March 1998 report, which proposed ten subjects that were "unsuitable" or "potentially harmful" for minors. To the four categories already identified by RSACi - "nudity," "sex," "language," and "violence" - the IWF added "personal details," " financial commitments," "tolerance" (actually meant to block intolerance), "potentially harmful subjects," "adult themes," and "context variables." This last category would consist of judgment calls by raters that material fitting into one of the previous nine groups was nevertheless sufficiently valuable from a scientific, journalistic, or literary point of view that users of the filter might want to override it.

To add to the complexity, within each of the IWF's ten categories of "potentially harmful" or "unsuitable" expression it proposed four or five gradations: thus, the IWF adopted RSACi's five levels of "nudity," ranging from "revealing attire" and "partial nudity" to "frontal nudity (qualifying as provocative display)." It likewise adopted RSACi's five levels for "language," from "mild expletive" to "crude, vulgar language" or "extreme hate speech." To these it added five gradations for "tolerance," from "neutral (non-prejudicial) reference to groups or attitudes about them," to advocacy of "action which would cause physical, psychological or economic harm or violence against the group." Its category for "potentially harmful subjects," also with five proposed levels, covered games, hobbies, sports, gambling, and "potential mind-disturbing material, including advocacy of suicide." "Adult themes" was a "catch-all category" that might include "abortion, fetishes, adultery, etc.": no gradations were proposed.

Despite its claims to noncensorial, purely informational intent, the IWF report recommended that browser software be shipped with the default setting to apply ratings. It did not say at which of the many possible levels of blocking the default should be set - if at the maximum, even mildly vulgar language, "kissing related romance," and "neutral (non-prejudicial) reference to groups or attitudes about them" would be blocked. Kerr had no answer when asked where precisely (out of the fifty or so possible permutations) the default should be set under the IWF's plan.[48]

Yaman Akdeniz, a researcher at the University of Leeds and founding director of an anticensorship group, Cyber-Rights and Cyber-Liberties, was one of the first to notice that IWF's materials were listing Mark Stephens as Liberty's nominee on the Advisory Committee, thus implying that Britain's major civil liberties organization supported filtering and other government-encouraged efforts at Internet content control. Akdeniz alerted Liberty, which, he said, "did not even know what the heck IWF was at the time when I phoned them." John Wadham agreed: "Liberty did not have its eye on the ball on this issue," and the initial "miscommunication" was "exploited by the IWF to our detriment." A meeting ensued in April 1998, at which a representative of the IWF, Clive Feather, was told that Liberty "is not involved with IWF nor supports private policing schemes."[49]

Yet the IWF continued to assert its civil liberties bona fides, and its Web site continued to identify Stephens as Liberty's nominee through 1998 and much of

1999.[50] David Kerr's explanation, in June 1999, was that Stephens never represented Liberty's views at the IWF, "nomination" not being equivalent to representation, and that "we have never pretended that Liberty supports IWF policies." He added apologies "that we have caused any confusion by not changing the Web site. This was delayed by other pressures and was not meant to deceive anyone. We will remove the reference forthwith."[51] Shortly thereafter, Wadham wrote to Kerr formally requesting the change. But Akdeniz and others protested that the IWF's March 1998 rating and filtering report was still being circulated with Liberty's name. Liberty, meanwhile, approved a statement at its 1999 annual meeting noting the "considerable flaws" in filtering/rating systems, opposing "the imposition of compulsory rating systems and filtering systems on adults" in libraries, and recognizing that children too "have a right to receive information."[52]

If Liberty did not, as Wadham said, have its eye on the ball regarding filtering in 1997, neither did most of the civil liberties world. The question of harm to minors is a difficult one even for people who otherwise oppose censorship; and Mark Stephens's disagreement with Liberty about rating and blocking evidenced a general ambivalence among civil libertarians regarding this politically seductive alternative to the more obviously coercive forms of Internet control. Even the ACLU, litigating *Reno I,* had touted privately marketed labeling and blocking schemes as "less restrictive alternatives" to criminal prohibitions; only later did it publish *Fahrenheit 451.2,* pointing out some of the more conspicuous shortcomings of filtering software. And in Liberty's 1999 book, *Liberating Cyberspace,* Wadham referred to "a legitimate need to ensure that people, including teenagers, are not exposed to offensive or potentially damaging material," and suggested that the need is "more appropriately and effectively" met "through self-regulation and the development of more sophisticated technology" - presumably ratings and filters. [53]

By early 1999, the IWF had helped form an international industry group, INCORE (Internet Content Rating for Europe), and had received a grant of 250,000 euros from the European Union to begin development of an international rating and blocking scheme. Nor was the IWF the only profiltering entity to benefit from EU largesse. The London-based Childnet International had received an EU grant to develop Internet complaint hotlines and promotional programs on the virtues of ratings and filters. Childnet was the creation of Nigel Williams, a former officer of the evangelical group CARE (Christian Action, Research and Education). Williams had previously written of pornography that it "trivialises and debases one of God's special gifts. Yet we need not be depressed - seeing through Satan's lies is half the battle."[54] The rhetoric was reminiscent of ideological conflicts over youth, sin, and sexuality going back at least to Victorian times.


## The European Union Weighs In

Continental Europe was, in general, less conflicted about youthful sexuality than Britain, but by the mid-1990s its governments were also anxious about sex in cyberspace. Not long after Congress passed the ill-fated 1996 Communications Decency Act, Western Europe was confronted with a Belgian pedophile scandal involving the deaths of four girls and implicating police and high officials in allegations of corruption. In this tense atmosphere, panic about uses of the Internet to entice children into sexual activity spilled over into initiatives that would control minors' simply *reading* pornography - or other "objectionable" content.[55]

The EU consisted by the late 1990s of fifteen Member States and was a maze of administrative, judicial, and legislative institutions that governed ever larger portions of Europe's economy.[56] The major administrative body, the European Commission, was headquartered in Brussels and Luxembourg and divided into various DGs (Directorates General) of which two, DG 10 and DG 13, would be most involved in censorship directed at the young. It was DG 10 that administered the 1989 "Television Without Frontiers" Directive, whose main purpose was to remove national barriers to the free flow of TV signals, but which also required Member States to block any shows that "might seriously impair the physical, mental or moral development of minors, in particular programmes that involve pornography or gratuitous violence."[57] The directive offered no guidance on how to distinguish pornography from other sexual expression, or gratuitous from justifiable depictions of violence; and as David Hughes, an official at DG 10, explained, the EU's Member States have extremely diverse ideas about what, if anything, on television "might seriously impair" youthful psyches.[58]

The "Television Without Frontiers" Directive did not stop at proscribing television that "might seriously impair" young minds; it also required the banning or time-channeling of shows "*likely* to impair" them.[59] With respect to the second, presumably less grievous, category of programming, it did not specify what was "likely to impair" minors' development. As the Court of the European Free Trade Association (EFTA) explained in 1997, the directive introduced no "common standard," for "the mental and moral development of minors forms an important part of the protection of public morality, an area where it is not possible to determine a uniform European conception." Thus, neither "serious impairment" nor "likely impairment" has an objective meaning; each country should impose its own version.[60]

The same year as the EFTA decision, the European Parliament directed DG 10 to commission a study of TV rating and blocking, with a focus on the same v-chip device that the U.S. Congress had mandated in 1996 for all TVs 13 inches or larger. The bulky *Final Report: Parental Control of Television Broadcasting,* was produced by the University of Oxford Programme in Comparative Media Law and Policy. Released in February 1999, it surveyed in mind-boggling detail the technical ramifications of TV ratings, the existing classification and censorship schemes in EU Member States, sociological research on the utility of ratings, and data on TV's psychological effects. Although its conclusions were ambiguous - the only clear one being that the v-chip was technologically unfeasible for Europe - the *Final Report* offered insights into European harm-to-minors politics.

The report noted that rating and blocking would suppress valuable information and entertainment for adults as well as youth. It confirmed that the Member States had "highly differentiated approaches" reflecting "their own internal media history" and "social construct," and therefore that "the foundation does not exist, at this point, for extensive harmonisation" in the form of a transnational rating system. France had developed "extremely elaborate" TV rating procedures, for example, while other countries such as Luxembourg had "not implemented any specific systems." The substantive differences, moreover, were striking: the film *Sex, Lies, & Videotape* was 18+ in the UK "while it obtained a 7+ certificate in Sweden and would have even been released within a general audience certificate if it had not contained a violent scene." Only Britain and Italy rated films for bad language; only Germany and the Netherlands rated for fascist ideology or political extremism. France labeled a film for age 12 and up if the national Classification Commission decided that it "might shock the sensitivity of children" through "horrible images" or "representation of traumatic relationship between parent[s] and children." In Britain, by contrast, "sex/nudity related content appears with very sophisticated gradations" in each category of the classification scheme. This concern with sexual content "is not expressed in such a detailed way, nor regulated so carefully in the other countries, and, indeed, in some of them sex is not even perceived as detrimental for minors."[61]

Given this diversity, the *Final Report* said it was "difficult to see how a European-wide classification system could be achieved." But ultimately, the problem with v-chips and other rating and blocking systems was even more basic. Such systems are based on "one dimensional criteria such as age or a basic content descriptor (e.g., sex, violence, incitement to immoral behaviour, crude language), possibly presented in a variety of forms (Sex Level 1, Sex Level 2, Sex Level 3)." Consequently, works are not "appreciated in their complexity and will be rated without an appreciation for context. Risk is also high that certain programmes that would have been of interest for children ... will fall under these too simplistic criteria and thus never be displayed on the screen." Children too are "individuals with the right to receive information and entertainment."[62]

Having pointed out the difficulties, however, the *Final Report* remained mindful of harm-to-minors politics. It recommended "informational rating systems," which it said would become more common with digital TV set-top boxes and program guides. Indeed, the report looked forward to an electronic world in which a thousand rating systems might bloom, reflecting "religious and cultural preferences, varying philosophies of child-rearing, language training and criteria far removed from the current emphasis on violence and sexually explicit images." Such "niche filtering" admittedly could "be viewed as quasi-censorial," it said, but the "interest in encouraging pluralistic third party and multiple rating approaches" should "take precedence over this concern."[63]

Finally, the report noted that factors other than the simple presence of media violence determine whether television viewing is harmful. Researchers had found that children "are capable of making varied and complex judgments about violent content," despite "a widespread belief" that they are much less able than adults "to comprehend the context in which violence is shown, and are therefore more susceptible to harm." To the extent bad messages are an issue, the report urged "the enhancement of children's media literacy and critical viewing skills." It noted that Austria, Denmark, England, Finland, France, Germany, Ireland, the Netherlands, Italy, Scotland, Spain, and Sweden all incorporated critical viewing skills into their public education.[64]

DG 10's David Hughes concurred in the *Final Report's* conclusions. It had been clear two years earlier, he said, that the v-chip was not feasible for Europe; politics had driven the commissioning of the study. The murder of a toddler, James Bulger, in Britain, by two older children, among other factors, "made the debate very passionate and not very rational." TV ratings would be impossible to impose in any standardized way on nations as diverse as those in the EU, said Hughes. Accommodating Muslim cultural values would require rigorous classification of female attire, a standard at odds, to say the least, with most of Western Europe. Yet none of this meant that DG 10 would abandon the ratings game. From the viewpoint of the EU bureaucracy, Hughes said, "it doesn't really matter what the justification" is.[65]

While the massive *Final Report* was in preparation, the European Commission was forging ahead with Internet filtering schemes. At an April 1996 meeting in Bologna, with the Belgian pedophile scandal still in the news, the EU's ministers for telecommunications and culture identified "illegal and harmful content on the Internet as an urgent priority for analysis and action."[66] The European Commission responded the following October with two documents - a *Communication* to the European Parliament and a *Green Paper on the Protection of Minors and Human Dignity in Audiovisual and Information Services.* Both touted filters as a way to protect youth from legal but "potentially harmful" online speech."[67]

The *Communication* started by distinguishing "illegal" from "harmful" but legal expression. Child pornography, for example, is criminal throughout the EU, as is "racist material or incitement to racial hatred," though the authors acknowledged that the "exact definition" of these crimes "varies from country to country." (In fact, there are large differences in the extent to which European nations outlaw racist speech.) As to "harmful" expression, the *Communication* did not essay a definition: it was simply material that "may offend the values and feelings of other persons" – "content expressing political opinions," for example, or "views on racial matters." Indeed, what is considered harmful "depends on cultural differences."[68] It was unclear whether the *Communication* meant to place speech "offensive" to adults in the same category as speech considered "harmful" or "unsuitable" for minors, but this seemed to be the assumption, even while acknowledging that all three concepts vary from one country to another. But if "unsuitable," "offensive," and "harmful" all mean the same thing, then the term "harmful" simply loses its ordinary meaning.

The *Communication* did not clarify these ambiguities but nevertheless recommended the creation of a European-wide Internet labeling and filtering system. It approvingly described the various programs available; and finessing the definitional problem once again, urged the development of European ratings instead of relying on programs devised in the United States, "where there may be a different approach on what is suitable content for minors."[69]

The *Green Paper* was a more discursive "think piece" beneath whose surface hovered a question of political turf: in the brave new world of the Internet, which DG (10 or 13) would administer the Internet censorship rules, and the ensuing funds? Like the *Communication*, the *Green Paper* took pains to distinguish between illegal speech in the new media, which the authors said "may be banned for everyone" regardless of age, and legal expression that cannot be banned but nevertheless "might affect the physical and mental development of minors" and so should be subject to rating and blocking. The paper used various terms to describe this second category of speech: "questionable," "liable to upset" children, possibly "pos(ing) a problem for minors," possibly "shock[ing] minors," and possibly "harmful to their development." The authors acknowledged not only that attitudes toward socialization of children "vary greatly" among the Member States, but that "a consensus does not necessarily exist, even in medical circles, as to what is likely to affect the moral and physical development of minors." Moreover, "the term 'minors' does not cover a uniform group and it is doubtful whether children of four have the same problems as adolescents of 15." The *Green Paper* nevertheless urged that the EU attempt to "identify shared values" and "areas where there may be a need for common standards" and promote PICS "or equivalent systems with a view to reaching - as quickly as possible - a critical mass of labeled material and navigation systems and parental control devices."[70]

In the next three years, the European Commission, Parliament, Council, and their various committees and working groups were to churn out reports, hold meetings, examine legal ramifications, network with online corporations, and start spending serious money on developing and promoting Internet rating and filtering. Yet all the while, they remained agnostic on the question whether any identifiable category of expression causes identifiable harm to youth. They continued to confuse "harm" with "unsuitability," or offense to moral or cultural values, and to press for standardized labels even while insisting that harm or offense are relative questions to be resolved separately by each Member State.

Thus, a European Commission "working party" reported in March 1997 that industry groups in a number of nations were generating self-regulation schemes not only to remove "illegal" content from their computers (without, however, any judicial determination of illegality) but to provide their customers with classification and filtering systems, develop codes of conduct, encourage online speakers to self-rate, and "deal with cases where the content provider fails to rate properly."[71] A report of the Commission's Legal Advisory Committee the same month applauded both self- and third-party ratings though admitting the difficulty of describing expression in a "value-free" manner.[72] An April 1997 *Resolution* by the European Parliament affirmed the importance of free speech and acknowledged that the notion of "harmful content ... appertains essentially to the domain of morals," but nevertheless called on the Commission "to encourage the development of a common international rating system compatible with the PICS protocol, and sufficiently flexible to accommodate cultural differences."[73]

Occasional objections were raised within the EU bureaucracy during this labor- and paper-intensive process. The European Parliament's Committee on Women's Rights commented that "parental control" can "be viewed negatively as a means of limiting access to information, thus excluding children and adolescents from a free choice of knowledge."[74] The Economic and Social Committee pointed out that an *Action Plan* proposed by DG 13 for funding rating and blocking schemes was "impracticable" because the information on the Internet was too vast to be classified and labeled, and systems like PICS, although presented as "user-empowering," could become "an instrument of control." Still another committee commented wryly on the amount of paper consumed by the largely duplicative *Green Paper* and *Communication,* suggesting that "as much as Internet content providers compete with each other, Commission DGs also seem to be competing."[75]

## "Les Dangers Ubuesques du Filtrage"

By 1998, the EU's plans for international Internet filtering seemed unstoppable, but civil liberties groups did voice their opposition. The Campaign Against Censorship of the Internet in Britain, Feminists Against Censorship, and Cyber-Rights and Cyber-Liberties were joined by Italy's Associazione per la Liberta nella Communicazione Elettronica Interattiva (Association for Freedom in Interactive Electronic Communication), France's Imaginons un Réseau Internet Solidaire (IRIS; loosely translated as Imagining Internet Network Solidarity), and about thirty others in Europe, the United States, Canada, Australia, and even Singapore in protesting the repressive potential of rating and blocking schemes.

IRIS was particularly imaginative. Its online publications outlined the dangers of rating and filtering, among them the *"liberticide"* that would result from forced self-rating, and the risk that linguistic and cultural minorities would be subject to the tastes and values of "dominant organisms, that is to say, essentially American."[76] IRIS's first *lettre electronique,* in January 1998, contained an *"alerte sur les dangers ubuesques du filtrage"*- that is, a suggestion that the grotesque dictator King Ubu in Alfred Jarry's comic play *Ubu the King* would be quite at home in the world of Internet blocking. IRIS illustrated its point with an *"exemple de blocage"*: the Web site of an association for the protection of animals. IRIS commented: *"Disney World s'internationalise, decidement: le pere Ubu y a aussi sa place"* (rough translation: Disney World goes decidedly international; King Ubu also belongs there). IRIS particularly objected to the EU's filtering recommendations; to a decision by the French Conseil d'État to make ISPs responsible for online content, and to U.S.-based efforts to suppress racist sites.[77]

In 1997, the civil liberties groups created a Global Internet Liberty Campaign (GILC) to publicize concerns ranging from encryption laws to rating and filtering. GILC protested new PICS rules promulgated by W3C (the World Wide Web Consortium) because they went "far beyond the original objective of PICS to empower Internet users," and instead facilitated "server/proxy-based filtering" that would permit "upstream censorship, beyond the control of the end user."[78] Nine months later, GILC published *"Regardless of Frontiers: Protecting the Human Rights to Freedom of Expression on the Global Internet,"* a pamphlet outlining the risks to free expression posed by blocking and labeling systems, particularly when implemented by government institutions like libraries and schools. But the report did not question the necessity of "protecting children from content that is permissible for adults"; it simply argued that the availability of filtering software for parents who want to use it rendered government regulation unnecessary.[79]

The civil liberties opposition did not make much headway against the combined force of the EU bureaucracy and the major online corporations, and by the end of 1998, DC 13's *Action Plan* was in place. The plan encompassed four main projects for 1999-2002 - hotlines, "support for self-regulation," "developing technical measures," and "awareness initiatives" - with a total budget of twenty-five million euros. "Technical measures" meant rating and filtering, whose purpose was variously described as dealing with "undesirable content on the Internet" "harmful content," or content "which could be harmful for children." "Awareness initiatives" were activities to persuade governments, Internet speakers, teachers, and parents of the benefits of a classified and filtered online world.[80]

DG 13 now devised "preparatory actions" that different organizations would be paid to undertake in furtherance of the *Action Plan.* INCORE, the industry group largely organized by Britain's Internet Watch Foundation, was the contracting organization for "Preparatory Action 2," a "feasibility study for a European system of content self-rating." Among other things, INCORE would evaluate different filtering programs to determine their respect for "European cultural and linguistic differences" and their ability to "deal with the issue of content which is not appropriately rated."[81] In May 1999, meanwhile, the major online corporations – Microsoft, Netscape, AOL, and Bertelsmann among them - formed yet another international filtering group, the Internet Content Rating Association, or ICRA. Its goal was to "try to create the first world standard" for rating and blocking based on the American RSACi system, whose assets it soon acquired. The new consortium acknowledged that global filtering was not feasible in a cyberworld where "only a tiny proportion - about 1% - of sites have rated themselves," but hoped to drum up enthusiasm "by developing an undisputed standard and boosting awareness of its use through major publicity campaigns." According to the IWF, the companies forming ICRA had "the technical and financial power to complete and implement" global filtering; and they would govern the "new international system" of "voluntary self-rating."[82]

At an "expert meeting" of rating and filtering promoters in Munich that September, Bertelsmann unveiled a new "layer cake" plan for Internet rating and filtering. Incorporated in a *Memorandum on Self-Regulation of the Internet,* the plan had been developed by Yale professor Jack Balkin, with funding from Bertelsmann. The proposed "layers" consisted, first, of PICS - compatible "voluntary" labels or "meta-tags" drawn from a "basic vocabulary" of keywords; then ideologically value-laden "templates" created by different organizations to rate the "meta-tags" based on their varying attitudes toward what is good, bad, or harmful for minors; and finally, third-party ratings of online sites, including whitelists and blacklists that would "provide for more contextualized judgements."[83] In an earlier memorandum, Balkin had proposed that the "common descriptive meta-tags" be "developed by a board of social scientists with reference to relevant and empirical sociological data as to what constitutes 'actual harm' to children." He acknowledged that this would require "difficult tradeoffs" and "adaptability to changing mores,"[84] but failed to note that there is no agreement among social scientists within cultures, no less across them, as to what if anything in the realm of speech or ideas predictably causes psychological harm. Balkin also acknowledged that "his common language will not cover every aspect of content. . . . "There can be no [common] description for blasphemy in Saudi Arabia.. . . Neither can hate speech or political speech be satisfactorily rated. 'It's a leaky system,'" he said. "'But it's the best you can do.'"[85]

GILC made an appearance in Munich to point out the drawbacks of filtering, whether in the form of layer cakes or self-rating. It warned that "the imposition of civil or criminal penalties for 'mis-rating'. . . is likely to follow any widespread deployment of a rating and blocking regime."[86] The online group netfreedom weighed in with an article arguing that if ISPs required self-rating, they would simply be replacing government censors. "Why is this going forward?" the reporters asked. "What happened is the government (the European Commission, in this case) decided to get serious. They buckled down, and at the end of 1998, allocated funds to be spent on the development of a global rating system." With all that money available, "the corporate participants can be reasonably assured of being reimbursed for all their plane fares and hotel costs. (Question: if it's so voluntary, how come the government is paying people to develop it?)"[87]

Even the CDT (the Center for Democracy and Technology), a champion of ratings, critiqued the Bertelsmann plan. It would "jeopardize free expression on the Internet," said the CDT, by "promoting a single, comprehensive, global rating system developed with government involvement or backed by government enforcement;" and "in the name of 'self-regulation,'" would encourage ISPs to collaborate in controlling speech that is legal but "considered offensive by some." ISPs would police the speech of their subscribers, while government regulators would define the standards to be applied.[88]

By early 2000, reports from the first phase of the Action Plan were filtering in. INCORE, surveying the European scene, found that too few sites were labeled - especially in languages other than English - to create the "critical mass" necessary for global blocking. It reiterated its view, however, that self-labeling advanced free expression by "reducing pressures on democratic governments to pursue censorship." A report on third-party rating from a French/Italian consortium found serious accuracy problems in the five filtering systems it examined (including Cyber Patrol, SurfWatch, and CyberSnoop). The "precise definition of what is illegal or harmful varies from one country to another," it said; and "the lack of localised versions" made it "difficult to filter slang or swear words." Sixty-four percent of respondents said the software "lacked coherency in terms of filtering results." Improvements - requiring more studies and more funds-were definitely needed.[89]

If INCORE, Bertelsmann, or the European Commission thought that industry-created layer cakes or other rating schemes would forestall direct government censorship, that illusion was soon dispelled by events in Australia. The Australian Broadcasting Authority (ABA) already had an elaborate system for rating TV, films, magazines, posters, and books in order to shield minors "from material likely to harm or disturb them" when, in early 1999, the government persuaded Australia's Internet Industry Association (IIA) to create a Code of Practice that extended the rating system to computers.[90] This "self-regulation" code was not free of official involvement; but even so, it did not satisfy those wanting more forceful controls. A month after the code's appearance, legislation was introduced requiring ISPs to remove "highly offensive or illegal material from their services" upon order of the ABA. The industry protested; the Australian Computer Society said the law would make

Australia "the laughing stock of the world"[91]; but in June 1999 Australia passed the Broadcasting Services Amendment (Online Services Act).

The law established a complex system for rating and removing "prohibited content" (defined as anything classified RC ["Refused Classification"] or X by the government's Classification Board), or "potential prohibited content" (anything online that has not been classified but if it were, "there is a substantial likelihood" that it would be "prohibited content"). Material would be rated or "potentially" rated as the result of either a private complaint or the ABA's own initiative. Once given the disapproved label, it had to be removed within fourteen hours by the "relevant Internet content host." There was a separate R category for expression that would be prohibited unless subject to a "restricted access system" designed to police Internet content that is "unsuitable for children"[92]- that is, the same age-screening found to be unfeasible two years earlier by the U.S. Supreme Court in *Reno v. ACLU*. By early 2000 the government was ordering ISPs to take down disapproved sites, some of which shifted to overseas servers to avoid the law.[93]

In contrast to the Australian government, the European Union says rating and filtering should be voluntary-for the content provider and the computer user. Yet Richard Swetenham, the DG 13 official in charge of filtering plans, acknowledged that "inducements" to self-rating under an ostensibly voluntary system would inevitably be necessary-and self-rating was the only real option because no third-party rating system could classify even a fraction of the Internet.

Swetenham was well aware of the problems with global ratings. Despite the EU's rhetorical genuflections to cultural diversity, rating systems by definition can only provide a preselected set of adverse labels; and Swetenham wondered how many different categories of potentially undesirable content - not to mention levels within categories - can be created before classifications become unworkable. As for the question of what, if any, online expression might actually harm youngsters, Swetenham was skeptical. "I'm not a psychologist," he said, "and at the end of the day, I don't really care."[94]

### Notes

1. *Reno v. ACLU*, 521 U.S. 844, 874, 870 (1997).
2. Press release, "SurfWatch Plays Crucial Role in Overturning Communications Decency Act," June 26, 1997; <http://www.surfwatch.com>.
3. Center for Democracy & Technology, "Internet Family Empowerment White Paper: How Filtering Tools Enable Responsible Parents to Protect Their Children Online*"* (July 16, 1997).

The White Paper was prepared with the help of America Online, AT&T, IBM, Microsoft, and other companies or industry groups with a commercial interest in blocking software.

4. *Resolution on the Use of Filtering Software in Libraries,* ALA Council, July 2, 1997, reprinted in ALA *Newsletter on Intellectual Freedom* (Sept. 1997), p. 119; ALA Intellectual Freedom Comm., *Statement on Library Use of Filtering Software, id., pp.* 119-20; Remarks of Harriet Silverstone, ALA *Newsletter, id., pp.* 154-55.

5. "Boston Public Library Censors Kids' Net," *Berkshire Eagle,* Mar. 29, 1997, p. A5; Amy Argetsinger, "Libraries Urged to Nip Internet in the Buff," *Washington Post*, Apr. 21, 1997, p. BI; Maria Seminerio, "Boston Schools Deploy Net Filters," *ZDNN Tech News*, Mar. 22, 1999, <http://www.zdnetcom/zdnn/stories/news/0,4586,2229381,00.html>. A similar controversy erupted in Austin, Texas, where the compromise solution was to allow four unrestricted, adults-only computers, which minors could not use even with parental permission. See Catherine Ross, "An Emerging Right for Mature Minors to Receive Information," 2 U. Pa. J. Con. Law 223, 235 (1999).

6. See Child Advocacy Working Group, Child Online Safety (prepared for the Internet Online Summit, Dec. 1-3, 1997), http://www.att.com/projects/tech4kids, p. 5.

7. Michael Krantz & Declan McCullagh, "Censor's Sensibility," *Time,* Aug. 11, 1997, p. 48; see also Andrew Shapiro, "The Dangers of Private Cybercops," *New York Times,* Dec. 4, 1997, p. A31; Gay & Lesbian Alliance Against Defamation (GLAAD), Access Denied: The Impact of Internet Filtering Software on the Lesbian & Gay Community (Dec. 1997); "An Internet Filter Is Eager to Zap the Starr Report," *New York Times,* Sept. 17, 1998, p. G3 (reporting CYBERsitter's announcement that its software would keep youngsters from reading the salacious details of Independent Counsel Ken Starr's report to Congress on the Clinton-Lewinsky affair).

8. See Jonathan Wallace, "The X-Stop Files: Self-Proclaimed Library-Friendly Product Blocks Quaker, Free Speech and Gay Sites," Oct 1997, <http://www.spectacle.org>.

9. Gordon Ross, "Censorship and the Internet," Nov. 19, 1997, "fight censorship" e-mail list, Nov. 22, 1997. Ross was the head of Net Nanny. By mid-2000, the number of Web pages was estimated to be more than one billion. Lisa Guernsey, "The Search Engine as Cyborg," New York Times, June 29, 2000, p. E1.

10. See Shawn Zeller, "A Shaky Deal on Internet Smut," *National Journal, Nov.* 22, 1997, p. 2383; *Fahrenheit 451.2: Is Cyberspace Burning? - How Rating and Blocking Proposals May Torch Free Speech on the Internet* (New York: ACLU, 1997), p. 2, reprinted in *Filters and Freedom: Free Speech Perspectives on Internet Content Controls* (David Sobel, ed.) (Washington, DC: EPIC, 1999).

11. Netparents.org, "Businesses, Public and Private Groups Unite Behind Initiative for Family-Friendly Internet Online World," July 16, 1997, <http://www. netparents.org>.

12. Jeremy Redmon, "Cyberporn at Libraries Has Smut Foes Furious," *Washington Times,* Oct. 30, 1997, p. C4; *Philanthropy* 4 (1997), describing Enough is Enough program in the context of a $160,000 grant from Fieldstead & Co. Family Friendly Libraries was the creation of a Christian-right activist, Karen Jo Gounaud, whose stated goals were to persuade libraries to filter the Internet, to stop promoting "homosexual ideology," and to replace the ALA's *Library Bill of Rights* with a "traditional family"-oriented acquisition policy. This meant according to Gounaud, more shelf space for material promoting "reparative therapy, ex-gay ministries, or the success stories of the thousands who have made that healing transition." Author's telephone interview with Karen Jo Gounaud, May 17, 2000; FFL Web site at http://fflibraries.org. Another group, Filtering Facts, published Dangerous Access, a collection of stories about youngsters (and adults) accessing pornography on library computers. See <http://wwww.filteringfacts.org>.

13. Declan McCullagh, "Why the Censorware Summit Is a Bad Idea," "fight censorship" e-mail list, Oct. 30, 1997 (commenting: "What' s wrong with this idea? Last I checked, the New York Times would never back a 'self-labeling' or 'self-censorship' scheme to stave off a federal censorship law. They'd have the balls to stand up and fight. When faced with presidential pressure to adopt an RSACi-type self-labeling system, the Net should do the same"); Declan McCullagh, "CyberPatrol Blocks Yahoo," "fight censorship" e-mail list Nov. 16, 1997.

14. Marc Rotenberg, "EPIC Letter to CNET and the Internet Community on Self-Labeling," , "fight censorship" e-mail list, July 26, 1997.

15. *Fahrenheit 451.2, supra* n. 10, p. 2.

16. *Id., pp.* 9-12 (noting also that minors have the right to access even "offensive" information - a view that "was considered controversial, even among our allies").

17. Lawrence Lessig, "What Things Regulate Speech: CDA 2.0 vs. Filtering," 38 *Jurimetrics* 629, 632 (1998).

18. Carl Kaplan, "Is a Better CDA Preferable to Opaque Censorship?" *New York Times Online,* Oct. 30,1997, http://www.nytimes.com (quoting Lessig in part); see also Irene Graham, "Will PICS Torch Free Speech on the Internet?" in *Filters & Freedom, supra* n. 9, p. 22.

19. Quotations are from press releases and brochures distributed at the Internet Online Summit, December 1-3, 1997, Renaissance Hotel, Washington, DC. Other companies advertising their wares included EdView, which offered a whitelist of "thousands of sites that have been reviewed and confirmed as being 'secure and smart'"; Microsoft, which touted the PICS-compatible RSACi system; and America Online, which described its "AOL Neighborhood Watch" as allowing separate restricted-access settings for "kids only," "young teens," and "mature teens."

20. Press releases distributed by Net Shepherd at Internet Online Summit, Dec. 1-3, 1997.

21. "Net Shepherd Responds to the EPIC Report 'Faulty Filters,'" http://www.netshepherd.com/fsEpicResponse.htm, Dec. 2, 1997; Amy Harmon, "Ideological Foes Meet on Web Decency," Now York Times, Dec. 1, 1997, p. DI (quoting Dan Sandford, Net Shepherd's chief executive). The press conference was the first event sponsored by a new coalition called IFEA (Internet Free Expression Alliance), which included, among others, the ACLU, the American Society of Newspaper Editors, PEN, the Society of Professional Journalists, and EPIC. See IFEA Mission *Statement, h*ttp://www.epic.org; Press Release on Internet Ratings and Filters, *Cyber-Liberties,* Nov. 25, 1997, http://www.aclu.org. Filtering companies did attempt to improve their accuracy by using "text strings" in place of single keywords, and sophisticated techniques for identifying nude images on the basis of flesh tones and curves. But the errors did not abate; see, e.g., Dick Kelsey, "Pom-Detection Software Scans Photos," Computer, June 1, 2000, http://www.currents.net/news/00/06/01/news2.html (describing Heartsoft, Inc.'s image-scanning software); Declan McCullagh, "Smart Filter Blocks All But Smut," *Wired News,* June 25, 2000, http://www.wired.com/news/technology/ 0,1282,36923,00.html (describing Exotrope, Inc.'s software, which "incorrectly blocked dozens of photographs including portraits, landscapes, animals, and street scenes"). Filters also sometimes openly discriminated: the same "fulminations against gays and lesbians" that went unfiltered by Cyber Patrol, SurfWatch, and other popular products when found on the conservative Web sites of Focus on the Family and Concerned Women for America were blocked when "duplicated and placed on personal Web pages." Declan McCullagh, "Filters Kowtowing to Hate?" *Wired News,* May 27, 2000, http://www.wired.com/news/print/ 0,1294,36621,00.html.

22. *Remarks by Vice President Al Gore at the Internet/Online Summit*, Dec. 2, 1997, "fight censorship" e-mail list, Dec. 4, 1997; author's notes.

23. Author's notes (Hughes quote); Aaron Pressman, "Voluntary Internet Measures Endorsed to Protect Kids," Reuters, Dec. 1, 1997, "fight censorship" e-mail list, Dec. 2, 1997.

24. Harmon, *supra n.* 21, p. D6.

25. *American Library Ass'n v. Pataki*, 969 F. Supp. 160 (S.D.N.Y. 1997).

26. *ACLU v. Johnson*, 4 F. Supp.2d 1029 (D.N.M. 1998), aff'd, 194 F.3d 1149 (10th Cir. 1999); *ACLU v. Miller*, 977 F. Supp. 1228 (N.D. Ga. 1997*); Cyberspace Comm'ns v. Engler*, 55 F. Supp. 2d 737 (D. Mich. 1999), aff'd without opinion (6th Cir. 2000); *PSINET, Inc. v. Chapman*, 108 F. Supp. 2d 611 (E.D. Va. 2000) (granting preliminary injunction).

27. Complaint in *Mainstream Loudoun v. Board of Trustees of Loudoun County Library*, No. 97-2049-A (E.D.Va. Dec. 22, 1997). The board called it a "Sexual Harassment Policy," though it did not address acts of harassment or noncomputer-based sexual material.

28. See *Mainstream Loudoun,* 24 F. Supp. 2d 553 (E.D. Va. 1998); Complaint in *Mainstream Loudoun,* ¶¶105, 119; Plaintiff-Intervenors' Complaint (Feb. 5, 1998); Jon Echtenkamp, "Library Picks Software," *Loudoun Times-Mirror,* Nov. 19, 1997, p. AI; Wallace, *supra* n. 8.

29. The other intervenor-plaintiffs were Banned Books On-line; *Ethical Spectacle* online magazine; Books for Gay and Lesbian Teens/Youth Page; artist Sergio Arau; and *San Francisco Examiner* columnist Rob Morse.

30. Brief in Support of Motion to Intervene, *Mainstream Loudoun,* Feb. 5, 1998, p. 13; Plaintiffs' Opposition to Defendants' Motion to Dismiss, p. 16. The Supreme Court's school library case was *Board of Ed. v. Pico,* 457 U.S. 853 (1982).

31. *Mainstream Loudoun v. Board of Trustees, 2* F. Supp. 2d 783, 794-95 (E.D.Va. 1998); 24 F. Supp. 2d at 561-57.

32. By the end of 1999, the profiltering group Filtering Facts reported that nearly 1,000 public library systems in the U.S. were using filters on all of their computer terminals. Associated Press, "Libraries Struggle with Pressure to Filter Internet," *Freedom Forum Online* (Dec. 10, 1999), http://www.freedomforum.org/speech/1999/12/10filters.asp. The next year, filtering became a ballot issue in southwestern Michigan, as the American Family Association invested $35,000 in a campaign in the small city of Holland to require library filters. Voters rejected the proposal 55% to 45%, after which the neighboring municipality of Hudsonville rescinded a filtering ordinance its city commissioners had passed the previous December. Keith Bradsher, "Town Rejects Bid to Curb Library's Internet Access," *New York Times,* Feb. 24, 2000, p. A12; Dave Yonkman, "Hudsonville Library Users Have Web Access Restored," *Holland Sentinel,* Feb. 24, 2000, http://www. thehollandsentinel.net/stories/022400/new_hudsonville. html.

33. Katie Hafner, "Library Grapples with Internet Freedom," *New York Times,* Oct. 15, 1998, pp. GI, G8; Wendy Leibowitz, "Shield Judges from Sex?" *National Law Journal,* May 18, 1998, p. A7; American Family Association Action Alert, "Cyber Patrol Filtering Software Blocks AFA Website," May 28, 1998, http://www.afa.net; see also *Censorship in a Box: Why Blocking Software Is Wrong for Public Libraries* (New York: ACLU, June 1998), p. 4, reprinted in *Filters and Freedom, supra* n. 10, p. 121; Courtney Macavinta, "Report Attacks SmartFilter's Blocking Criteria," *CNET News.com,* Mar. 23, 1999, http://www.news.com/ News/Item/0,4,34154,00. html; The Censorware Project, *Censored Internet Access in Utah Public Schools and Libraries,* Mar. 1999, (reporting also that SmartFilter censored music lyrics with terms such as "tap" and "surveillance," a scholarly paper about Nazi Germany, a court decision in a drug case, the Iowa State Division of Narcotics Enforcement, and a government brochure, *Marijuana: Facts for Teens),* reprinted in *Filters and Freedom,* p. 67. The Peacefire Web site eventually published reports on massive overblocking by most filters, *e.g.,* http://www.peacefire.org/censorware/FamilyClick/familyclick-blocked.html (report on AIDS blocked, along with advice for victims of pulmonary disease). The ZapMe Company's computers, provided free to schools, limited students to sites chosen by ZapMe and forced them "to view everything through the ZapMe 'Netspace,' a bordered frame containing a constantly rotating series of ads" for Frito-Lay and Topps bubble gum, among other sponsors. Steven Manning, "Reading, Writing and Candy Ads," *Salon.com,* Aug. 15, 2000, http://www.salon.com/tech/feature/2000/08/15/zapme/index.html.

34. *Statement of American Library Ass'n to U.S. Senate Commerce, Science & Transportation Comm. on Indecency on the Internet,* Feb. 10, 1998, reprinted in *Newsletter on Intellectual Freedom* (May 1998), p. 94; see also "Filtering the Internet," *New York Times,* Mar, 16, 1998, p. A24, noting distinction between parents' choice to install software and government's mandating its use.

35. White House Press Release, Statement of the Vice President on Protecting Our Children from Inappropriate Material on the Internet, Mar. 23, 1998.

36. "Children's Internet Protection Act," Title XVII of the Labor, HHS and Education Appropriations Act, P.L. 106-954, 114 Stat. 2763, 106th Cong., 2nd Sess. (2000); see "Federal Filtering Mandate Moves Toward Enactment," *EPIC Alert* Vol. 7.19 (Oct. 31, 2000); "A Misguided Pornography Bill," *New York Times* Week in Review, Nov. 12, 2000, p.14 (editorial on inadvisability of mandated filtering and host of educational sites blocked by

filters). In 1999, three states (Arizona, South Dakota, and Michigan) passed laws requiring public libraries to install filters or otherwise develop policies restricting minors' computer access.

37. David Hudson, "Company to Filter Internet Access for All Tennessee Public Schools," *Freedom Forum Online,* Nov. 11; 1998, http://www.freedomforum.org/speech/1998/11/ 11ena.asp.

38. Anemona Hartocollis, "Board Blocks Student Access to Web Sites," *New York Times,* Nov. 10, 1999, pp. B1, B8. A Commerce Department report earlier in 1999 obliquely made the same point: lower-income youths (who are disproportionately minorities) depend more heavily on public Internet access at community centers, schools, and libraries. National Telecomm'ns & Information Admin., *Falling Through the Net: Defining the Digital Divide* (Washington, DC: U.S. Dep't of Commerce, July 1999).

39. 390 U.S. 629 (1968).

40. The other plaintiffs were the ACLU; American Booksellers Foundation for Free Expression; Blackstripe (an online forum for gay and lesbian African Americans); Electronic Frontier Foundation; Electronic Privacy Information Center; Free Speech Media (an online host for independent audio and video); Internet Content Coalition (an association of content providers including *The New York Times* and *Time, Inc.);* Philadelphia Gay News, PlanetOut Corporation (a Web site for "gay, lesbian, bisexual and transgendered persons"); Salon Internet, Inc. (publisher of the popular online magazine); and West Stock, Inc. (a Web site for the display and sale of stock photographs). All said they engaged in commercial activity, thus subjecting them to COPA.

41. *ACLU v. Reno ("Reno II"),* 31 F. Supp. 2d 473, 498 (E.D.Pa. 1999), aff'd, 217 F.3d 162 (3d Cir. 2000).

42. Brief for the Appellant, *ACLU v. Reno,* No. 99-1324 (3d Cir. July 26, 1999); Reply Brief for the Appellant (Sept. 13, 1999), p. 24.

43. *Reno II,* 217 F.3d. at 173-77. COPA also mandated the creation of a commission to study technological solutions to the problem of online sexual content. Among the witnesses at the commission's hearings in 2000 were anti-pornography advocates and filtering manufacturers touting their wares, but also EPIC attorney David Sobel, who testified that because the definition of "harmful to minors" is so vague, any discussion of blocking "treads on thin constitutional ice." David McGuire, "Online Porn Panel Wrestles with Age Verification," *Computer,* June 11, 2000, http://www. currents.net/news/00/06/10/news5.html; see also http://www.copacommission.org. As this book went to press, the Supreme Court had not yet ruled on COPA.

44. "Dear Sir/Madam" Letter from Chief Inspector Stephen French, Metropolitan Police Service, London, to "All Internet Service Providers," Aug. 9, 1996, http://www.liberty.org.uk/cacib/ theMet.html; Angus Hamilton, 'The Net Out of Control: A New Moral Panic - Censorship and Sexuality," in *Liberating Cyberspace: Civil Liberties, Human Rights and the Internet (*ed. Liberty) (London: Pluto, 1999), pp. 174-75. The French Letter arrived in ISP mailboxes about a month after the House of Lords had issued a major report, *Agenda for Action in the UK,* which urged "voluntary" industry self-regulation of Internet content in order to "meet public concerns" about violent, sexual, or extremist online speech and "avoid demands for inappropriate legislation." *Agenda for Action in the UK,* 1995-96, 5th Report (July 23, 1996), http://www.parliament.the-stationery-office.co.uk/pa/ldl99596/ldselect/inforsoc/inforsoc.htm. The UK Internet Service Providers Association responded by agreeing to "collaborate in removing 'obscene' material" from online newsgroups. Adam Newey, "Freedom of Expression: Censorship in Private Hands," in *Liberating Cyberspace, supra,* p. 32.

45. See *R-3 Safety-Net: An Industry Proposal,* Sept. 23, 1996, http://dtiinfol.dti.gov.uk/safety-net/ r3.htm; KPMG/Denton Hall, *Review of the Internet Watch Foundation* for the Dep't of Trade and Industry and the Home Office, Jan. 22, 1999, http://www.dti.gov.uk/CII/iwfreview/index.html, §§ 2.1.1-2.1.2; Internet Watch Foundation, *Rating and Filtering Internet Content: A United Kingdom Perspective,* http://www. internetwatch.org.uk/rating/rating-r.htmI (March 1998); Yaman Akdeniz, "Governance of Pornography and Child Pornography on the Global Internet: A Multi-Layered Approach," in

*Law and the Internet: Regulating Cyberspace* (Lilian Edwards & Charlotte Waelde, eds.) (Oxford: Hart, 1997), p. 235.

46. E-mail from John Wadham to author, June 14, 1999; author's interview with John Wadham, Mar. 16, 1999; author's telephone interview with John Wadham, Apr. 7, 1999; author's telephone interview with Alex Hamilton, treasurer and executive committee member of Liberty, Apr. 13, 1999; author's interview with Mark Stephens, Mar. 17, 1999 (recalling that Peter Dawe, a foundation executive who had given the IWF its start-up funding, approached him out of concern that there was "nobody representing civil liberties" on the Advisory Committee, and "asked me if I would do it and would Liberty nominate me").

47. Wendy Grossman, "Europe Readies Net Content Ratings," *Wired News,* July 7, 1997, http://www.wired.com/news/news/politics/story/5002.html.

48. *Rating and Filtering, supra* n. 45; author's interview with David Kerr, Mar. 15, 1999. Kerr indicated during the interview that the "adult themes" category might be dropped.

49. E-mail from Yaman Akdeniz to author, Mar. 19, 1999; author's telephone interview with Alex Hamilton, Apr. 13, 1999; author's interview with John Wadham, Mar. 16, 1999; author's interview with Malcolm Hutty, Mar. 24, 1999. In 1997, Cyber-Rights and Cyber-Liberties published a critique of the IWF's filtering plans: "Who Watches the Watchmen: Internet Content Rating Systems, and Privatised Censorship," http://www.leeds,ac.uk/law/pgs/yaman/watchmen.htm, reprinted in *Filters and Freedom: Free Speech Perspectives on Internet Content Controls* , p. 33.

50. Internet Watch Foundation, *Rating Legal Material,* http://www.iwf.org.uk/rating/rating.html; *Rating and Filtering, supra* n. 45.

51. E-mail from David Kerr to author, June 15, 1999. The author's inquiries in early 1999 precipitated the removal of Liberty's name as a sponsoring organization from the IWF's Web site.

52. E-mail correspondence between Yaman Akdeniz and Clive Feather, Nov. 23, 1999, distributed via http://www.cyberrights.org; Liberty Policy on *Internet Encryption and Rating Systems, July* 1999. In 2000, Malcolm Hutty, director of CACIB (Campaign Against Censorship of the Internet in Britain), agreed to join the IWF board, explaining: "The IWF does constitute a base from which the pro-censorship lobby can work to achieve their goals. I think by having a civil liberties person on the inside many, though probably not all, such poor decisions can be averted." E-mail from Malcolm Hutty to author, May 23, 2000.

53. Liz Parratt & John Wadham, "Introduction," in *Liberating Cyberspace, supra* n. 44, p. 4. One of the contributors to the volume did mention "serious concerns about the effect that centralised rating might have on free expression online": Adam Newey, "Freedom of Expression: Censorship in Private Hands," *Liberating Cyberspace,* p. 44.

54. Nigel Williams, "Pornography," *Nucleus* (Oct. 1997), http::/www.cmf.org.uk/ pubs/nucleus/nucoct97/pornog.htm; see also Nigel Williams & Claire Wilson-, Thomas, *Laid Bare: A Path Through the Pornography Maze* (London: Hodder & Stoughton, 1996), p. 81 (urging prayer and confession as cures for pornography use). Williams should not be confused with the English novelist Nigel Williams.

55. See Penny Campbell & Emmanuelle Machet, "European Policy on Regulation of Content on the Internet," in *Liberating Cyberspace,* p. 140.

56. See Nicholas Rengger, *Treaties and Alliances of the World* (6th ed.) (London: Cartermill Int'l, 1995), p. 252; David Goldberg *et al., EC Media Law and Pol*icy (London: Addison-Wesley Longman, 1998), p. 8, n. 2; Robert Cottrell, "Europe: So Far, It Flies," *New York Review of Books,* Apr. 8, 1999, pp. 66-73 (describing agreements beginning with the Treaty of Rome that set up the EC or Common Market in 1957-not to be confused with the 1950 Treaty of Rome that produced the European Convention on Human Rights-and continuing through the Treaty of Maastricht that created the EU in 1993).

57. *Television Without Frontiers Directive,* European Parliament & Council, 89/552/EEC (Oct. 3, 1989), as amended by Eur. Parl. & Council Dir. 97/36/EC, reprinted in *Audiovisual Policy of the European Union* (European Commission, DG 10, 1998); see Oxford University Programme in Comparative Media Law & Policy, *Final Report: Parental Control of*

*Television Broadcasting* (1999), pp. 41-44, http://europa.eu.int/comm/dg10; Goldberg et al., *supra* n. 56, pp, 56-75.

58. Author's interview with David Hughes, Mar. 3, 1999; e-mail from David Hughes to author, Mar. 25, 1999.

59. *Television Without Frontiers, supra* n. 57, Art. 22 (emphasis added).

60. Case E-8/97, *TV 1000 Sverige AB & Norwegian Gov't* (June 12, 1998), ¶¶ 24, 26.

61. *Final Report, supra* n. 57, Executive Summary; ch. 2.

62. *Id.*, Executive Summary.

63. *Id.*

64. *Id.*, ch. 3.

65. Author's interview with David Hughes, Mar. 3, 1999.

66. European Commission working party on illegal and harmful content on the Internet, Report (1997), Introduction, http: //www 2.echo.lu/legal/en/internet/wpen.html.

67. *Communication* to the European Parliament, the Economic & Social Committee, & the Committee of the Regions, *Illegal and Harmful Content on the Internet* (Oct. 16, 1996), http://www2.echo.lu/legal/en/intemet/communic.html; *Green Paper on the Protection of Minors and Human Dignity in Audiovisual and Information Services* (Oct. 16, 1996), http://www2.echo.lu/legal/en/internet/gpen.txt.html, or http://www.europa.int/en/record/green/gp9610/protec.htm.

68. *Communication, supra* n. 66, Introduction, §§ 3, 5.

69. Id., § 5(f).

70. *Green Paper, supra* n. 67, Introduction & Summary; ch. 1, § 1, ch. 2, §§ 2, 2.2, 2.2.2, ch. 3, § 3.2.

71. Working party *Report, supra* n. 66.

72. European Commission Legal Advisory Board, *Response to the Green Paper on the Protection of Minors and Human Dignity in Audiovisual and Information Services*, http://www2.echo.lu/legal/en/internet/gplabrep.html, § 3.5.2.

73. *Resolution on the Commission Communication on Illegal and Harmful Content on the Internet*, COM(96), 0487-C4-0592/96 (Apr. 24, 1997), http://www.europarl.eu.int.

74. *Opinion of the Committee on Women's Rights, Letter from the Chairperson of the Committee (Nel van Dijk) to Mrs. Hedy dAncona, Chairperson of Comm. on Civil Liberties & Internal Affairs*, Jan. 24, 1997 (appended to the Resolution, *supra* n. 73).

75. Economic and Social Comm., *Opinion on the "Proposal for a Council Decision Adopting a Multiannual Community Action Plan on Promoting Safe Use of the Internet,"* Official Journal C 214, July 10, 1998; Comm. on Culture, Youth, Education and the Media, *Opinion for the Comm. on Civil Liberties & Internal Affairs on the Commission Communication on Illegal and Harmful Content on the Internet*; Nov. 19, 1996, and Feb. 27, 1997 (appended to the Resolution, *supra* n. 73).

76. IRIS, *Libertés individuelles et libertés publiques sur Internet*, Oct. 1997, Annexe VI, François Archimbaud, *Étiquetage et filtrage: possibilités, dangers, et perspectives*, http://www.iris.sgdg/documents/rapport-ce/annex6.html.

77. *La Lettre electronique d'Iris*, No. 1 (Jan. 19, 1998), http://www.iris.sgdg.org/lesiris/li1.html. The Conseil d'État's 1998 report on the Internet surveyed a range of legal issues (privacy, consumer protection, cryptology, domain names); with respect to industry self-regulation, it tended to agree with IRIS that rating and blocking reflected "an Anglo-Saxon behavioural influence that does not correspond to the French ways of thinking and traditions." Council of State, *The Internet and Digital Networks* (1998), http://www.ladocfrancaise.gouv.fi.

78. *GILC Submission on PICS*, Dec. 1997, http://www.gilc.org/speech/ratings/gilc-pics-submission.html, reprinted in *Filters and Freedom, supra* n. 10, p. 103.

79. Global Internet Liberty Campaign, *"Regardless of Frontiers": Protecting the Human Rights to Freedom of Expression on the Global Internet* (Sept. 1998); http://www.gilc.org.

80. *Action Plan on Promoting Safer Use of the Internet: The European Union Adopts Action Plan*, OJ L 98/560/EC Official Journal L 270 (Oct. 7, 1998), p. 48; Decision No. 276/1999 of the European Parliament & Council, Jan. 25, 1999, http://www2.echo.lu/legal/en/internet/actplan.html.

81. *Action Plan Preparatory Actions*, DG 13 Web site, http://www2.echo.lu/iap.

82. IWF press release, "IWFA Founding Member of New Rating Body-ICRA," May 12, 1999; Don Jellinek, "Web Warning on X-Rated Material," *The Guardian*, Online, Apr. 29, 1999, p. 5; ICRA press release, "Committee to Help Revise International Filtering and Labeling System to Protect Children from Harmful Internet Content," Apr. 4, 2000, http://www.icra. org/press/p6.htm (asserting that "to date, more than 130,000 Web sites have rated with the RSACi system, including a great number of the top 100 sites which account for 80% of the web's traffic," and announcing new advisory board members, including Jerry Berman of the Center for Democracy & Technology, Jack Balkin of Yale Law School, and Nigel Williams of Childnet International).

83. Bertelsmann Foundation, *Memorandum on Self-Regulation of the Internet*, and *Comments on the Memorandum*, http://www.stiftung.bertelsmann.de/internetcontent/english/ frameset_nojs.htm; Pamela Mendels, "Plan Calls for Self-Policing of the Internet" *New York Times*, Sept 20, 1999, p. C5; Matthew Yeomans, "The World's Wide Web: The Rating Came," *Industry Standard*, Sept. 30, 1999, http://www.thestandard.com/articles/display/ 0,1449,6705,00. html.

84. Information Society Project ("an international project, sponsored by the Bertelsmann Foundation"), Yale Law School, *Draft Recommendations for Initiative for Self-Regulation on the Internet: Rating and Filtering*, Apr. 16, 1999, http://www.law.yale.edu/infosociety/ filtering_recommendations.html, offering as examples of possible "meta-tag" creators the Catholic Church and the National Abortion Rights Action League.

85. Yeomans, *supra* n. 83.

86. Global Internet Liberty Campaign, *Member Statement Submitted to the Internet Content Summit*, Munich, Germany, Sept. 9-11, 1999, http://www.gilc.org/speech/ratings/gilc-munich. html, see also Mendels, *supra* n. 83; Courtney Macavinta, "AOL, Others Plan Global Net Content Rating System,"CNET News.com, Sept. 2, 1999, http://www.news.com/News/Item/ Textonly/0.25,41248.00.html.

87. Michael Sims & Jamie McCarthy, "Munich: The Censors' Convention," *Internet Freedom*, Sept. 18, 1999, http://www.netfreedom.org/news.asp?item+87.

88. Center for Democracy & Technology, *First Amendment and Free Expression: An Analysis of the Bertelsmann Foundation Memorandum on Self-Regulation of Internet Content: Concerns from a User Empowerment Perspective*, Oct. 24, 1999, http://www.cdt.org/speech/ bertelsmannmemo.shtml.

89. David Kerr, *Final Report: Self-Labelling and Filtering* (INCORE, Apr. 2000), http://www.ispo.cec.be/iap/INCOREexec.html; *Final Report: Review of European Third-Party Filtering and Rating Software Services* (IDATE, Dec. 1999), http://www.ispo. cec.be/iap.IDATEexec.html; Katharine Schmidt, "Babysitter or Big Brother?" *Wall Street Journal*, June 13, 2000, http://interactive.wsj.com/public/current/articles/ SB96032339330267771.htm. ICRA also began to have doubts about the viability of global ratings. A report by its advisory board in August 2000 expressed frustration at "the failure" of RSACi to achieve wide acceptance among either online publishers or parents, and recommended more reliance on third-party blacklists, especially for difficult categories like nudity, language, and sports violence. *Report of the Advisory Board*, Aug. 4, 2000, http://www.icra.org/adreport.htm. In Britain, meanwhile, the IWF announced that, at the behest of the government, it would begin to police online racism. But because it was often difficult to determine the legality of offensive speech about race, the IWF would not "ask anyone to remove material unless government prosecutors 'say they would be able to get a result in court.'" David Kerr said: " 'Quite frankly, to an extent this is a hot potato for the government and we are not going to allow them to dump it on us.'" Lakshmi Chaudhry, "British ISPs Crack Down on Hate," Jan. 25, 2000, http://www.wired.com/news/polifics/ 0,1283,33906.00.html; Alan Travis, 'Watchdog Moves to Curb Racist Websites," *The Guardian*, Jan. 26, 2000, http://www.newsunlimited.co.uk/uk_news/story/ 0,3604,128923.00.html.

90. See Office of Film & Literature Classification, *Guidelines for the Classification of Films and Videotapes* (Sydney, July 1996) (mandatory classification system); *Printed Matter*

*Classification Guidelines* (Sydney, July 1992) (voluntary classification system for "printed matter," which nevertheless mandated that unclassified publications had to "observe requirements" regarding display and access by youngsters "that would attach to such publications if classified"); Internet Industry Association, Internet Industry Code of Practice, Feb. 12, 1999, http://www.IIA.net.au/Code4.html (agreeing that companies would label and segregate "content, the possession of which while not illegal . . . , is nevertheless determined by the Relevant Authority to be unsuitable for minors in accordance with the National Classification Code"; "Relevant Authority" meant any group authorized by "statute, ministerial direction or parliamentary intent" to assign classifications, "including the Telecommunications Ombudsman, the Australian Broadcasting Authority, and the Federal or State Police).

91.  James Glave, "No Smut Please, We're Australian," *Wired News,* Apr. 22, 1999, http://www.wired.com/news/news/politics/story/19268.html; see also Adam Creed, "Australian Net Regulation Plans Draw Industry Fire," *Newsbytes,* Mar. 21, 1999, http://www.newsbytes.com; "Stop! Police!" *Sydney Morning Herald* online, May 8, 1999, wysiwyg://73/http://www.smh.com.au/icon/ 990508/cover.html.

92.  Broadcasting Services Amendment (Online Services Act); Pt. 3, Div. 1, cl. 10-11; Pt. 4, Div. 1-3; Pt 1, cl. 4. The law also provided for industry self-censorship codes, to be supplemented or replaced by governmental standards if not considered adequate, *id.,* Pt. 5.

93.  Stewart Taggart, "Australian Net Censor Law Passes," *Wired News,* July 7, 1999, http://www.wired.com/news/print_version/politics/story/20499html (reporting Electronic Frontiers Australia's description of the law as "political posturing, designed to create the illusion that the government was 'cleaning up the Internet,' while in fact the amendments have done nothing to stop any end-user accessing anything they please"); Luisa Bustos, "ABA Starts Cleaning Up the Web," *Network Today World*, Jan. 21, 2000, http://www2.idg.com.au/ nww; Simon Hayes & James Riley, "Censor to Face High Court Test," *Australian IT*, Jan. 31, 2000, http://www.australianit.com.au/com (reporting Eros Foundation's plan to bring a constitutional challenge to the law); Jamie Murphy, "Australia Using Law to Go After Objectionable Sites," *New York Times on the Web,* Feb. 19, 2000, http://www.nytimes. com/library/tech/00/02/cyber/articles/19australia.html

94.  Author's interview with Richard Swetenham, Mar. 2, 1999.

# A Brief History of Censorship

**Christopher Hunter**

The urge to censor that which is new, unpopular, and uncomfortable is one of the oldest and most basic of human urges. The desire to censor largely grows out of a perceived need to protect a community (especially children) from the supposedly harmful ideas espoused by those who dissent from conventional community norms. This sets up the classical debate between the rights of the community to preserve its norms and the rights of the individual to self-determination. As Garry (1993) frames the problem:

> There has historically existed a fear that individual liberties and community control are incompatible and even destructive of each other. Libertarians who seek expansion of individual freedom see censorship as the effort of an intolerant community to impose conformity and to diminish the range of freedom available to its individual members. Those who believe that too much individual freedom undermines community see censorship as a means of empowering community to deal with the destructive excesses of individual freedom. (p. 107)

Perhaps the oldest and most famous example of censorship best illustrates this dilemma. Ancient Greece is often held up as a progressive and democratic society which valued free thought, and even political dissent. However, in 399 B.C. Socrates severely challenged these ideals. For questioning the existence of the gods and denouncing Athenian democracy, Socrates was charged with corrupting youth and offending the gods. Sticking to his ideals, Socrates chose hemlock and death, rather than bend to the mores of Athenian society (Stone, 1987; Riley, 1998).

---

This essay is excerpted from Hunter's MA thesis "Filtering the Future?" Available online: http://www.ala.org/alaorg/oif/hunterthesis.html.

Running contrary to Socrates truth seeking individuality, his philosophical counterpart, Plato, argued for the near total protection of the community from dissenting opinions. In *The Republic*, Plato argues the need for extensive censorship to protect the education of children, the morals of citizens, and to generally achieve a good and just society (Wolfson, 1997: p. 23). Indeed, Plato notes, "Then the first thing will be to establish a censorship of the writers of fiction, and . . . reject the bad (1977)." Plato goes on to argue for the censorship of playwrights, poets, and music. Warning of the influence of storytellers Plato comments:

> Children cannot distinguish between what is allegory and what isn't, and opinions formed at that age are usually difficult to eradicate or change; it is therefore of the utmost importance that the first stories they hear shall aim at producing the right moral effect. (1977)

Based on these arguments Plato even called for the censorship of Homer's *Odyssey*.

Yet another Greek philosopher, Aristotle, also laid the foundation for the suppression of ideas based on a concern for community. To Aristotle, the state was the ultimate embodiment of man's desire for the good life. Thus the state is the highest representation of community, and is therefore justified in curbing speech which detracts from the good life. As Smolla (1992) notes:

> When this Aristotelian impulse is the dominant mode of thinking in a society, there will be an inexorable tendency to think it reasonable for the state to exercise control over speech. Speech that promotes the good life, speech that affirms values of community, justice, and the rule of law, will be fostered and nurtured by the state, speech destructive of those ends will be condemned. (p. 71)

While it is clear that Greek philosophers laid the foundation for, and even practiced censorship, it was the Romans who brought us the term, and bureaucratized its enforcement. In 443 B.C. the Romans established the office of the censor (from the Latin "censere") whose duty was to count citizens for political, military, and taxation purposes (Hoyt, 1970: p. 9). Additionally, Censors, appointed by the state to five year terms, established standards for citizenship. These included moral standards such as religious worship and general public conduct. Censors had the power to strip Romans of citizenship if they disapproved of public or private behavior. Cato the Elder was the most famous of Roman Censors (Jansen, 1988: p. 41). Under subsequent Roman rulers, the office of the censor was used to persecute Jews, Catholics, and the unpopular works of various Greek and Roman authors. Under the reign of Nero, censorship of Christian proselytizers reached a bloody new peak. As recounted by Tacitus (cited in Jansen, 1988):

> They died in torments, and their torments were embittered by insult and derision. Some were nailed on crosses; others sewn up in the skins of wild beasts and exposed to the fury of dogs; others again, smeared over with combustible materials, were used as torches to illuminate the darkness of night. (p. 43)

Following the rise of Christianity the Church became the main force behind the censorship of materials. Contrary to popular belief, the early Church primarily censored literature deemed dangerous to religious or political authority, not immoral, filthy, or depraved writing. For example, the first act of Church censorship, the banning of *Acti Pauli* (about the life of St. Paul) in 150 A.D., was justified on doctrinal grounds (Jansen, 1988: p. 47). When the Church of Rome laid down its rules for the censorship of books in the fourth century A.D. it made no mention of public morals, but rather forbade Christians from circulating or possessing writings of the old pagans — the unbelievers (Hoyt, 1970: p. 12).

Under this censorship regime, the Church came to control the vast majority of books in pre-printing press Europe. Lists of forbidden books would occasionally be distributed, again, largely aimed at religious heresies such as Gnosticism. The Church also maintained its control over the written word through its monopoly of medieval education. For the few who sought higher education in religion, philosophy, and science, the only books available were hand copied manuscripts (often transcribed by monks) already deemed acceptable by the Church (Hoyt, 1970: p. 12).

All of this radically changed when Johann Gutenberg invented the printing press and published his first bible around 1450. Within 20 years, some 255 European towns had printing presses churning out thousands of pamphlets and books. The Church's monopoly over the written word, and thus its monopoly over the dissemination of ideas was destroyed. The printing press and Luther disintermediated the Catholic priest and laid the seeds for mass literacy, and mass political and religious dissent (Grendler, 1984; Eisenstein, 1980).

Responding to this new technology of freedom, the Church developed one of the most comprehensive and long lasting censorship regimes in human history. In 1524, under Church guidance, Charles V of Belgium published a list of censored books. Forty years later in 1564, the Church formalized the listing of banned books by publishing the *Index librorum prohibitum* (*Index of Prohibited Books*). The *Index* consisted of several parts: 1.) a listing of outright banned authors (Luther, Zwingli, Calvin, etc.), 2.) a listing of banned titles, 3.) rules for expurgation of books with some "error" which were not all bad (for example the substituting of court nobility for clerics and priests in bawdy books such as Chaucer's *Canterbury Tales*), and 4.) sweeping rules for the dissemination of printed works (Grendler, 1984: 30). Generally, the *Index* continued to punished doctrinal error, but it also expanded to include immoral and obscene works (from the Latin root, *obscensus*, meaning "filthy" or "repulsive"). As rule number eight of the original *Index* notes:

> Books which professedly deal with, narrate or teach things lascivious or obscene are absolutely prohibited, since not only the matter of faith but also that of morals, which are usually easily corrupted through the reading of such books, must be taken into consideration, and those who possess them are to be severely punished by the bishops. Ancient books written by heathens may by reason of their elegance and quality of style be permitted, **but may by no means be read to children**. (emphasis added, Modern History Sourcebook, 1999)

The *Index*, updated every fifty years and to eventually include more than 4,000 banned works (publication of the *Index* ceased in 1966), was disseminated to Catholic countries like France who implemented licensing and distribution controls over all printed material. Violators were jailed, tortured, and often put to death. Indeed, just before the French Revolution, the Bastille imprisoned more than 800 authors, printers, and book dealers (Cate, 1998). Despite these controls, and the prospect of death for violating them, a vast underground press flourished in Europe. For example, books banned by Catholic France were either published in France under the name of a foreign press, or were published in a foreign country like the Netherlands and smuggled in. In this way Europeans were exposed to the new political ideas of Locke, Milton, Rousseau, and other Enlightenment writers. Works that laid the theoretical and political foundations for the French Revolution, and other similar uprisings throughout Europe (Alter, 1984: p. 17).

Following the French Revolution, censorship entered a new phase in both its enforcement, and its favored topic. First, the late 18th century revolutions sweeping Europe and the new world severely curbed the political authority of the church. Thus the power of censorship was passed to secular parliaments and rulers. In doing so, the major target of censorship also changed (Hoyt, 1970: p. 14).

Concurrent with the revolutions mentioned above, was the rise of mass literacy and a flourishing press. Newspapers helped aggregate what was previously only separate local communities and opinions into a nationally "imagined community" with a collective voice expressed via public opinion (Tarde, 1898: Anderson, 1991: Carey 1995). No longer could rulers ignore the "will of the people." As such, they became obsessed with the potentially dangerous moral and ideological ideas spread though public media. Goldstein (1989) summarizes this trend in his book about 19th century political censorship:

> Censorship of the press and arts above all reflects the fact that, in an age of urban industrialization, widespread literacy and rapid transportation and communications, what average citizens think matters to political leaders. Much of the political struggle therefore consists of a battle for control of the minds of the population. (xiv)

Evidence of this shift away from religious censorship and towards state sponsored moral control of the public first emerged in 18th century England. In 1727, Richard Curl was convicted by an English court for publishing *Venus in the Cloister, or the Nun in Her Smock*. The lord chief justice, declared that "obscene libel" previously handled only by religious courts, was indeed a problem for secular authorities if it "reflects on religion, virtue, or morality" or "if it tends to disturb the civil order of society (Tedford, 1993: p. 12)." Thus obscenity became a crime under English common law. In 1857, Parliament officially recognized the crime of obscenity by passing the Obscene Publications Act which laid down the rules for the search, seizure, and destruction of obscene materials (Tedford, 1993: p. 13).

Helping English obscenity prosecutions along was one of the most famous censors of all time. Thomas Bowdler was an English doctor who sought to purify literature which might corrupt the morals of his fellow citizens. Bowdler took his cue from his father, who would orally "bowdlerize" morally questionable passages while reading from famous works of literature. Bowdler fondly remembers listening to his father read Shakespeare, "without knowing that those matchless tragedies containing expressions improper to be pronounced and without having any reason to suspect that any parts of the plays had been omitted (cited in Hoyt, 1970: p. 20)."

Following his desire to purify English morals, in 1802 Bowdler helped found the Society for the Suppression of Vice, whose goal was "To prevent the profanation of the Lord's Day, prosecute blasphemous publications, bring the trade in obscene books to a halt, close disorderly houses and suppress fortune tellers (in St. John-Stevas, 1962: p. 104)." From 1802 to 1807, the Society successfully prosecuted between thirty and forty obscenity cases (Tedford, 1993: p. 13).

Bowdler's high point of "delicate" censorship was the 1807 publication of *The Family Shakespeare*, "bowdlerized" to exclude profanity, indecency, and blasphemy. A second edition published in 1817 went on to become a best seller (Hoyt, 1970: p. 21).

During this period of English obscenity prosecutions, one case in particular had a great impact upon the development of U.S. ideas about censorship and the constitutional protection of books. In 1868 Lord Cockburn ruled in the obscenity case of *Regina v. Hicklin*, and enunciated the "*Hicklin* rule" for determining obscenity: "Whether the tendency of the matter charged as obscenity is to deprave and corrupt those whose minds are open to such immoral influences, and into whose hands a publication of this sort may fall (cited in Bosmajian, 1976: p. 3)." This definition, latter adopted by U.S. courts, clearly appeals to protection of the community from "dangerous" and "impure" expression.

Like Bowdler in England, America's most infamous 19th century censor, Anthony Comstock, crusaded to save the morals of his fellow citizens. However, unlike Bowdler, Comstock didn't bother editing works he disagreed with, instead he lobbied for their outright censor.

Comstock's crusade against indecent literature began in 1867 when he moved to New York City where he worked in a dry-goods store. Appalled by the filthy literature his fellow employees were reading and passing around, he tracked down the supplier of the material in question, and had him arrested. Encouraged by his early success, Comstock set about on a censorious tizzy that would last nearly fifty years.

In 1872, at age 27, Comstock founded the New York Society for the Suppression of Vice, whose state given mandate was to suppress "obscene literature" including "vile weekly newspapers" and "licentious books (Hoyt, 1970: p. 22)."

The Society received the support of several prominent New York industrialists including soap magnate Samuel Colgate, and financier J.P. Morgan (who ironically had one of the most extensive private collections of erotica in the nation).

One year after founding the New York Society, Comstock lobbied Congress to pass federal legislation outlawing the sending of "obscene or crime-inciting matter" through the mails. Prohibited material under what became known as the Comstock Law included, "every obscene, lewd, lascivious, or filthy book, pamphlet, picture, paper, letter, writing, print, or other publication of an indecent character" not to mention any material regarding contraception or abortion (Hoyt, 1970: p. 23). The Comstock Law, and the Vice Suppression Society served as models for similar laws and organizations in other U.S. cities like the New England Watch and Ward Society of Boston, and vice suppression societies in Philadelphia, Cincinnati, Chicago, and San Francisco. Many of these organizations continued their moral and legal crusades against obscenity until WW II.

Following passage of his federal anti-obscenity law, Comstock was appointed a special agent of the Post Office, a position which carried police powers. In this position, where he worked until his death in 1915, Comstock lived up to his crusading image by, according to his account, "convicting persons enough to fill a passenger train of 61 coaches, 60 coaches containing 60 passengers each, and the sixty-first almost full . . . and destroying over 160 tons of obscene literature (cited in Hoyt, 1970: p. 26)." During his reign, the U.S. Supreme Court in 1896 ruled that the Comstock Law was constitutional. In doing so, the court accepted the *"Hicklin* Rule" for defining obscenity, and thus laid the legal foundation for the future banning of great literature like James Joyce's *Ulysses*, D.H. Lawrence's *Lady Chatterly's Lover*, and Hemingway's *For Whom the Bell Tolls* (Tedford, 1993: p. 40).

Debates about the banning of obscene material continued well into the 20th century. New groups like the National Organization for Decent Literature (founded in 1955) and The Citizens for Decent Literature (1956) gained widespread support. New types of media, including paperback books, comics, and films, also came under the scrutiny of these organizations. However, in the wake of two landmark obscenity cases *Roth v. United States* (1957) and *Miller v. California* (1973) which made the legal prosecution of obscenity much more difficult, morality crusaders had to turn to new censorship tactics. These new tactics mostly consisted of community pressure against distributors of "objectionable" material, and boycotts of offending book stores and movie theaters. Such community driven efforts often ended in promises of industry self regulation via conduct codes and content rating systems such as the Motion Picture Association of America's G, PG, PG-13, R, NC-17 system. Indeed today's debate over violence on television and pornography on the Internet have resulted in similar calls for industry regulation via the labeling and filtering of content.

## The Mechanisms of Censorship

From the above discussion of the history of censorship it is possible for us to isolate out a number of elements, or mechanisms, by which censorship is bureaucratized and implemented:

*Categorization* — this is the first and most difficult mechanism of censorship. Its aim is to identify broad or narrow categories of content which are deemed off limits. As seen above, these content categories can change over time, for example from an early concern with heresy to a more recent concern with obscenity and immorality. Additional categorizations can be added (violence), or old ones dropped (heresy) as social norms change over time.

*Listing* — once authors and titles have been categorized as off limits, they must be listed and distributed to censors who can then enforce regulations against the enumerated offending works. Of great importance to the long term success of a censorship regime is the continued update of these lists to include the latest works created by pesky new authors. As a result of continual updating, lists can become extremely long (4,000 banned works in the *Index*) thus making them unwieldy and inflexible in their implementation.

*Word Filtering* — for those works categorized as "not all bad," rules must be laid down for the expurgating, or "bowdlerizing" of offending passages. Word filtering rules may require simple omission, or more extensive character or plot modification.

*Access and Distribution Control* — all points of access to content categorized as off limits must be controlled so as not to allow the censored material to be distributed to the public in its unadulterated form. For the Church and many European nations this meant licensing the use of the printing press, and for Comstock it meant controlling the mails.

It is rather interesting that the mechanisms of censorship developed some 400 years ago by the *Index*, have changed so little over time. What the *Index* was to the printing press, software filters like CyberPatrol, CYBERsitter, Net Nanny, etc. are to the digital printing press of our age, the World Wide Web. Filter makers, despite advertising their use of "advanced artificial intelligence," still rely on the age-old censorship techniques of categorization, listing, word filtering, and access controls. These techniques did not prove terribly effective in defeating the spread of the printed word, and they are sure to fail again in a digital environment where everyone is a potential publisher capable of reaching a world-wide audience.

## References

Alter, A. I. (1984). An introduction to the exhibit. in *Censorship: 500 years of conflict*. New York: New York Public Library.

Anderson, B. (1991). *Imagined communities*. New York: Verso.

Bosmajian, H. A. (1976). *Obscenity and freedom of expression*. New York: Burt Franklin.

Carey, J. (1995). The press, public opinion, and public discourse. in T. Glasser and C. Salmon (Eds.) *Public opinion and the communication of consent*. New York: Guilford. 373-403.

Cate, F.H. (1998). *The Internet and the First Amendment: Schools and sexually explicit expression*. Bloomington, IN: Phi Delta Kappa.

Eisenstein, E. (1980). *The Printing press as an agent of change: Communications and cultural transformations in early-modern Europe*. Cambridge: Cambridge University Press.

Garry, P. (1993). *An American paradox: Censorship in a nation of free speech*. Westport, CT: Praeger.

Goldstein, R. J. (1989). *Political censorship of the arts and the press in nineteenth-century Europe*. New York: St. Martin's.

Grendler, P. E. (1984). The Advent of printing. in *Censorship: 500 years of conflict*. New York: New York Public Library.

Hoyt, O. G. & Hoyt, E. P. (1970). *Censorship in America*. New York: Seabury.

Jansen, S. C. (1988). *Censorship: The Knot that binds power and knowledge*. New York: Oxford.

Modern History Sourcebook. (1999). *Rules on prohibited books*. Available via the World Wide Web at http://www.fordham.edu/halsall/mod/trent-booksrules.html.

Plato. (1977). *The Republic*. S. Buchanan Ed., New York: Penguin.

Riley, G. B. (1998). *Censorship*. New York: Facts on File.

Smolla, R. (1992). *Free speech in an open society*. New York: Vintage.

St. John-Stevas, N. (1962). The Church and censorship. in J. Chandos (Ed.). *To deprave and corrupt*. New York: Associated Press.

Stone, I. F. (1987). *The Trial of Socrates*. Boston: Little, Brown.

Tarde, G. (1898/Unpublished translation). Opinion and Conversation. in *L'opinion et la Foule*. Paris: Alcan.

Teford, T. L. (1993). *Freedom of speech in the United States*. Second Edition. New York: McGraw Hill.

Wolfson, N. (1997). *Hate speech, sex speech, free speech*. Westport, CT: Praeger.

# Statement on Library Use of Filtering Software

**American Library Association, Intellectual Freedom Committee**

On June 26, 1997, the United States Supreme Court in *Reno, Attorney General of the United States, et al. v. American Civil Liberties Union, et al.*, issued a sweeping reaffirmation of core First Amendment principles and held that communications over the Internet deserve the highest level of Constitutional protection.

The Court's most fundamental holding was that communications on the Internet deserve the same level of Constitutional protection as books, magazines, newspapers, and speakers on a street corner soapbox. The Court found that the Internet "constitutes a vast platform from which to address and hear from a world-wide audience of millions of readers, viewers, researchers, and buyers," and that "any person with a phone line can become a town crier with a voice that resonates farther than it could from any soapbox."

For libraries, the most critical holding of the Supreme Court is that libraries that make content available on the Internet can continue to do so with the same Constitutional protections that apply to the books on libraries' shelves. The Court's conclusion that "the vast democratic fora of the Internet" merit full constitutional protection serves to protect libraries that provide their patrons with access to the Internet. The Court recognized the importance of enabling individuals to receive speech from the entire world and to speak to the entire world. Libraries provide those opportunities to many who would not otherwise have them. The Supreme Court's decision protects that access.

The use in libraries of software filters to block constitutionally protected speech is inconsistent with the United States Constitution and federal law and may lead to legal exposure for the library and its governing authorities. The American Library Association affirms that the use of filtering software by libraries to block access to constitutionally protected speech violates the Library Bill of Rights.

---

ALA Intellectual Freedom Committee, July 1, 1997; Rev. November 17, 2000.

## What is Blocking/Filtering Software

Blocking/filtering software is a mechanism used to:

restrict access to Internet content, based on an internal database of the product, or; restrict access to Internet content through a database maintained external to the product itself, or; restrict access to Internet content to certain ratings assigned to those sites by a third party, or; restrict access to Internet content by scanning text, based on a keyword or phrase or text string, or; restrict access to Internet content by scanning pixels, based on color or tone, or; restrict access to Internet content based on the source of the information.

## Problems with the Use of Blocking/ Filtering Software in Libraries

Publicly supported libraries are governmental institutions subject to the First Amendment, which forbids them from restricting information based on viewpoint or content discrimination.

Libraries are places of inclusion rather than exclusion. Current blocking/filtering software not only prevents access to what some may consider "objectionable" material, but also blocks information protected by the First Amendment. The result is that legal and useful material will inevitably be blocked.

Filters can impose the producer's viewpoint on the community.

Producers do not generally reveal what is being blocked, or provide methods for users to reach sites that were inadvertently blocked.

Criteria used to block content are vaguely defined and subjectively applied.

The vast majority of Internet sites are informative and useful. Blocking/filtering software often blocks access to materials it is not designed to block.

Most blocking/filtering software was designed for the home market and was intended to respond to the preferences of parents making decisions for their children. As these products have moved into the library market, they have created a dissonance with the basic mission of libraries. Libraries are responsible for serving a broad and diverse community with different preferences and views. Blocking Internet sites is antithetical to library missions because it requires the library to limit information access.

Filtering all Internet access is a one-size-fits-all "solution," which cannot adapt to the varying ages and maturity levels of individual users.

A role of librarians is to advise and assist users in selecting information resources. Parents and only parents have the right and responsibility to restrict their own children's access—and only their own children's access—to library resources, including the Internet. Librarians do not serve in loco parentis.

Library use of blocking/filtering software creates an implied contract with parents that their children will not be able to access material on the Internet that they do not wish their children to read or view. Libraries will be unable to fulfill this implied contract, due to the technological limitations of the software.

Laws prohibiting the production or distribution of child pornography and obscenity apply to the Internet. These laws provide protection for libraries and their users.

**What Can Your Library Do to Promote Access to the Internet?**

Educate yourself, your staff, library board, governing bodies, community leaders, parents, elected officials, etc., about the Internet and how best to take advantage of the wealth of information available. Information on libraries and the Internet is available on the OIF Web site at www.ala.org/alaorg/oif/filtersandfiltering.html.

Uphold the First Amendment by establishing and implementing written guidelines and policies on Internet use in your library in keeping with your library's overall policies on access to library materials. Information on Internet Use Policies is available on the OIF Web site at www.ala.org/alaorg/ oif/internetusepolicies.html. (See also "Internet Filtering Statements of State Library Associations" at www.ala.org/alaorg/oif/stateresolutions.html and "Access to Electronic Information, Services, and Networks: An Interpretation of the Library Bill of Rights" at www.ala.org/alaorg/oif/electacc.html.)

Promote Internet use by facilitating user access to Web sites that satisfy user interest and needs.

Create and promote library Web pages designed both for general use and for use by children. These pages should point to sites that have been reviewed by library staff.

Consider using privacy screens or arranging terminals away from public view to protect a user's confidentiality.

Provide Internet information and training for parents and children on internet use which will include; the wide variety of useful resources on the internet, child safety on the Internet, limitations of filtering software and library rules regarding time, place and manner restriction.

Establish and implement user behavior policies.

# Statement of the American Library Association to the Senate Commerce, Science and Transportation Committee on Indecency on the Internet

**ALA Washington Office, February 10, 1998**

---

The American Library Association submits this statement to the Senate Commerce, Science and Transportation Committee to express our grave concerns about proposed legislation which, as we understand it, would create a federal mandate for schools and libraries applying for universal service discounts to install filtering and blocking software in order to participate in the universal service program.

The American Library Association (ALA) is the nation's oldest and largest association of librarians with approximately 56,000 members, including members of the American Association of School Librarians (AASL), the Association of Library Services to Children (ALSC), the Young Adult Library Services Association (YALSA) and the Public Library Association (PLA).

We recognize the serious issues raised by this hearing and acknowledge that as new technologies proliferate, we must balance the extraordinary value they bring to communications and learning with responsible use and careful guidance. However, we are concerned that a federal mandate to filter intrudes unnecessarily into the prerogatives of local community-based institutions — our public schools and public libraries — as well as into the professional expertise and judgement of public and school librarians.

We are also concerned about the constitutional implications of a filtering mandate. In 1997, the Supreme Court, in *ACLU v Reno*, unanimously struck down the Communications Decency Act which sought to limit minors access to "indecent" and "patently offensive" material on the Internet. That sweeping decision bestowed on the Internet the highest level of constitutional protection, equal to that provided books, newspapers and speakers on the street corner. The Court recognized that both children and adults have a constitutional right to access the vast majority of information on the Internet, and that while children's rights to information are not coextensive with adults, broad measures to keep them away from all "indecent" material are both unconstitutionally vague and over broad. Before the Committee considers any specific legislation, it must be carefully measured against the high barrier to further content regulation of the Internet erected by the Reno court.

We respectfully disagree with the premise that filtering software is the only effective way to guide children away from "questionable" material on the Internet. Libraries serve as a community's principal source of information. For many in a community, the public library provides the only access to the vast resources of the Internet. School libraries are integral to the curriculum and serve as resources for educating our children. The use of blocking software deprives the community of access to many sites that provide valuable as well as constitutionally protected information for both adults and children on subjects ranging from AIDS and breast cancer to religion and politics. Very often, blocking software also fails to provide "protection" from other materials that others may find "objectionable," however defined.

While blocking and filtering products can be useful tools for parents to use at home, their use in a library setting is questionable at best. Libraries serve all the families and all library users in a given community. As public institutions supported primarily by local public tax monies, libraries are obligated to meet the information needs of the entire community or school population, while upholding the basic principles of the First Amendment. Within the same community, within the same school district or library system, indeed, even within the same library or school building, users have vastly different needs. Federally mandated blocking software cannot responsibly anticipate the information and curricular needs of a community or determine the best sources of information for any particular public or school library user. This is the responsibility of library and school boards who reflect the values and standards of their constituencies and who are in the best position to know how to responsibly guide children's Internet access.

When a library installs commercial filters or blocking software, it transfers the professional judgement about the information needs of the community from the librarian to anonymous third parties — often part time workers with no credentials and no ties to the community — who evaluate sites for the software manufacturer. But it is the librarian, not the software manufacturer, who has professional skill to serve the community's information needs, the obligation to acquire materials that fulfill those needs, and the responsibility to work with governing boards to help develop policies to assure appropriate Internet use. It is also the librarian who must respond to community complaints and potential legal action over improper or inadequate blocking.

Today's children are growing up in a global information society. It is imperative that they learn critical viewing and information skills that will help them make good judgments about the information they encounter. Students of all ages must be able to assess as well as access information — i.e., be able to distinguish between information that is useful and valuable and that which is not. Children must learn to handle and reject content that may be offensive to their values and to adhere to online safety rules when confronted with uncomfortable situations. They must learn to make wise use of new information technologies and to be accountable for safe and responsible online behavior. Simply blocking offensive and unwanted content will not teach students those critical skills.

Librarians engage in many different activities aimed at helping children make wise and responsible use of the Internet. First, many libraries provide training for children, parents and teachers on appropriate use of the Internet. Second, and perhaps most importantly, libraries develop use policies for children and other library users which establish the rules for appropriate online behavior which must be followed in order to maintain on-line privileges. National professional associations, state library and education agencies and other entities also provide guidance on how to assess Internet resources and how to develop and enforce good use policies. In many libraries and schools, such use policies require both parents and children to read, discuss and sign use agreements that commit them to follow those policies and to refrain from inappropriate conduct. Supervision and guidance is provided to children using on-line resources by librarians, teachers and others whose presence assures a more valuable online experience.

Most important, librarians assure safe and positive online experiences for children through guidance to sites that are educational, entertaining and valuable based upon each child's needs. In addition to providing direct advice and guidance to children seeking to research particular topics or find certain information many individual libraries as well as the American Library Association, have developed children's web sites and home pages that lead children directly to the best the Internet has to offer. The library community is also an active source for information for parents, teachers and others in the community about assessing sources of information on the Internet.

Notwithstanding the many concerns about the use of filtering in libraries, some communities have made the judgment to install blocking software in libraries. Others have tried blocking and eventually removed the software because the blocking software has proved to be ineffective, overly broad and difficult to maintain. Still others have carefully studied the costs and benefits of filtering with their library or school boards and decided to use other methods to guide children's Internet use. But all in the library community who have looked at children's Internet access have made their decision based on professional judgement and local community circumstances and norms, not on the basis of federal mandates.

## CONCLUSION

We understand that the increased access to the Internet in schools and libraries that will accompany universal service has heightened concerns about children's access to inappropriate and illegal material. Those concerns are serious, but they are not new. Communities have been developing many different and effective ways to guide children's access that are informed by professional research and judgment and local norms and values. We urge this Committee not to interfere with local control and decision making by mandating a single approach to a multifaceted problem. There is no one right solution; there are many. We stand ready to work with this Committee to provide additional information on local policies and practices.

## REFERENCES:

1. American Library Association Selection Criteria: How to Tell if You Are Looking at A Great Web Site (http://www.ala.org/parentspage/greatsites/criteria)

2. Indiana Department of Education Requirements for Acceptable Use Policies ( http://www.siec.k12.in.us/aup/require.html)

3. American Library Association 700+ Great Sites (http://www.ala.org/parentspage/greatsites)

4. ALA American Association of School Librarians - ICONnect: Get Connected to Learning: Using the Internet (http://www.ala.org/ICONN/index.html)

5. ALA Kids Connect @ the Library: A Sampling of Library Web Sites for Parents and Kids

# Statement Before the Commission on Online Child Protection

**Electronic Privacy Information Center**

**David L. Sobel, June 9, 2000 Washington, DC**

Thank you for providing me with the opportunity to appear before the Commission to address the privacy implications of age verification technologies that might be used to restrict access to certain material on the Internet. The Electronic Privacy Information Center (EPIC), as an organization committed to the protection of both privacy rights and free expression, has a longstanding interest in this issue and has participated in relevant legislative and judicial proceedings since its inception in 1994. We also co-founded and coordinate the Internet Free Expression Alliance (www.ifea.net), a coalition of more than two dozen organizations committed to the continuation of the Internet as a forum for open, diverse and unimpeded expression with particular emphasis on both legal and technological impediments to free expression.

As an initial matter, I note that the Commission has invited me to discuss the rather limited question of whether age verification systems pose threats to personal privacy. While I welcome the opportunity to address that issue, my testimony would be incomplete if I did not say a word about the underlying premise of the Commission's inquiry, namely "to identify technological or other methods that . . . will help reduce access by minors to material that is harmful to minors on the Internet." Given the inherent subjectivity of terms such as "harmful to minors" or "indecent," I believe that efforts to mandate restrictions on access to such material are prohibited by the First Amendment, particularly in a medium like the Internet, which makes content available in every community in the nation. For that reason, EPIC participated as plaintiff and co-counsel in the constitutional challenge to the Communications Decency Act and is currently acting in a similar capacity in the pending challenge to the criminal provisions of the Child Online Protection Act (COPA). Every federal judge (including the Justices of the Supreme Court) who has considered the issue has agreed that content-based restrictions on Internet "indecent" or "harmful to minors" speech are unconstitutional.

First Amendment considerations are an important aspect of my testimony today, because I believe the privacy issues we are discussing are inseparable from the free speech issues. Any requirement that Internet users identify themselves in some way (or even take additional steps to establish that they are entitled to receive the information they seek) as a condition of access to online content necessarily chills free speech. The courts have recognized that the exercise of First Amendment rights may not be conditioned upon a surrender of personal privacy. For instance, a federal appeals court invalidated a state's requirement that citizens provide their Social Security numbers when registering to vote, finding that such requirements "compel a would-be voter . . . to consent to the possibility of a profound invasion of privacy when exercising the fundamental right to vote."[1] Likewise, mandated age verification systems impose a similar condition on an adult's right to access information on the Internet. Such requirements also infringe on the First Amendment right to communicate anonymously. As the Supreme Court stated in *McIntyre v. Ohio Elections Commission*, anonymity "exemplifies the purpose behind the Bill of Rights, and of the First Amendment in particular: to protect unpopular individuals from retaliation — and their ideas from suppression — at the hand of an intolerant society."[2]

The privacy impacts of age verification — and therefore the free speech implications — are felt by both consumers and providers of online content. From a consumer perspective, a new regime for the collection of personal data in the name of "child online protection" would impose yet another burden on the privacy of Internet users. The American people, when they go online, are already acutely aware of the fact that they are being over-monitored and over-profiled. Polling results consistently show that many Americans are "concerned" or "very concerned" about the loss of privacy, particularly with regard to commercial transactions that take place over the Internet.[3] One recent poll has indicated that the "loss of personal privacy" is the number one concern facing the United States in the twenty-first century. These results are not surprising when an Internet advertising firm such as DoubleClick reportedly has compiled approximately 100 million online user profiles to date.

Given the public concern over online privacy, it seems apparent that age verification requirements will deter most adults from accessing restricted content, because Web users are increasingly unwilling to provide identifying information in order to gain access to online content. Web users who wish to access sensitive or controversial information are even less likely to register to receive it.[4] The district court recognized this fact when it found COPA to be unconstitutional, noting that "the implementation of credit card or adult verification screens in front of material that is harmful to minors may deter users from accessing such materials."[5] Indeed, the uncontroverted evidence presented to the court established that COPA's age verification requirements would prevent or deter Web users from accessing a wide range of constitutionally protected speech.[6]

There is little doubt that all effective age verification technologies require consumers, at some stage of the verification process, to divulge personally identifiable information, whether a credit card number, driver's license, birth certificate or other documentation. The Adult Check system, for instance, claims that it has the ability to verify independently the age of an applicant and, in order to prevent "password sharing," resorts to "originating IP address verification." While some of these technologies (such as some digital certificate systems) are less invasive than others, they all require the consumer to provide personal data to a third party.[7] On a truly voluntary basis, some consumers may choose to avail themselves of such technologies in order to conduct online transactions, and when carefully implemented they can play a useful role in facilitating electronic commerce. But any governmental mandate to obtain and use such an age verifier as a condition of access to information suffers from the constitutional defects that I have discussed.

As I have noted, the use of age verification systems impacts providers of online content as well as consumers. Given the apprehension that many consumers have about obtaining an adult ID or password, content providers who would be required to impose such requirements as a condition of access to their Web sites will suffer a loss of traffic and, consequently, revenue. Indeed, the inhibiting effect of such systems formed the basis for the district court's discussion of the issue when it considered the constitutionality of COPA:

Evidence presented to this Court is likely to establish at trial that the implementation of credit card or adult verification screens in front of material that is harmful to minors may deter users from accessing such materials and that the loss of users of such material may affect the speakers' economic ability to provide such communications. The plaintiffs are likely to establish at trial that under COPA, Web site operators and content providers may feel an economic disincentive to engage in communications that are or may be considered to be harmful to minors and thus, may self-censor the content of their sites.[8]

The court's finding underscores the clear relationship between the privacy and free speech aspects of age verification requirements; one simply cannot be separated from the other. For that reason, such requirements would introduce a troubling new component into the Internet's architecture, one that would hasten the demise of both personal privacy and freedom of expression. I submit that such a result is not in the long-term interests of the emerging online industry or of an American public that is increasingly turning to this medium as a vital source of information and entertainment. Rather than focus on approaches that seek to block access to information and compromise privacy, I strongly urge both the Commission and Congress to emphasis and support educational initiatives that will help young people learn to responsibly and safely navigate this exciting and enriching medium.

## Notes

1. *Greidinger v. Davis*, 988 F.2d 1344, 1354 (4th Cir. 1993).

2. 115 S. Ct. 1511, 1524 (1995) (striking down an Ohio statute prohibiting anonymous distribution of campaign literature). *See also Lamont v. Postmaster General*, 381 U.S. 301, 307 (1965) (finding unconstitutional a requirement that recipients of communist literature notify the post office that they wish to receive it); *Talley v. California*, 362 U.S. 60, 64-65 (1960) (declaring unconstitutional a California ordinance that prohibited the distribution of anonymous handbills); *ACLU of Georgia v. Miller*, 977 F. Supp. 1228 (N.D. Ga. 1997) (striking down Georgia statute that would have made it a crime for Internet users to "falsely identify" themselves online).

3. A recent poll conducted by Newsweek asked respondents how they would feel about a Web site that "tracked your movements when you browsed the site, but didn't tie that information to your name or real-world identity." Even that relatively anonymous kind of tracking led 28 percent to say they would feel "not very comfortable" and 35 percent to feel "not at all comfortable." If the site "merged your browsing habits and shopping patterns into a profile that was linked to your real name and identity," 21 percent would feel "not very comfortable" and 68 percent "not at all comfortable." http://www.businessweek.com/2000/00_12/b3673010.htm.

4. In a related context, the Supreme Court has recognized that identification requirements can have a chilling effect on access to sexually-explicit material. In *Denver Area Educ. Telecomms. Consortium, Inc. v. FCC*, 518 U.S. 727 (1996), the Court struck down a statutory requirement that viewers provide written notice to cable operators to obtain access to certain sexually oriented programs because the requirement "restrict[s] viewing by subscribers who fear for their reputations should the operator, advertently or inadvertently, disclose the list of

those who wish to watch the . . . channel." 518 U.S. at 754. In considering the precursor to COPA, the Supreme Court found that the credit card and adult access code requirements of the CDA would also unconstitutionally inhibit adult Web browsers. *Reno v. ACLU*, 521 U.S. at 857 n.23 ("There is evidence suggesting that adult users, particularly casual Web browsers, would be discouraged from retrieving information that required use of a credit card or password.")

5. *American Civil Liberties Union v. Reno* ("*ACLU II*"), 31 F. Supp.2d 473, 495 (E.D. Pa. 1999).

6. The evidence also showed that Internet users would be deterred by adult access code services that cater to the pornography industry, and would not want to affiliate with such services in order to gain access to material deemed to be "harmful to minors."

7. Digital certification technologies can lessen the privacy and First Amendment implications of age verification systems, but not remove them entirely. Such approaches can separate personal identity from a particular certified characteristic; age, for instance. But they still impose upon the user the burden of providing information to the third party certificate issuer, a burden that raises constitutional problems when imposed as a condition of accessing a particular category of information.

8. *ACLU II*, 31 F. Supp.2d at 495.

# Member Statement on Rating and Filtering Systems

## Global Internet Liberty Campaign

Submitted to the Internet Content Summit,
Munich, Germany, September 9-11, 1999

## Summary

The creation of an international rating and filtering system for Internet content has been proposed as an alternative to national legislation regulating online speech. Contrary to their original intent, such systems may actually facilitate governmental restrictions on Internet expression. Additionally, rating and filtering schemes may prevent individuals from discussing controversial or unpopular topics, impose burdensome compliance costs on speakers, distort the fundamental cultural diversity of the Internet, enable invisible "upstream" filtering, and eventually create a homogenized Internet dominated by large commercial interests. In order to avoid the undesirable effects of legal and technical solutions that seek to block the free flow of information, alternative educational approaches should be emphasized as less restrictive means of ensuring beneficial uses of the Internet.

* * * * *

A number of serious concerns have been raised since rating and filtering systems were first proposed as voluntary alternatives to government regulation of Internet content. The international human rights and free expression communities have taken the lead in fostering more deliberate consideration of so-called "self-regulatory" approaches to Internet content control. Members of the Global Internet Liberty Campaign have monitored the development of filtering proposals around the world and have previously issued two statements on the issue -- "Impact of Self-Regulation and Filtering on Human Rights to Freedom of Expression" in March 1998 and a "Submission to the World Wide Web Consortium on PICS Rules" in December 1997. These joint statements reflect the international scope of concern over the potential impact that "voluntary" proposals to control on-line content could have on the right to freedom of opinion and expression guaranteed by Article 19 of the Universal Declaration of Human Rights. The undersigned organizations now reiterate those concerns on the occasion of the Internet Content Summit.

Originally promoted as technological alternatives that would prevent the enactment of national laws regulating Internet speech, filtering and rating systems have been shown to pose their own significant threats to free expression. When closely scrutinized, these systems should be viewed more realistically as fundamental architectural changes that may, in fact, facilitate the suppression of speech far more effectively than national laws alone ever could.

First, the existence of a standardized rating system for Internet content -- with the accompanying technical changes to facilitate blocking -- would allow governments to mandate the use of such a regime. By requiring compliance with an existing ratings system, a state could avoid the burdensome task of creating a new content classification system while defending the ratings protocol as voluntarily created and approved by private industry.

This concern is not hypothetical. Australia has already enacted legislation which mandates blocking of Internet content based on existing national film and video classification guidelines. The Broadcasting Services Amendment (Online Services) Bill places sweeping restrictions on adults providing or gaining access to material deemed unsuitable for minors as determined by Australian film and video classification standards. The Australian experience shows that even developed democracies can engage in Internet censorship, given the necessary technical tools. An international content ratings system would be such a tool, creating a ratings regime and blocking mechanisms which states could impose on their citizens.

Australia is not alone in its support of mandatory Internet content ratings systems. The United States government, in its unsuccessful defense of the Communications Decency Act, argued that the use of an Internet "tagging" scheme would serve as a defense to liability under the Act. The scenario advanced by the U.S. government would have required online speakers to "tag" material as "indecent" in a manner that would facilitate blocking of such content. That argument failed in the face of evidence that Web browsers were not yet configured to recognize and block material bearing such "tags." If the sort of "voluntary" rating systems being advocated today had been widely used in 1996, the government's argument may have prevailed.

In sum, the establishment and widespread acceptance of an international rating and blocking system could promote a new model of speech suppression, shifting the focus of governmental censorship initiatives from direct prohibition of speech to mandating the use of existing ratings and blocking technologies.

Second, the imposition of civil or criminal penalties for "mis-rating" Internet content is likely to follow any widespread deployment of a rating and blocking regime. A state-imposed penalty system that effectively deters misrepresentations would likely be proposed to facilitate effective "self-regulation." Proposed legislation creating criminal and civil liability for mis-rating Internet content has already been discussed in the United States.

In addition to their potential to actually encourage government regulation, rating and filtering systems possess other undesirable characteristics. Such systems are likely to:

> prevent individuals from using the Internet to exchange information on topics that may be controversial or unpopular;

> impose burdensome compliance costs on non-commercial or relatively small commercial speakers;

> distort the fundamental cultural diversity of the Internet by forcing Internet speech to be labeled or rated according to a single classification system;

> enable invisible "upstream" filtering by Internet Service Providers or other entities; and

> eventually create a homogenized Internet dominated by large commercial speakers.

In light of the many potential negative effects of rating and filtering systems, the movement toward their development and acceptance must be slowed. If free speech principles are to be preserved on the Internet, thoughtful consideration of these initiatives and their potential dangers is clearly warranted. Although generally well-intentioned, proposals for "self-regulation" of Internet content carry with them a substantial risk of damaging the online medium in unintended ways.

The rejection of rating and filtering systems would not leave the online community without alternatives to state regulation. In fact, alternative solutions exist that would likely be more effective than the legal and technical approaches that have created a binary view of the issue of children's access to Internet content. Approaches that emphasize education and parental supervision should receive far more attention than they have to date, as they alone possess the potential to effectively direct young people toward beneficial and appropriate uses of the Internet. Ultimately, the issue is one of values, which can only be addressed properly within a particular family or cultural environment. Neither punitive laws nor blocking technologies can ensure that a child will only access online content deemed appropriate by that child's family or community. While the Internet is a global medium, questions concerning its appropriate use can only be addressed at the most local level.

For these reasons, we urge a re-orientation of the ongoing debate over Internet content. We submit that a false dichotomy has been created, one that poses state regulation or industry "self-regulation" as the only available options. We urge a more open-minded debate that seriously explores the potential of educational approaches that are likely to be more effective and less destructive of free expression.

## For More Information

1. American Civil Liberties Union, "Fahrenheit 451.2: Is Cyberspace Burning? -- How Rating and Blocking Proposals May Torch Free Speech on the Internet"

2. Center for Democracy and Technology, Blocking and Filtering Content on the Internet after the CDA: Empowering Users and Families Without Chilling the Free Flow of Information Online"

3. Computer Professionals for Social Responsibility, "Filtering FAQ"

4. Cyber-Rights & Cyber-Liberties, "Who watches the Watchmen: Internet Content Rating Systems, and Privatised Censorship"

5. Electronic Privacy Information Center, "Faulty Filters: How Content Filters Block Access to Kid-Friendly Information on the Internet"

6. Imaginons un Réseau Internet Solidaire (IRIS), "Labeling and Filtering: Possibilities, Dangers, and Perspectives"

7. Global Internet Liberty Campaign Submission on the Illegal and Harmful Use of the Internet to the Irish Minister for Justice

8. Global Internet Liberty Campaign Member Statement on "Impact of Self-Regulation and Filtering on Human Rights to Freedom of Expression"

## List of Signatories

> ALCEI - Electronic Frontiers Italy
> American Civil Liberties Union
> Canadian Journalists for Free Expression
> Cyber-Rights & Cyber-Liberties (UK)
> Electronic Frontiers Australia
> Electronic Frontier Foundation
> Electronic Privacy Information Center
> Fsrderverein Informationstechnik und Gesellschaft (FITUG)
> Fronteras Electronicas Espana (FrEE)
> Human Rights Watch
> Imaginons un Réseau Internet Solidaire
> Index on Censorship
> Internet Freedom
> Internet Society
> Liberty (National Council for Civil Liberties)
> NetAction
> Privacy International
> Quintessenz User Group
> xs4all

61

# Blacklisting Bytes

Seth Finkelstein & Lee Tien, for the
Electronic Frontier Foundation

The Electronic Frontier Foundation's (EFF) thesis is simple: The quest for a technical solution to the alleged problem of minors' access to "harmful" material on the Internet is both misguided and dangerous to civil liberties. While we don't want to overstate our concerns, we believe that it's impossible to prevent minors from accessing large amounts of material that is accessible to adults on the Internet. Moreover, we believe that attempting to do so will build into the Internet mechanisms that can and will be used for other types of censorship. Although our discussion will focus on censorware, Prof. Lawrence Lessig has persuasively analyzed the architecture of "filtering" in terms that place censorware and ratings-based systems on the same spectrum.

Criticism of censorware isn't new. Many have argued that censorware is caught on the horns of a dilemma: if it blocks too little, it's ineffective and therefore unconstitutional; if it's effective, it blocks too much and again is unconstitutional. This White Paper will highlight what we believe is a novel aspect of the dilemma. For censorware to effectively block minors' access to "harmful" material, it must block material that isn't itself "harmful." For instance, the censorware product SmartFilter blacklists two broad classes of websites that publish no "harmful" content: privacy/anonymity service sites and language-translation services.

We don't use the term "censorware" instead of "filter" lightly or for partisan reasons. The term "filter" implies that impurities are extracted, leaving a purified result. This frames the issues in terms of content alone. We believe that "filter" euphemistically hides the real, architectural issue, control of people: censorware is about an authority preventing those under its control from reading forbidden information.

---

Originally produced as an Electronic Frontier Foundation White Paper for the National Research Council Project on Tools and Strategies for Protecting Kids from Pornography and Their Applicability to Other Inappropriate Internet Content.

That privacy, anonymity, and language-translation sites are blacklisted illustrates our point. Why are they blacklisted? Because they offer capabilities that can be used to escape the control-system. There's nothing obscene or pornographic about language translators or a web relay that shields reader identity. These are useful services. But because they let people read forbidden material, they must be blacklisted.[1] More generally, the debate over censorware is one example of the larger debate over architecture and social control.

## I. The Analytical Structure of the Censorware Debate

The inherent difficulty of effective, constitutional censorware is, we believe, both logical and practical. Ordinary or general censorship tries to stop anyone from publishing or receiving certain types of speech. Censorware attempts something harder: preventing minors from getting material that lawfully can be published to and accessed by many American adults. However categorized, government cannot constitutionally eliminate such speech from the Internet, because government cannot reduce the adult population to reading only what children may read.

### a) Toxicity and the hermetic seal

Much of the debate regarding minors, sex, and censorware has taken place between two vastly different and thoroughly incompatible theories. Civil-liberties advocates frequently espouse what might be dubbed the control-rights theory, which is concerned with determining whether, according to some ideology, politics, or philosophy, some person or organization has the legal right to exercise control over another in a certain context. As a paper submitted to the Congressional COPA Commission argued:

> [T]he decision by a third party that a person may not use a computer to access certain content from the Internet demands some sort of justification. The burden should be on the filterer to justify the denial of another persons's access. The most plausible justifications for restricting access are that the third party owns the computer or that the third party has a relation of legitimate authority over the user.

The reasoning of many censorship advocates is dramatically different. The American Family Online page states:

CAUTION: This is not to say we want you to go looking for trouble. Pornography is dangerous, and viewing it (even for a moment) can set off a terrible chain of events.

In short, "pornography" is toxic material. Not even a moment's viewing is safe. This idea is reflected in official language, like the Children's Internet Protection Act or material "harmful to minors." This toxic-material theory isn't concerned with an involved determination regarding justification, with who/what/where. It's focused on exposure of anyone, any time, anywhere.

To someone who believes in the toxic-material theory, that pornography is dangerous, telling them that they should accept the constraints of the control-rights theory is nonsensical. The subject can't ever be allowed out of the blinder-box. Not at a school, not at a library, not anywhere. Censorware may not work well, but they'll take it for what it does. Indeed, the ineffectiveness of censorware is an argument for stronger legal regulation, as Morality in Media told the Congressional COPA Commission.

*b) Censorware as control*

Censorware isn't a "filter"; it is software designed and optimized for use by an authority to prevent another person from sending or receiving information. The word "filter" implies a model whereby impurities are extracted, yielding a purified result. But a focus on content is both distracting and misleading. The basic aim is control of people. The architectural issue is how an authority can prevent those under its control from reading forbidden information.

There are many arguments about such control, with ideological positions usually depending on whether the authority relationship is parent-child, employer-employee, or government-citizen. But that's a debate of philosophy, not technology. The technical requirements for instituting such control are independent of views of its moral correctness.

What do we mean by "architectural control" or "architecture of censorship"? The general point is that the design and deployment of technical systems promotes and even embodies norms. Both censorware and technologically implemented ratings systems, we believe, promote a norm of censorship.

We believe that architectural censorship is harmful to free speech norms. It's plausible to hypothesize a "critical mass" model in which expectations "depend[] on how many are behaving a particular way, or how much they are behaving that way." In this model, what game theorists call "common knowledge" is crucial

— to reach critical mass, people need to know a lot about what others do. To develop public norms about censorship, we at least need to know a lot about it and how other people feel about it. The invisibility of architectural censorship obstructs the production of common knowledge about its flaws, while its implementation probably cultivates censorship.

Thus, while technological solutions seem to promote individual choice, their architectural implementation weakens collective choice.

### c) Transparency and First Amendment principles

EFF's concern about architectural control leads us to enunciate two principles or values that should govern censorware and any proposed technological solution with the same objective.

### i) Transparency

Any technological solution must operate and be implemented transparently. End-users must know what censorware does, when, and why. For example, censorware shouldn't deny access to sites without expressly stating that access was denied. Not displaying a forbidden site as though it did not exist or merely displaying a generic error messages violates this principle.

Censorware should also make clear the criteria or categories under which information was blocked. It should show where the blocking occurred, whether at the user's own browser or somewhere upstream, like at an OSP, intranet, or proxy-server. More generally, all information relevant to user choice should be publicly available. Such information includes: blacklists of banned sites or words; rules or other criteria for rating banned sites; the formulas or algorithms for applying the rules and ratings. We also think that transparency requires user ability to alter default configurations.

The legal justification for transparency is the right to receive information from willing speakers, which government may not unduly burden. Transparency is needed for informed user choice. The deeper reason, however, is the need to counteract the weakening of collective choice processes caused by invisible or opaque architectural censorship. We need common knowledge.

### ii) Privacy and anonymity

Censorware raises enormous privacy and anonymity issues as well. The very process of browsing both generates a list of visited sites at the client end and passes information about the client to visited sites. Censorware exacerbates matters by paying special attention to "bad" sites. When censorware is implemented in a hierarchical environment, it's likely that browsing will be monitored.

Second, proposed alternatives to censorware often rely on some sort of identification architecture, like age verification, Internet IDs, and so on. It's often argued that these alternatives are easily evaded. Our point, however, is that identification architectures enable greater social control. As the sociologist Erving Goffman noted, identity differentiates people, and "[a]round this means of differentiation a single continuous record of social facts can be attached, entangled, like candy floss, becoming then the sticky substance to which still other biographical facts can be attached." The First Amendment, however, clearly protects the right to speak anonymously.[2] If so, then the right to read anonymously should be even more clearly protected. For instance, nearly all states protect the identities of library patrons.

## II. The reality of censorware

*a) A quick introduction to the fundamentals of censorware: Blacklisting by name, blacklisting by address, blacklisting by word*

Despite the mystique of the computer, almost all censorware operates very simplistically: they compare URLs (host and paths) against a blacklist. Sometimes the blacklist is local to the machine (client implementation). Sometimes it's stored remotely on a proxy server (server implementation). The client-side programs (e.g., CyberSitter, NetNanny) are typically home-based products, while the server programs (e.g., Bess, SmartFilter, WebSense,) are used by large organizations. Some programs have both client and server versions (e.g., CyberPatrol).

When a person types in a URL indicating material they wish to read, the censorware examines various parts of the URL against its internal blacklist to see if the URL is forbidden. Take the following URL as an example:

http://www.eff.org/Censorship/Internet_censorship_bills/2000/
20001222_eff_hr4577_statement.html

Typically, censorware first checks the host, here <www.eff.org>, in two different ways:

1. By name - the name of the host is in the blacklist
2. By address - the IP address of the host in the blacklist

In the case of matching by-name, the program would search the blacklist to find entries matching the string <www.eff.org>. For matching by-address, the program would first determine the IP address associated with <www.eff.org>, which is 204.253.162.16, and see if there are entries matching that address. This is an important distinction, because host names and addresses can be quite different. A host can have many equivalent names, and also multiple IP addresses. Worse, different hosts can all have the same IP address ("virtual hosting").

If the host is found on the blacklist (either by-name or by-address), then the program looks to see how extensively it should be banned. Conceptually, this is just how much of the URL is on the blacklist. Items can range from:

1. Blacklisting the whole domain - everything on http://www.eff.org
2. Blacklisting a directory on the site - everything below http://www.eff.org/Censorship/
3. Blacklisting a particular file on the site - http://www.eff.org/Censorship/Internet_censorship_bills/2000/ 20001222_eff_hr4577_statement.html

We emphasize that there is no deep artificial intelligence here. It's merely looking up a host and path, and deciding if they match an entry on a huge blacklist.

Note that blacklists which work by-name typically also contain numeric representations of the IP address of the most popular sites. This is completely unlike blacklisting by-address. The typical numeric representation of an IP address (e.g., 204.253.162.16) is just one way of many of connecting to that IP address. For example, the URLs http://www.eff.org, http://www.eff.net, and http://www.eff.com, will all reach the same host at the same IP address. The URL http://204.253.162.16 is similar. A blacklist that worked by-name, but only banned http://www.eff.org and http://204.253.162.16, would ignore http://www. eff.net or http://www.eff.com, even though all four eventually reach the same IP address. A blacklist that worked by-address would ban all four, but would also ban any other domain that has the misfortune to share that address via virtual hosting.

This simple distinction, by-name or by-address, is sometimes described in very confusingly . The X-Stop censorware blacklist has been extensively analyzed, due to its role in the precedent-setting *Mainstream Loudoun* case. It's entirely by-name. However, the ads for X-Stop trumpet "Direct Address Block (DAB)," which merely means that the typical numeric representations of some IP addresses are on the blacklist, too. The simple checking of blacklist text is described with almost comical marking spin: "Because this is done with numbers instead of letters (there are only 10 digits as opposed to 255 characters) the response is nearly instantaneous."

Less commonly, the path in the URL itself may be examined for forbidden words ("keyword filtering"). For example, if "censorship" were on the list of forbidden words, any attempt to read the material at http://www.eff.org/Censorship/ would be rejected.

Blacklists can have multiple categories of banned sites, (e.g. one for "Sex," another for "Drugs," perhaps another for "Rock And Roll," and so on), which often leads to discussion of tuning the censorware by selecting categories. But blacklists are almost always secret, so there's no way to know what sites are actually in the category. This secrecy is zealously guarded by almost all censorware manufactures. In *Microsystems v Scandinavia Online AB*, the company that makes CyberPatrol sued two programmers who reverse-engineered and cryptanalyzed the CyberPatrol blacklist and published their results.

The whole list-matching process above may be repeated all over again against exception lists or "whitelists." A few products consist only of whitelists, or can work in whitelist-only mode. For example, CyberPatrol named its blacklist the "CyberNOT" list, and called its whitelist "CyberYES." It can be set (in both client and server versions) so that everything not prohibited is permitted (blacklist-only), or only that which is explicitly allowed is permitted (whitelist-only). And of course the whitelist can override the blacklist. In general, such blacklist/whitelist settings are standard in server-level programs, along with the ability to create additional organization-specific blacklists or whitelists. These options shouldn't obscure the fact that they are nothing more complex than matching a string against lists of items deemed naughty or nice.

Some censorware programs try to implement more exotic approaches to determining bans, based on scanning images or words on a page. These products or features work so poorly that they are barely worth discussing.

*b) The mathematics of censorware*
It's instructive to consider just how large are some of the numbers involved in censoring the web.

As of February 2001, there were more than 35 million domain names registered in the world. More than 20 million of these were ".com" domains. Web server surveys have shown there were more than 27 million web servers in operation as of January 2001. One study estimated the Web to have approximated 800 million pages in February 1999.

Many censorware companies claim their blacklists are human-reviewed. How long it would take to evaluate the whole web? How fast can a person evaluate a web page? Does it take 1 second? 10 seconds? Co-author Finkelstein's experience in preparing evidence for *Mainstream Loudoun* suggests that a reasonable overall estimate is one page per minute. While people can work faster for brief periods, extended viewing is boring and fatiguing. One page per minute is a good order-of-magnitude number (one page per 6 seconds, or one page per hour, are certainly unreasonable).

One page per minute is 60 pages per hour. That's 480 pages per eight-hour workday. Let's call it 500 pages per workday for ease of calculation. At 200 workdays per year, we have 100,000 pages per work-year. So one person doing only censorware evaluation could only do .01 million pages in a year. Compare this to the above numbers about the size of the web and number of domains. Evaluating the whole web at a per-page level — 800 million pages at 0.1 million pages per work-year would take 8,000 workyears.

We don't claim that the above result is precise. The idea is to get a reasonable estimate of the size of the task. Even if we're off by a factor of 10, it's still an enormous number. Thus consider some very generous assumptions. If pages are evaluated twice as fast, and 100 people working full-time doing nothing else, it still takes 40 workyears.

To make matters worse, the web isn't static. It's constantly changing. A simple way to see the impossibility of evaluating the whole web is as follows: For every single day's changes, a significant fraction of that total change would have to pass through the censorware company. Again, every day, including weekends and holidays, as the Internet is international and worldwide in scope.

Further, let's consider roughly how much of the web consists of sex sites. Some well-researched estimates here are "Only 1.5% of sites contain pornographic content" or 1.9% to 2.3% "Percent of Public Web" is "Adult Sites." This small relative number (about 2%) of commercial sex sites answers a key objection to the above estimate of the work needed to examine the web. Certainly, it's not necessary to look at every web page of a website avowedly dedicated to selling sexual content. However, the proportion of those sites is almost a rounding error in the estimation of the overall web size. Approximately 98% of the web is not so easy to dismiss.

These size statistics are relevant from another angle. While 2% of 27 million web servers is tiny in relative terms, it yields more than half a million in absolute numbers ($2*10^\wedge-2 * 27*10^\wedge6 = 54 * 10^\wedge4 = 0.54 * 10^\wedge6$). It's to follow the links where commercial sex sites and commercial sex lists refer to each other. This can easily generate a blacklist of (as an order of magnitude) 100,000 commercial sex sites. Compiling such a blacklist would not represent any significant sampling or coverage of the entire web. Rather, it's a comparatively simple task, given the directories of such sites.

But given the estimate above that a person can evaluate perhaps 100,000 pages per work-year, it would take an entire work year for one person to evaluate a 100,000 item blacklist. It is utterly impossible for ordinary people to attempt to validate these blacklists, even if they weren't almost always secret in the first place. In sum, neither the web, nor large censorware blacklists, can be human-reviewed.

*c) Artificial Idiocy*

Given the inability to human-review the web, a censorware blacklist necessarily must be created largely by a computer program. Often extravagant claims are made regarding such programs, usually involving the buzzwords "Artificial Intelligence." It is important to debunk this myth of intelligent censorware, both empirically and theoretically.

Whenever censorware blacklists have been examined, the so-called intelligence has turned out to be nothing more than looking for simple keywords. The canonical example is the phrase "breast cancer" triggering bans because of the occurence of the word "breast." Now, this example has become so well-known and much-discussed that it's likely censorware companies make sure that keyword searching programs treat it as a very special case. But it's just one example. Any extensive investigation of an actual blacklist tends to produce many other instances.[3]

From a theoretical point of view, the claimed abilities would require a computer-science breakthrough of Nobel-Prize magnitude. Consider the legal test for "obscenity," which requires that an obscene work "taken as a whole[..] lack[..] serious literary, artistic, political or scientific value." It is hard to see how anyone can seriously assert that computer programs could make such a judgment when humans endlessly debate these concepts.

Moreover, "obscenity" is typically discussed as if it were an intrinsic property. But the "contemporary community standards" prong of the obscenity test makes it a geographical variable. Standards vary considerably from Memphis to San Francisco. Whether material is obscene or not depends on location. The concept of "harmful to minors" is doubly variable. It involves dimensions of both location and age. The combination 7-year-old/Memphis will be extremely different from 17-year-old/San Francisco. Such complex determinations are beyond any computer in the foreseeable future.

Of all claims made about censorware's abilities, the most ludicrious is the claim that a program can evaluate images for nudity. First, people often don't think that it suffers from the same problem that afflicts the "flesh-colored" band-aid. Human beings come in a wide variety of hues (commonly ranging from light pink to yellow to brownish to nearly black). Any program that claims to scan for "skin color" is either being obnoxiously racist in its implicit definition, or will be counting far too much to be meaningful. Second, gray-toned images present an even greater problem. No censorware alleged to have such fantastic image-recognition capability has ever stood up to serious evaluation.

*iv*

*d) The inherent under- and over-inclusiveness of censorware*
Given the mathematical constraints addressed above, it should come as no surprise that censorware ends up banning both too little and too much with regard to its supposed main target. Too little, in that many commercial sex sites will not be on the blacklist. Too much, as the attempts to construct such an overarching blacklist are an invitation to everything from deliberate agendas to shoddy work.

Moreover, that the blacklist will likely have a large collection of commercial sex sites leads to a kind of statistical masking. Imagine if a blacklisting company simply took a list of people who had been in prison (getting 100,000 such names would be fairly easy), then added its own personal enemies, and claimed it to be a list of harmful-people. As much of that list would undeniably be convicted criminals, the claim would be statistically accurate. But the opportunities for everything from deliberate malice to random error is obvious.

Further, suppose that such a list was kept by either looking up a person's name or home address. If by-name, even a slight variation in a name would result in not matching the list. But if kept by home address, many people could be living at that address. In fact, "virtual hosting," an arrangement in which many different (and usually unrelated) websites share the same IP address, perfectly exemplifies this problem. Blacklisting methods are either too narrow (by-name) or too broad (by-address).

Virtual hosting is only one illustration of a general principle. Any simple rules for banning material have similar problems. Consider the methodology for matching the word "sex" in a URL. Should all directories named "/sexstuff" or "/sexsites" qualify? If not, then simple variations will render the ban useless. But if so, the same rule will also ban directories named "/sextet," "/sextant" or "/sexton." Thus, there's no way to match enough variants to have a high assurance of excluding all "/sexual" material, without blacklisting a sextillion innocuous items. These problems have been repeatedly documented in reports from Peacefire (http://peacefire.org), Censorware Project (http://censorware.net), and Seth Finkelstein's Anticensorware Investigations (http://sethf.com/anticensorware/). But this work is sometimes dismissed as too partisan. It is corroborated, however, by experiments from the much more widely known Consumer Reports and similar results from the UK Consumer's Assocation .Yet the overinclusiveness of censorware is even worse, and in hindsight is quite obvious from the perspective of architectural control. Certain categories of sites that themselves contain no "toxic" material must also be censored.

The following subsections are based on co-author Finkelstein's[4] empirical investigation of the censorware product SmartFilter, made by Secure Computing. He explains: "Often, blacklists are subdivided into many categories - hypothetically, Sex, Drugs, Rock-and-Roll, etc. Rather than finding some feminist websites banned under Sex, or medical-marijuana political advocacy considered Drugs, I decided to take a different approach for a change. Consider the number of categories under which a site is blacklisted to be a type of evilness-index. I wanted to know which sites did SmartFilter consider to be of greatest evil? Which URL's were ranked as so vile, so corrupting, that they achieved a kind of censorware academy-award sweep, appearing in as many categories as possible?"

### i) Privacy and anonymity sites
Censorware is designed to control access to information. Thus, the subject can never be let out of the blinder-box. It follows that all privacy and anonymity services, all websites that let a user receive material via an encrypted or private form, represent a threat to that control. Since the blacklist could be thwarted by using such privacy/anonymity services, these services must then be on the blacklist in almost every SmartFilter category (the NonEssential category, reserved for user-defined entries, was the only one not found below). And

indeed, a who's-who of privacy and anonymity service sites turned out to be blacklisted virtually everywhere.  This is a non-exhaustive list:

* http://anonymouse.home.pages.de
* http://proxy.magusnet.com/proxy.html
* http://www.aixs.net
* http://www.anonymiser.com
* http://www.anonymizer.com
* http://www.cyberpass.net
* http://www.freedom.net
* http://www.i-safetynet.com
* http://www.i-safetynet.net
* http://www.idzap.com
* http://www.iprive.com
* http://www.mywebproxy.com
* http://www.private-server.com
* http://www.rewebber.de
* http://www.safeweb.com
* http://www.silentsurf.com
* http://www.spaceproxy.com
* http://www.the-cloak.com
* http://www.ultimate-anonymity.com

To be concrete, these are all blacklisted by SmartFilter as all of the following categories:

Sex Related, Illegal Drugs, Hate Speech, Criminal Skills, Worthless, On-line Sales, Gambling, Personal Pages, Job Search, Sports, Games and Fun, Humor, Alternative Journals, Entertainment, Alternative Lifestyle, Extreme/Gross Content, Chat/Web-mail, Investments Information, General News, Poltics/ Opinion/Religion, Dating and Introduction Services, Art/Culture, Cult/Occult, Usenet News Site, Self Help, Travel.

Simply put, privacy and anonymity are inimical to the goal of control.  The point of censorware is to prevent a person from reading banned material.  But privacy and anonymity web sites are dedicated to allowing people to escape monitoring and constraints of authorities.  Thus, in order not to have a break in the blinder-box, they must be blacklisted.  Everywhere.

*ii) Language translation sites*

The second broad group of websites that SmartFilter considered to be of greatest evil was slightly more surprising — translation services, i.e., sites that enable users to read webpages written in a different language. Here's a non-exhaustive list:

* http://babelfish.altavista.com/translate.dyn
* http://www.babelfish.org
* http://www.onlinetrans.com
* http://www.systransoft.com
* http://www.voila.com
* http://www.voycabulary.com
* http://www.wordbot.com
* http://www.worldlingo.com

What could be so offensive about the poor Babelfish? A moment's reflection revealed that it raised the same issue as the privacy or anonymity services listed above. Even something as prosaic and useful as a web-page translation system permits escape from censorware's information restrictions. Indeed, a language translation site can be used as a way of reading any other content whatsoever. So these websites also must be blacklisted everywhere, again in virtually all categories.

## III. Censorware and its law, in light of reality

Government may not regulate speech based on its substantive content or message, and may not favor one private speaker over another or impose financial burdens on certain speakers based on the content of their expression. Discrimination based on speakers' views on a subject is an egregious form of content discrimination. Even in a non-public forum, government regulation must be viewpoint-neutral when directed against speech otherwise within the forum's limitations. In short, "power in government to channel the expression of views is unacceptable under the First Amendment." Thus, in general, government use of censorware must be subject to strict scrutiny.

*a) Censorware and minors*

The constitutionality of technological solutions used by government entities depends on what they block. Absent special circumstances, the outer limit of constitutionally permissible blocking is so-called "harmful to minors" (HTM) speech. HTM speech may be fully protected by the First Amendment as to adults, yet "unprotected" as to minors.

Speech is "harmful to minors" if it (i) is "patently offensive to prevailing standards in the adult community as a whole with respect to what is suitable . . . for minors"; (ii) appeals to the prurient interest of minors; and (iii) is "utterly without redeeming social importance for minors."

Courts have narrowly tailored HTM-based access restrictions to its constitutional boundaries. This point was made clear in *Reno v. ACLU*, where the Supreme Court held unconstitutional a general prohibition of indecent speech on the Internet. First, parents may disseminate HTM speech to their children. Second, the HTM concept only applies to commercial transactions. Third, for HTM purposes, minors are those under the age of 17. Fourth, the government may not simply ban minors' exposure to a full category of speech, such as nudity, when only a subset of that category can plausibly be deemed HTM. Fifth, the government interest is not equally strong throughout the HTM age range.

Finally, an entirely separate problem is that HTM speech is not defined monolithically, but rather varies from community to community. This inherent variation requires that governments tailor any technological solution intended to block HTM speech to local community standards.

*b) Applying the analysis to technological solutions*
In short, HTM-based regulation is subject to many constitutional limits. Accordingly, the very existence of a government interest in regulating minors' access to the Internet turns upon the extent of censorship. The state's interest does not extend beyond HTM speech, slightly modified for schools. Thus, if censorware or any technological means substantially transgresses this constitutional boundary, it will not survive First Amendment scrutiny under either the substantive strict scrutiny test or formal tests like vagueness and overbreadth.[5]

It is widely recognized, of course, that existing technologies like censorware block much protected speech that is not HTM. Censorware proponents have argued that technology can be improved, but we have shown that this is highly unlikely. First, there is too much information on the Internet to censor with the constitutionally required precision. Second, because the definition of HTM speech varies both with age and location, any constitutionally satisfactory HTM-based censorship must be tailored to both variables. Censorware does not scale well.

Third, the example of SmartFilter's censorship of sites that are blocked for what they do, not what they say, demonstrates that censorware is necessarily caught between over-inclusiveness and ineffectiveness. Equally important, it demonstrates that the real issue here is control, not content. In simple terms, with censorware, people cannot be permitted to read anonymously. Privacy, anonymity, and even language translation sites constitute a security hole to the control system of censorware. If not banned themselves, they allow people to escape the blacklist, and this is unacceptable as a matter of control.

## IV.    Conclusion: censorware, ratings, and architectural censorship

The search for a technical solution is fundamentally misguided, because it has been guided by unstated and unsupportable assumptions. For censorware, the hope has been that the problem of overinclusiveness can, over time, be technologically solved. We have shown that there is an inherent tradeoff between effectiveness in controlling minors' access and inclusiveness or fit: for effective censorware must block sites that do not offer "offensive" material but do offer "tools," such as privacy, anonymity, and language-translation utilities.

This example also illustrates our more general point about architectural censorship: the evils of invisibility. We are not aware of any public documentation of the blacklisting of privacy, anonymity, and translation sites other than co-author Finkelstein's work. EFF believes that the use of censorware is not only legally unjustifiable, but corrosive of free speech values and public debate over First Amendment rights. As Prof. Lessig put it, "[o]nly when regulation is transparent is a political response possible." Censorware hides blacklists in black boxes.

### Notes

1.  Seth Finkelstein, "SmartFilter - I've Got A Little List" <http://sethf.com/anticensorware/smartfilter/gotalist.php>.
2.  See generally Lee Tien, *Who's Afraid of Anonymous Speech? McIntyre and the Internet*, 75 Or. L. Rev. 117 (1996).
3.  For a case study, see Seth Finkelstein, *supra* n.2.
4.  Mr. Finkelstein formerly was chief programmer for the Censorware Project, which analyzed many censorware products in order to investigate what they actually censored. The work presented here, however, is independent and associated with no organization, including EFF. After EFF learned of his paper *SmartFilter's Greatest Evils*, EFF asked him to co-author this

White Paper. EFF thanks Mr. Finkelstein for doing so; virtually all the non-legal discussion here is his contribution. *SmartFilter's Greatest Evils* is at <http://sethf.com/anticensorware/ smartfilter/greatestevils.php>.

5. We do not address an even stronger argument against censorware — that it operates as a prior restraint — because it was well analyzed in *Mainstream Loudoun.* Our point that effective censorware must block privacy, anonymity, and translation sites also strengthens that argument.

# Amnesty Intercepted: Global human Rights Groups Blocked by Web Censoring Software

**Peacefire**

**Bennett Haselton, December 12, 2000**

Prompted by numerous student reports of being unable to access Amnesty International and other human-rights-related Web sites from school computers, Peacefire tested several popular blocking programs used in schools, to see which of these sites were blocked. We configured the programs to block only the kinds of Web sites that would be blocked in a typical school setting (pornography, drugs, violence, etc.), so that purely political sites should have been accessible. But we found several Amnesty-related sites blocked by the software we tested, including several documents on Amnesty.org itself blocked by CYBERsitter, chapters of Amnesty International Israel blocked by Cyber Patrol and SurfWatch, and several human rights groups blocked by Bess.

**Notes on testing:** Our method of collecting "test sites" was unscientific (running Web searches to find human-rights-related Web sites). Of the sites that we found to be blocked, not all of these were relevant enough to be listed here. Also, this is obviously not an exhaustive list of all political sites blocked by these products. For a more scientific study of percentage error rates for blocking software, see Peacefire's Study of average error rates for censorware programs, published 10/23/2000.

We have included screen shots of the sites being blocked by the different programs; in the description of each site, the words "blocked by [productname]" are linked to a screen shot of the "blocked site" message. Sites listed as blocked by Cyber Patrol as "sexually explicit" are blocked in one of the three Cyber Patrol categories "Full Nudity," "Partial Nudity" or "Sexual Acts/Text." (SurfWatch has a single category for "sexually explicit" sites.)

Although Cyber Patrol and SurfWatch are now both owned by SurfControl Corporation and blocked many of the same sites, the lists of sites blocked by the two programs are not identical. (SurfWatch is no longer being sold, but existing SurfWatch customers can still pay for weekly updates to the SurfWatch blocked-site list.)

## Blocked sites

"It's extremely unfortunate that students in schools across the United States are inadvertently being denied access to portions of Amnesty International Web sites by these software programs. These students should be lauded — not thwarted — for their efforts to obtain important human rights information." — Karen Schneider, Director of Communications, Amnesty International USA

http://www.amnesty.org.il/
*Amnesty International Israel*
The English portion of the site includes information on the Junior Urgent Action Network, for Israeli youth aged 13 to 18, to educate Israeli teenagers on issues related to human rights. The Amnesty International Israel page is currently blocked by Cyber Patrol.

http://www.lawstudents.org/amnesty/
*Amnesty International at New York University*
The student-run chapter of AI at the NYU school of law. (SurfWatch currently blocks all of http://www.lawstudents.org/ as "sexually explicit"; LawStudents.org the home page of the Law Students Network, which is an online legal studies information center created by an NYU law student.)

http://www.clc-ctc.ca/
*Canadian Labour Congress*
A coalition of Canadian labor unions promoting health care and job safety within Canada and abroad, the CLC worked with Amnesty International in creating the International Tribunal on Workers' Human Rights. The CLC Youth Committee focuses on youth involvement and rights of young workers. The Canadian Labour Congress site is currently blocked by Cyber Patrol as "sexually explicit."

http://www.algeria-watch.de/
*Algeria Watch*
Algeria Watch monitors human rights violations in Algeria. The site includes a November 2000 report from Amnesty International on the Algerian human rights

situation. The Algeria Watch Web site is currently blocked by SurfWatch as "sexually explicit."

http://www.kurdistan.org/
*American Kurdish Information Network (AKIN)*
A U.S.-based nonprofit organization that raises awareness of human rights violations committed against Kurds in Iraq, Iran, Turkey and Syria, and documented by groups including Human Rights Watch and Amnesty International. AKIN's Web site is currently blocked by Cyber Patrol as "sexually explicit."

http://www.spanweb.org/
*Strategic Pastoral Action Network*
An non-violence advocacy organization that publishes action alerts pertaining to human rights abuses in different countries. SpanWeb.org is blocked by SurfWatch in the "Drugs/Alcohol" category.

http://www.iglhrc.org/
*International Gay and Lesbian Human Rights Commission*
IGLHRC is based in the U.S. but spotlights human rights abuses against gays and lesbians abroad, with regularly published news bulletins and action alerts. IGLHRC.org is currently blocked by I-Gear in the category "Sex/Acts."

http://www.dalitstan.org/
*Dalitstan*
Dalitstan works to defend the human rights of Dalits, the class of "Black Untouchables" living in India, who are the victims of widespread discrimination and oppression under the Indian caste system. Dalitstan.org is currently blocked by SurfWatch under the category "Violence/Hate Speech."

http://www.senser.com/
*Human Rights for Workers*
An online campaign against sweatshops and supporting job safety as a fundamental human right. The Human Rights for Workers site is currently blocked by SurfWatch as "sexually explicit."

http://www.mumia.de/
*Mumia Solidaritäts Index (in German only)*
A German site opposing the execution of American death row prisoner Mumia Abu Jamal, with links to Amnesty International documents that have called

attention to Mumia's case. Mumia.De is currently blocked by Cyber Patrol and by SurfWatch as "sexually explicit."

http://www.milarepa.org/
*The Milarepa Fund*
The Milarepa Fund raises awareness of violence against civilians and other human rights violations in Tibet. The site's mission statement calls for more non-violent action and states, "we support the youth of the world who represent a powerful vehicle to achieve that change." The Milarepa Fund Web site is currently blocked by Cyber Patrol as "sexually explicit."

http://www.peacemagazine.org/
*Peace Magazine*
A bi-monthly magazine that chronicles efforts to bring peace to areas such as Kosovo and Palestine, and contains editorials arguing against military intervention. The Peace Magazine site is currently blocked by Cyber Patrol as "sexually explicit."

http://www.bicc.de/
*Bonn International*
Center for Conversion BICC promotes and facilitates the processes whereby people, skills, technology, equipment, and financial and economic resources can be shifted away from the defense sector and applied to alternative civilian uses. The BICC site is currently blocked by Cyber Patrol as "sexually explicit."

http://www.caprn.bc.ca/
*Canada Asia Pacific Resource Network*
CAPRN promotes solidarity among labor unions and non-governmental organizations in the Asia Pacific, and is allied with groups such as Amnesty International on issues such as CAPRN's campaign against violence in East Timor. The CAPRN site is currently blocked by Cyber Patrol as "sexually explicit."

http://www.sigi.org/
*Sisterhood Is Global Institute*
SIGI promotes human rights issues at a global level, with focuses on women's rights issues in countries where violence against women is widespread. SIGI.org is currently blocked by Cyber Patrol and by SurfWatch as "sexually explicit."

http://www.mnsj.org/

*Metro Network for Social Justice*
MNSJ is a non-partisan alliance of groups promoting anti-poverty campaigns and other causes in the Toronto area. MNSJ observed International Human Rights Day 1998 by inviting speakers from Amnesty International to talk about getting involved with AI. MNSJ.org is currently blocked by Cyber Patrol as "sexually explicit."

http://www.spur.asn.au/
*Society for Peace, Unity, and Human Rights for Sri Lanka*
SPUR documents "ethnic cleansing" and violence between the majority Buddhist Sinhalese and the mostly Hindu Tamils in Sri Lanka. The SPUR Web site is currently blocked by Cyber Patrol as "sexually explicit." (This blocked site focuses almost exclusively on violence by Tamils against Sinhalese, but N2H2's Bess program makes up for this by blocking TamilRights.org, which describes the conflict from the Tamil perspective.)

http://www.tamilrights.org/
*Human Rights & Tamil People*
Documents government and police violence against the minority Hindu Tamils living in Sri Lanka. TamilRights.org is currently blocked by Bess under the "minimal filtering" configuration.

http://www.casa-alianza.org/
*Casa Alianza*
Documents the poverty and danger facing street children in Central America. Casa Alianza is currently blocked by Bess under the "minimal filtering" configuration.

http://www.seansellers.com/
*Friends of Sean Sellers*
A memorial to a writer with Multiple Personality Disorder (MPD) who was executed in 1999 for murders that he committed at the age of 16; the site includes links to Sean's writings but also takes a political stance against the death penalty (specifically, execution for crimes committed by a minor, which is legal only in Yemen, Saudi Arabia, Pakistan, and the United States). SeanSellers.com is currently blocked by Bess under the "typical school filtering" configuration (but not under the "minimal filtering" configuration, which blocks fewer sites).

http://www.copts.com/
*The International Coptic Congress*

Chronicles violence against Coptic Christians living in Egypt, with documentation from outside groups including Amnesty International and foreign news agencies. The International Coptic Congress web site is currently blocked by Cyber Patrol and by SurfWatch as "sexually explicit," and also by Bess. (Bess only blocks the site under the "typical school filtering" configuration, not the "minimal filtering" configuration.) In a compromise with censors, the webmasters have put pictures of victims of police violence on a separate page labeled "not suitable for children," although none of the pictures would be illegal for people under 18 — even in the U.S. which has some of the most restrictive laws in the developed world regarding what people under 18 can view. (Ironically, other human rights sites that are listed in this report, criticize the U.S. for being the only industrialized democracy that considers minors old enough to be executed under the law, even though American laws also come closest to prohibiting minors from viewing footage of police violence.) In any case, SurfWatch and Cyber Patrol block the site as a "sexually explicit" site, which is obviously incorrect (click for a screen shot of categories enabled when testing with Cyber Patrol, or a screen shot of categories enabled when testing with SurfWatch).

http://www.stop-childpornog.at/
*The International Conference Combating Child Pornography on the Internet*
The official site for an anti-child-pornography conference that took place from 29 September to 1 October 1999 in Vienna. The conference Web site is currently blocked by I-Gear in the category "Sex/Acts."

http://www.liberte-aref.com/
*Liberte Aref*
A site documenting human rights abuses from the Djibouti government and supporting Aref Mohamed Aref, a Djibouti lawyer at risk of imprisonment for criticisms of the government. The Liberte Aref site is currently blocked by SurfWatch as "sexually explicit."

http://charter97.org/
*Charter 97*
A site chronicling human rights abuses in Belarus and criticizing the current government led by Alexander Lukashenko. (The English version of the site can be found at http://charter97.org/English/.) Charter97.org is currently blocked by SurfWatch in the "Drugs/Alcohol" category.

http://www.cbss-commissioner.org/

*Commissioner of the Council of the Baltic Sea States*
The Commissioner, based in Denmark, publishes an annual report on the state of human rights and democratic development in Baltic nations. The CBSS Commissioner site is currently blocked by SurfWatch as "sexually explicit."

http://www.gbr.org/
*Green Brick Road*
A directory of resources for students and teachers of global environmental education. Their catalog of books related to global education includes titles on human rights and environmental protection. The Green Brick Road site is currently blocked by SurfWatch as "sexually explicit."

http://www.parish-without-borders.net/
*Parish Without Borders*
A global network of Catholic communities focusing on outreach in developing nations. The site includes a section for action alerts pertaining to human rights abuses in different countries. SurfWatch currently blocks Parish Without Borders in the "Violence/Hate Speech" category.

http://www.kosova.dk/
*Kosova Web*
Home page of the Kosova Committee in Denmark, an organization of Kosova expatriates and supporters of peacemaking and self-determination in the former Yugoslavia. Kosova Web is currently blocked by SurfWatch in the "Drugs/Alcohol" category.

Finally, two Web sites which have nothing to do with human rights, but were discovered to be blocked after running a search for Web sites that support Amnesty International:

*ArtDogs* (http://www.artdogs.com/) and
*The Official Website of Suzanne Vega* (http://www.vega.net/)
Two musical artists whose Web sites state that a portion of their proceeds go to benefit Amnesty International. (Suzanne Vega is best known for her song "Luka," about a victim of domestic violence.) Bess currently blocks ArtDogs.com and blocks Vega.net both under the "typical school filtering" configuration.

## Documents on Amnesty.org blocked due to keyword filtering

Of the programs that we tested, all of them use some degree of keyword filtering (i.e., blocking a page based on its content, rather than because the page URL is on the program's blacklist), but most programs only block a page if a banned word appears in the URL or in the page title. CYBERsitter was the only program we tested that actually blocked entire pages based on keywords appearing in the middle of the page.

CYBERsitter keeps an internal database of "banned" words and phrases. If one of these words appears on a given page, CYBERsitter blocks the rest of the page from loading. (CYBERsitter blocks the page silently, so that the user gets a "Network error" message in their browser, without knowing that the page was blocked by CYBERsitter. But the CYBERsitter administrator can view the log file to see what words caused the page to be blocked.)

CYBERsitter promotional materials state:

> One of CYBERsitter's most unique features is its state of the art phrase filtering function. Rather than block single words or pre-defined phrases, CYBERsitter actually looks at how the word or phrase is used in context. Not only does this provide an excellent blocking method for objectionable text, but it eliminates the possibility that words with double meanings will be inadvertently blocked.
>
> http://www.cybersitter.com/bellsouth.htm [the page was taken down after this report was originally published]

Our tests found no basis for this claim; for example, a page containing the sentence: "Reports of shootings in Irian Jaya bring to at least 21 the number of people in Indonesia and East Timor killed or wounded ..." was blocked because CYBERsitter detected the phrase "LEAST 21" and blocked the document as "sexually explicit."

The following is a non-exhaustive list of documents on Amnesty International web sites that were blocked by CYBERsitter, and the keywords which caused them to be blocked:

http://www.amnesty.org/news/1998/32107198.htm
keywords: "LEAST21"

http://www.amnesty.org/ailib/aireport/ar98/asa12.htm
keywords: "SEXUALACTS"

http://www.amnesty.org/ailib/intcam/chad/chad2.htm
keywords: "FOROVER18," "BONG"

http://www.amnesty.org/ailib/intcam/juvenile/appeals_isr.htm
keywords: "AGEOF18"

http://www.amnesty.org/ailib/intcam/juvenile/appeals_ind.htm
keywords: "AGEOF18"

http://www.amnesty.org/ailib/intcam/women/igualdad.txt
keywords: "SEXUALY" [sic]

http://www.amnesty.org/ailib/intcam/tunion/1999/uganda.htm
keywords: "KILLTHEM," "HAVESEX", "FORUNDER18"

http://www.amnesty.org/ailib/intcam/children/kids99/kidappe.htm
keywords: "AGEOF18"

http://www.amnesty.org/ailib/intcam/juvenile/appeals_usa.htm
keywords: "AGEOF18"

http://www.amnesty.org/ailib/aireport/ar99/eur14.htm
keywords: "STRIPSHOW," "HAVESEX"

http://www.amnesty.org/ailib/aireport/ar99/eur50.htm
keywords: "LEAST21"

http://www.amnesty.org/ailib/aireport/ar97/MDE16.htm
keywords: "LEAST21"

http://www.amnesty.org/ailib/aireport/ar98/asa13.htm
keywords: "FOROVER18"

http://www.amnesty.org/ailib/aipub/1999/MDE/51401099.htm
keywords: "AGEOF18"

http://www.amnesty.org/aiweek/aiweek97/appeals/what.htm

keywords: "AGEOF18"

http://www.amnesty.org/news/1998/44500298.htm
keywords: "SEXUALNATURE," "SEXUALACTS," "INTERCOURSE"

http://www.amnesty.org/news/1998/30401298.htm
keywords: "AGEOF18"

http://www.amnesty.org.uk/press/arepfaqs.html
keywords: "LEAST21"

http://www.amnesty.org.uk/news/mag/nov98/usa.html
keywords: "SEXUALACTS"

http://www.amnesty.org.uk/childrights/cuganda.htm
keywords: "KILLTHEM," "HAVESEX," "18YEARSOFAGE"

http://www.amnesty.org.au/wwappeal.htm
keywords: "AGEOF18"

## Final Notes

The makers of Bess, Cyber Patrol, and SurfWatch all claim that sites are not blocked by their products unless they have been reviewed by employees first to ensure that the sites meet the company's criteria. The CEO of Bess testified to this before a Congressional committee in 1998:

> All sites that are blocked are reviewed by N2H2 staff before being added to the block lists. — Written testimony submitted by N2H2 CEO Peter Nickerson, September 11, 1998

and the statement also appears on the company's Web site:

> N2H2 employs a full time staff to compile its extensive database of inappropriate sites with a combination of technology and human review processes. This process reduces frustrations associated with "key-word blocking" methods including denied access to sites regarding breast cancer, sex education, religion, and health. Human review is the only way to ensure that

appropriate sites are separated from the inappropriate sites.
http://www.n2h2.com/products/c_gn_filtering.htm

SurfWatch similarly claims:

> Before adding any site to our database, each site 'candidate' is reviewed by a SurfWatch Content Specialist. Deciphering the gray areas is not something that we trust to technology; it requires thought and sometimes discussion. We use technology to help find site candidates, but rely on thoughtful analysis for the final decision.
> http://www.surfcontrol.com/support/surfwatch/filtering_facts/how_we_filter. html

(Cyber-lawyer James Tyre actually published an essay for The Censorware Project in May 1999, called Sex, Lies, and Censorware, quoting a SurfWatch spokeswoman as saying that sites are often blocked by SurfWatch without being viewed by staff first. However, 18 months later, the opposite claim is still posted on the SurfWatch Web site: "Before adding any site to our database, each site 'candidate' is reviewed by a SurfWatch Content Specialist.")

And Cyber Patrol stated in a recent press release:

> This list of inappropriate sites, called the CyberNOT list, has been compiled by a team of professional researchers which over the last five years has reviewed more than one million Web pages. The researchers look at every site, seeking to assure that the filtered material meets the published criteria defining what content is unsuitable for kids. http://www.surfcontrol.com/news/press_releases/content/10_26_2000.html

Our past studies have concluded it is extremely unlikely that these claims by Bess, Cyber Patrol, and SurfWatch are true (see, for example, our study on percentage error rates of different blocking programs), and is is more likely that blocking companies are using automated machines ("spiders") to find Web sites and add them to their blocked-site databases without reviewing them first.

I-Gear and CYBERsitter, on the other hand, do not claim that all sites in their databases have been reviewed for accuracy.

In the days after this report is published, it is likely that the companies mentioned will go into "damage control mode" and remove these mistakes from their lists. This report, however, only examines a minute fraction of sites on the Web; the findings reflect the underlying accuracy rate of the products examined. Since each product blocks at least several hundred thousand sites, the accuracy rate won't change significantly as a result of fixing the errors listed here.

# Blind Ballots: Web Sites of U.S. Political Candidates Censored by Censorware

Peacefire

Bennett Haselton & Jamie McCarthy, November 7, 2000

> *"I just went back to my website to re-read what I wrote nine months ago. That will be gone. I am incensed with what is going on here."*

- Jeffery Pollock, candidate for the 3rd Congressional District seat in Oregon, after hearing his site was blocked by Cyber Patrol. Pollock's Web site stated until today: "We should demand that all public schools and libraries install and configure Internet Filters." (That sentence was removed after this report was published.)

## Abstract

Two blocking software, or censorware, products were tested to see if they filter out political candidates. Settings typically used in a library or school were tested. Numerous politicians were found to be censored by this software, which collectively is used in tens of thousands of schools and libraries across the country.

## Introduction

Today, many U.S. high school students will be voting for the first time. For non-voting students, classroom discussions of current events will be dominated by election news and student opinions about the views of different political candidates. For many of these students, the Internet will be the source of much of the information they have gathered about those running for office.

Peacefire tested the Web sites of political candidates from a variety of parties, to see which were blocked by N2H2 Bess and Cyber Patrol, two of the most popular blocking software programs used in schools.

The URLs for candidates' campaign homepages were taken from NetElection.org, an informational site about 2000 election campaigns in the U.S.

N2H2 claims that their product is used in 17,000 schools, blocking the web access of thirteen million students across the United States. Cyber Patrol also claims that "17,000 schools and school districts across the nation" use their product.

Both companies claim that all sites blocked by their product, are reviewed by company employees first, to ensure that the sites meet their published criteria. We evaluated this claim against the evidence of the political sites which were blocked.

Both companies keep secret the list of sites that they block, but third-party researchers can discover blocked sites through trial and error.

### Candidates' sites blocked by Cyber Patrol

Cyber Patrol blocked four Republicans' Web sites, five Democrats' Web sites, and one Libertarian candidate's Web site. (Of course, this is not an exhaustive list of candidate's Web sites that are blocked by Cyber Patrol; these are just the sites we happened to find.)

Cyber Patrol claims: "In evaluating a site for inclusion in the list, we consider the effect of the site on a typical twelve year-old searching the Internet unaccompanied by a parent or educator" [emphasis added], but the program is also heavily marketed to schools and libraries, where of course many Internet users are registered voters.

The following sites were all blocked by Cyber Patrol with only the "Full Nudity", "Partial Nudity" and "Sexual Acts/Text" categories enabled, except for http://www.doggettforcongress.com/, which was blocked under "Questionable/ Illegal/Gambling". (Cyber Patrol's official definitions for these categories are published online, but none of the sites we found to be blocked contained anything remotely "pornographic.")

Some of the Democratic candidates' sites blocked by Cyber Patrol include:

> Pat Casey, 10th District, Pennsylvania;
> Linda Chapin, 8th District, Florida;
> Lloyd Doggett, Texas;
> Mark Greene, 12th District, Texas; and
> Joan Johnson, Colorado.

Some of the Republican candidates' sites blocked by Cyber Patrol include:

> Grant Garrett, 9th District, Michigan;
> Jeffery Pollock, 3rd District, Oregon (After hearing about this report, Mr. Pollock removed a sentence from his position page on Internet issues which stated, "We should demand that all public schools and libraries install and configure Internet Filters.");
> Jim Ryun, 2nd District, Kansas; and
> Chris Vance, 9th District, Washington.

Only one Libertarian candidate was found to be blocked by Cyber Patrol:

> Joe Whelan, West.

### Candidates' sites blocked by N2H2 Bess

In Federalist Paper 57, Alexander Hamilton remarked that our Congressmen need not come from the ranks of the landed gentry:

> Who are to be the objects of popular choice? Every citizen whose merit may recommend him to the esteem and confidence of his country. No qualification of wealth ... is permitted to fetter the judgement or disappoint the inclination of the people.

The landowners of the 21st century are those with great domain names for their websites. But many of our political candidates run their campaigns on a shoestring, and use free-hosting services to save money.

Unfortunately, it is exactly this class of candidate which N2H2 discriminates against on its self-described "Typical School Filtering" setting. This setting blocks all free-hosting services.

However, the program's Help information does not describe this fact, leaving the parents or school administration to believe that all blocked sites are similar to Playboy, or the racist group National Association for the Advancement of White People.

And we have discovered that this type of blocking discriminates disproportionately against conservative and third-party candidates. Five Republicans and six Libertarians are blocked because of this setting, but only one Democrat. And thirteen other third-party candidates have their websites blocked as well.

Take for example Robert Canales, "An Independent Minded Republican," who is running for the House in California Congressional District 34. His site looks professional and is loaded with information, including online chat, news from the AP wire, and position papers. His website has been blocked from thirteen million U.S. students.

Other blocked Republican websites include:

> Bob Levy, 18th District, Houston, Texas;
> Stephen A. Urban, 11th District, Wilkes-Barre, Pennsylvania;
> Arneze Washington, 9th District, Oakland, California; and
> Kathy Williamson, 32nd District, Los Angeles, California.

Only two Democratic candidates were blocked in our random sample:

> Brian Pedigo, 2nd District, Bowling Green, Kentucky; and
> Ed Markey, 7th District, Medford, Massachusetts.

It should be noted that Ed Markey is the incumbent, having held office for over twenty years, and that his website is blocked on the "minimal filtering" setting (i.e. it is categorized as Hate, Illegal, Pornography, and/or Violence).

The Libertarian Party was especially hard-hit in Missouri. Not only were their candidates from the 2nd, 4th, and 5th District blocked, but the Missouri Libertarian Party website was itself blocked.

The blocked Libertarian Party websites include:

> Fred Foldvary, 9th District, Berkeley, California;
> Keith D. Gann, 39th District, Orange County, California;
> Jim Higgins, 2nd District, Creve Coeur, Missouri;
> Thomas Knapp, 4th District, Lebanon, Missouri;
> Al Newberry, 5th District, Missouri;
> Wayne L. Parker, 5th District, Saucier, Mississippi; and
> and the Missouri Libertarian Party.

Other blocked political candidates include:

> Alan R. Barreca, Natural Law Party, California;
> Clifton Byrd, Reform Party, Texas;
> Dennis Carriger, Reform Party, Missouri;
> Bruce Currivan, Natural Law Party, D.C.;
> Ellen Jefferds, Natural Law Party, D.C.;
> Edmon V. Kaiser, American Independent Party, California;
> Jon Kurey, Natural Law Party;
> Rob Penningroth, Reform Party, Missouri;
> David J. Schaffer, Natural Law Party, Ohio;
> Douglas Schell, Reform Party, North Carolina;
> Frank Taylor, Minnesota.;
> Martin Lindstedt, Reform Party, Missouri; and
> Nikki Oldaker, Independent write-in, Florida (her website design was praised by ABC news).

Nikki Oldaker released this statement to Peacefire regarding the blocking of her Web site (which we reproduce here without taking a position for or against):

> This type of software can be very useful in private organizations to keep employees from engaging in non-work related web surfing on company time. The software is also useful in schools and public learning facilities (like libraries) to prevent children from accessing pornography. The fact that it is being used to filter out a website for legitimate candidates speaking about the issues and their candidacies is a disservice to the American voters and the FEC and Secretary of the Senate should be fully investigating the matter to find the responsible persons behind the censorship...The guilty party should be brought to trial and prosecuted under the FEC election laws for tampering.

## Conclusion

While blocking software companies often justify their errors by pointing out that they are quickly corrected, this does not help any of the candidates listed above. Their campaigns have been sabotaged in our public schools and libraries, and corrections made after Election Day do not help them at all.

Both companies claim that all sites blocked by their product are reviewed by company employees first, to ensure that the sites meet their published criteria. We believe that this claim is false, in light of the numerous Web sites of political candidates that were blocked by the two programs.

Peacefire is a group representing the free-speech rights of internet users under 18, and is located at www.peacefire.org. Its last report examined censorship of political speech (not candidates specifically) by N2H2 Bess. Peacefire members Haselton and McCarthy are also co-founders of The Censorware Project, which is in the process of moving to a new website.

# Fahrenheit 451.2: Is Cyberspace Burning? How Rating and Blocking Proposals May Torch Free Speech on the Internet

American Civil Liberties Union

## Executive Summary

In the landmark case *Reno v. ACLU*, the Supreme Court overturned the Communications Decency Act, declaring that the Internet deserves the same high level of free speech protection afforded to books and other printed matter.

But today, all that we have achieved may now be lost, if not in the bright flames of censorship then in the dense smoke of the many ratings and blocking schemes promoted by some of the very people who fought for freedom.

The ACLU and others in the cyber-liberties community were genuinely alarmed by the tenor of a recent White House summit meeting on Internet censorship at which industry leaders pledged to create a variety of schemes to regulate and block controversial online speech.

But it was not any one proposal or announcement that caused our alarm; rather, it was the failure to examine the longer-term implications for the Internet of rating and blocking schemes.

The White House meeting was clearly the first step away from the principle that protection of the electronic word is analogous to protection of the printed word. Despite the Supreme Court's strong rejection of a broadcast analogy for the Internet, government and industry leaders alike are now inching toward the dangerous and incorrect position that the Internet is like television, and should be rated and censored accordingly.

Is Cyberspace burning? Not yet, perhaps. But where there's smoke, there's fire.

> "Any content-based regulation of the Internet, no matter how benign the purpose, could burn the global village to roast the pig."
>
> U.S. Supreme Court majority decision, *Reno v. ACLU* (June 26, 1997)

## Introduction

In his chilling (and prescient) novel about censorship, Fahrenheit 451, author Ray Bradbury describes a futuristic society where books are outlawed. "Fahrenheit 451" is, of course, the temperature at which books burn.

In Bradbury's novel – and in the physical world – people censor the printed word by burning books. But in the virtual world, one can just as easily censor controversial speech by banishing it to the farthest corners of cyberspace using rating and blocking programs. Today, will Fahrenheit, version 451.2 – a new kind of virtual censorship – be the temperature at which cyberspace goes up in smoke?

The first flames of Internet censorship appeared two years ago, with the introduction of the Federal Communications Decency Act (CDA), outlawing "indecent" online speech. But in the landmark case *Reno v. ACLU*, the Supreme Court overturned the CDA, declaring that the Internet is entitled to the highest level of free speech protection. In other words, the Court said that online speech deserved the protection afforded to books and other printed matter.

Today, all that we have achieved may now be lost, if not in the bright flames of censorship then in the dense smoke of the many ratings and blocking schemes promoted by some of the very people who fought for freedom. And in the end, we may find that the censors have indeed succeeded in "burning down the house to roast the pig."

### Is Cyberspace Burning?

The ashes of the CDA were barely smoldering when the White House called a summit meeting to encourage Internet users to self-rate their speech and to urge industry leaders to develop and deploy the tools for blocking "inappropriate" speech. The meeting was "voluntary," of course: the White House claimed it wasn't holding anyone's feet to the fire.

The ACLU and others in the cyber-liberties community were genuinely alarmed by the tenor of the White House summit and the unabashed enthusiasm for technological fixes that will make it easier to block or render invisible controversial speech. (Note: see appendix for detailed explanations of the various technologies.)

Industry leaders responded to the White House call with a barrage of announcements:

- Netscape announced plans to join Microsoft – together the two giants have 90% or more of the web browser market – in adopting PICS (Platform for Internet Content Selection) the rating standard that establishes a consistent way to rate and block online content;

- IBM announced it was making a $100,000 grant to RSAC (Recreational Software Advisory Council) to encourage the use of its RSACi rating system. Microsoft Explorer already employs the RSACi ratings system, Compuserve encourages its use and it is fast becoming the de facto industry standard rating system;

- Four of the major search engines – the services which allow users to conduct searches of the Internet for relevant sites – announced a plan to cooperate in the promotion of "self-regulation" of the Internet. The president of one, Lycos, was quoted in a news account as having "thrown down the gauntlet" to the other three, challenging them to agree to exclude unrated sites from search results;

- Following announcement of proposed legislation by Sen. Patty Murray (D Wash.), which would impose civil and ultimately criminal penalties on those who mis-rate a site, the makers of the blocking program Safe Surf proposed similar legislation, the "Online Cooperative Publishing Act."

But it was not any one proposal or announcement that caused our alarm; rather, it was the failure to examine the longer-term implications for the Internet of rating and blocking schemes.

What may be the result? The Internet will become bland and homogenized. The major commercial sites will still be readily available they will have the resources and inclination to self-rate, and third-party rating services will be inclined to give them acceptable ratings. People who disseminate quirky and idiosyncratic speech, create individual home pages, or post to controversial news groups, will be among the first Internet users blocked by filters and made invisible by the search engines. Controversial speech will still exist, but will only be visible to those with the tools and know-how to penetrate the dense smokescreen of industry "self-regulation."

As bad as this very real prospect is, it can get worse. Faced with the reality that, although harder to reach, sex, hate speech and other controversial matter is still available on the Internet, how long will it be before governments begin to make use of an Internet already configured to accommodate massive censorship? If you look at these various proposals in a larger context, a very plausible scenario emerges. It is a scenario which in some respects has already been set in motion:

- First, the use of PICS becomes universal; providing a uniform method for content rating.

- Next, one or two rating systems dominate the market and become the de facto standard for the Internet.

- PICS and the dominant rating(s) system are built into Internet software as an automatic default.

- Unrated speech on the Internet is effectively blocked by these defaults.

- Search engines refuse to report on the existence of unrated or "unacceptably" rated sites.

- Governments frustrated by "indecency" still on the Internet make self-rating mandatory and mis-rating a crime.

The scenario is, for now, theoretical – but inevitable. It is clear that any scheme that allows access to unrated speech will fall afoul of the government-coerced push for a "family friendly" Internet. We are moving inexorably toward a system that blocks speech simply because it is unrated and makes criminals of those who mis-rate.

The White House meeting was clearly the first step in that direction and away from the principle that protection of the electronic word is analogous to protection of the printed word. Despite the Supreme Court's strong rejection of a broadcast analogy for the Internet, government and industry leaders alike are now inching toward the dangerous and incorrect position that the Internet is like television, and should berated and censored accordingly.

Is Cyberspace burning? Not yet, perhaps. But where there's smoke, there's fire.

### Free Speech Online: A Victory Under Siege

On June 26, 1997, the Supreme Court held in *Reno v. ACLU* that the Communications Decency Act, which would have made it a crime to communicate anything "indecent" on the Internet, violated the First Amendment. It was the nature of the Internet itself, and the quality of speech on the Internet, that led the Court to declare that the Internet is entitled to the same broad free speech protections given to books, magazines, and casual conversation.

The ACLU argued, and the Supreme Court agreed, that the CDA was unconstitutional because, although aimed at protecting minors, it effectively banned speech among adults. Similarly, many of the rating and blocking proposals, though designed to limit minors' access, will inevitably restrict the ability of adults to communicate on the Internet. In addition, such proposals will restrict the rights of older minors to gain access to material that clearly has value for them.

### Rethinking the Rush to Rate

This paper examines the free speech implications of the various proposals for Internet blocking and rating. Individually, each of the proposals poses some threat to open and robust speech on the Internet; some pose a considerably greater threat than others.

Even more ominous is the fact that the various schemes for rating and blocking, taken together, could create a black cloud of private "voluntary" censorship that is every bit as threatening as the CDA itself to what the Supreme Court called "the most participatory form of mass speech yet developed."

We call on industry leaders, Internet users, policy makers and parents groups to engage in a genuine debate about the free speech ramifications of the rating and blocking schemes being proposed.

To open the door to a meaningful discussion, we offer the following recommendations and principles:

### Recommendations and Principles

- Internet users know best. The primary responsibility for determining what speech to access should remain with the individual Internet user; parents should take primary responsibility for determining what their children should access.

- Default setting on free speech. Industry should not develop products that require speakers to rate their own speech or be blocked by default.

- Buyers beware. The producers of user-based software programs should make their lists of blocked speech available to consumers. The industry should develop products that provide maximum user control.

- No government coercion or censorship. The First Amendment prevents the government from imposing, or from coercing industry into imposing, a mandatory Internet ratings scheme.

- Libraries are free speech zones. The First Amendment prevents the government, including public libraries, from mandating the use of user-based blocking software.

### Six Reasons Why Self-Rating Schemes Are Wrong for the Internet

To begin with, the notion that citizens should "self-rate" their speech is contrary to the entire history of free speech in America. A proposal that we rate our online speech is no less offensive to the First Amendment than a proposal that publishers of books and magazines rate each and every article or story, or a proposal that everyone engaged in a street corner conversation rate his or her comments. But that is exactly what will happen to books, magazines, and any kind of speech that appears online under a self-rating scheme.

In order to illustrate the very practical consequences of these schemes, consider the following six reasons, and their accompanying examples, illustrating why the ACLU is against self-rating:

### Reason #1: Self-Rating Schemes Will Cause Controversial Speech To Be Censored.

Kiyoshi Kuromiya, founder and sole operator of Critical Path Aids Project, has a web site that includes safer sex information written in street language with explicit diagrams, in order to reach the widest possible audience. Kuromiya doesn't want to apply the rating "crude" or "explicit" to his speech, but if he doesn't, his site will be blocked as an unrated site. If he does rate, his speech will be lumped in with "pornography" and blocked from view. Under either choice, Kuromiya has been effectively blocked from reaching a large portion of his intended audience – teenage Internet users – as well as adults.

As this example shows, the consequences of rating are far from neutral. The ratings themselves are all pejorative by definition, and they result in certain speech being blocked.

The White House has compared Internet ratings to "food labels" – but that analogy is simply wrong. Food labels provide objective, scientifically verifiable information to help the consumer make choices about what to buy, e.g. the percentage of fat in a food product like milk. Internet ratings are subjective value judgments that result in certain speech being blocked to many viewers. Further, food labels are placed on products that are readily available to consumers – unlike Internet labels, which would place certain kinds of speech out of reach of Internet users.

What is most critical to this issue is that speech like Kuromiya's is entitled to the highest degree of Constitutional protection. This is why ratings requirements have never been imposed on those who speak via the printed word. Kuromiya could distribute the same material in print form on any street corner or in any bookstore without worrying about having to rate it. In fact, a number of Supreme Court cases have established that the First Amendment does not allow government to compel speakers to say something they don't want to say – and that includes pejorative ratings. There is simply no justification for treating the Internet any differently.

### Reason #2: Self-Rating Is Burdensome, Unwieldy, and Costly.

Art on the Net is a large, non-profit web site that hosts online "studios" where hundreds of artists display their work. The vast majority of the artwork has no sexual content, although there's an occasional Rubenesque painting. The ratings systems don't make sense when applied to art. Yet Art on the Net would still have to review and apply a rating to the more than 26,000 pages on its site, which would require time and staff that they just don't have. Or, they would have to require the artists themselves to self-rate, an option they find objectionable. If they decline to rate, they will be blocked as an unrated site even though most Internet users would hardly object to the art reaching minors, let alone adults.

As the Supreme Court noted in *Reno v. ACLU*, one of the virtues of the Internet is that it provides "relatively unlimited, low-cost capacity for communication of all kinds." In striking down the CDA, the Court held that imposing age-verification costs on Internet speakers would be "prohibitively expensive for noncommercial – as well as some commercial – speakers." Similarly, the burdensome requirement of self-rating thousands of pages of information would effectively shut most noncommercial speakers out of the Internet marketplace.

The technology of embedding the rating is also far from trivial. In a winning ACLU case that challenged a New York state online censorship statute, *ALA v. Pataki*, one long-time Internet expert testified that he tried to embed an RSACi label in his online newsletter site but finally gave up after several hours.

In addition, the ratings systems are simply unequipped to deal with the diversity of content now available on the Internet. There is perhaps nothing as subjective as a viewer's reaction to art. As history has shown again and again, one woman's masterpiece is another woman's pornography. How can ratings such as "explicit" or "crude" be used to categorize art? Even ratings systems that try to take artistic value into account will be inherently subjective, especially when applied by artists themselves, who will naturally consider their own work to have merit.

The variety of news-related sites on the Web will be equally difficult to rate. Should explicit war footage be labeled "violent" and blocked from view to teenagers? If along news article has one curse word, is the curse word rated individually, or is the entire story rated and then blocked?

Even those who propose that "legitimate" news organizations should not be required to rate their sites stumble over the question of who will decide what is legitimate news.

### Reason #3: Conversation Can't Be Rated.

You are in a chat room or a discussion group – one of the thousands of conversational areas of the Net. A victim of sexual abuse has posted a plea for help, and you want to respond. You've heard about a variety of ratings systems, but you've never used one. You read the RSACi web page, but you can't figure out how to rate the discussion of sex and violence in your response. Aware of the penalties for mis-labeling, you decide not to send your message after all. The burdens of self-rating really hit home when applied to the vibrant, conversational areas of the Internet. Most Internet users don't run web pages, but millions of people around the world send messages, short and long, every day, to chat rooms, news groups and mailing lists. A rating requirement for these areas of the Internet would be analogous to requiring all of us to rate our telephone or streetcorner or dinner party or water cooler conversations.

The only other way to rate these areas of cyberspace would be to rate entire chatrooms or news groups rather than individual messages. But most discussion groups aren't controlled by a specific person, so who would be responsible for rating them? In addition, discussion groups that contain some objectionable material would likely also have a wide variety of speech totally appropriate and valuable for minors – but the entire forum would be blocked from view for everyone.

### Reason #4: Self-Rating Will Create "Fortress America" on the Internet.

You are a native of Papua, New Guinea, and as an anthropologist you have published several papers about your native culture. You create a web site and post electronic versions of your papers, in order to share them with colleagues and other interested people around the world. You haven't heard about the move in America to rate Internet content. You don't know it, but since your site is unrated none of your colleagues in America will be able to access it.

People from all corners of the globe – people who might otherwise never connect because of their vast geographical differences – can now communicate on the Internet both easily and cheaply. One of the most dangerous aspects of ratings systems is their potential to build borders around American- and foreign-created speech. It is important to remember that today, nearly half of all Internet speech originates from outside the United States.

Even if powerful American industry leaders coerced other countries into adopting American ratings systems, how would these ratings make any sense to a New Guinean? Imagine that one of the anthropology papers explicitly describes a ritual in which teenage boys engage in self-mutilation as part of a rite of passage in achieving manhood. Would you look at it through the eyes of an American and rate it "torture," or would you rate it "appropriate for minors" for the New Guinea audience?

### Reason #5: Self-Ratings Will Only Encourage, Not Prevent, Government Regulation.

The webmaster for Betty's Smut Shack, a web site that sells sexually explicit photos, learns that many people won't get to his site if he either rates his site "sexually explicit" or fails to rate at all. He rates his entire web site "okay for minors." A powerful Congressman from the Midwest learns that the site is now available to minors. He is outraged, and quickly introduces a bill imposing criminal penalties for mis-rated sites.

Without a penalty system for mis-rating, the entire concept of a self-ratings system breaks down. The Supreme Court that decided *Reno v. ACLU* would probably agree that the statute theorized above would violate the First Amendment, but as we saw with the CDA, that won't necessarily prevent lawmakers from passing it.

In fact, as noted earlier, a senator from Washington state (home of industry giant Microsoft, among others) has already proposed a law that creates criminal penalties for mis-rating. Not to be outdone, the filtering software company Safe Surf has proposed the introduction of a virtually identical federal law, including a provision that allows parents to sue speakers for damages if they "negligently" mis-rate their speech.

The example above shows that, despite all good intentions, the application of ratings systems is likely to lead to heavy-handed government censorship. Moreover, the targets of that censorship are likely to be just the sort of relatively powerless and controversial speakers, like the groups Critical Path Aids Project, Stop Prisoner Rape, Planned Parenthood, Human Rights Watch, and the various gay and lesbian organizations we represented in *Reno v. ACLU.*

### Reason #6: Self-Ratings Schemes Will Turn the Internet into a Homogenized Medium Dominated by Commercial Speakers.

Huge entertainment conglomerates, such as the Disney Corporation or Time Warner, consult their platoons of lawyers who advise that their web sites must be rated to reach the widest possible audience. They then hire and train staff to rate all of their web pages. Everybody in the world will have access to their speech.

There is no question that there may be some speakers on the Internet for whom the ratings systems will impose only minimal burdens: the large, powerful corporate speakers with the money to hire legal counsel and staff to apply the necessary ratings. The commercial side of the Net continues to grow, but so far the democratic nature of the Internet has put commercial speakers on equal footing with all of the other non-commercial and individual speakers.

Today, it is just as easy to find the Critical Path AIDS web site as it is to find the Disney site. Both speakers are able to reach a worldwide audience. But mandatory Internet self-rating could easily turn the most participatory communications medium the world has yet seen into a bland, homogenized, medium dominated by powerful American corporate speakers.

### Is Third-Party Rating the Answer?

Third-party ratings systems, designed to work in tandem with PICS labeling, have been held out by some as the answer to the free speech problems posed by self-rating schemes. On the plus side, some argue, ratings by an independent third party could minimize the burden of self-rating on speakers and could reduce the inaccuracy and mis-rating problems of self-rating. In fact, one of the touted strengths of the original PICS proposal was that a variety of third-party ratings systems would develop and users could pick and choose from the system that best fit their values. But third party ratings systems still pose serious free speech concerns.

First, a multiplicity of ratings systems has not yet emerged on the market, probably due to the difficulty of any one company or organization trying to rate over a million web sites, with hundreds of new sites – not to mention discussion groups and chat rooms – springing up daily.

Second, under third-party rating systems, unrated sites still may be blocked.

When choosing which sites to rate first, it is likely that third-party raters will rate the most popular web sites first, marginalizing individual and non-commercial sites. And like the self-rating systems, third-party ratings will apply subjective and value-laden ratings that could result in valuable material being blocked to adults and older minors. In addition, available third-party rating systems have no notification procedure, so speakers have no way of knowing whether their speech has received a negative rating.

The fewer the third-party ratings products available, the greater the potential for arbitrary censorship. Powerful industry forces may lead one product to dominate the marketplace. If, for example, virtually all households use Microsoft Internet Explorer and Netscape, and the browsers, in turn, use RSACi as their system, RSACi could become the default censorship system for the Internet. In addition, federal and state governments could pass laws mandating use of a particular ratings system in schools or libraries. Either of these scenarios could devastate the diversity of the Internet marketplace.

Pro-censorship groups have argued that a third-party rating system for the Internet is no different from the voluntary Motion Picture Association of America ratings for movies that we've all lived with for years. But there is an important distinction: only a finite number of movies are produced in a given year. In contrast, the amount of content on the Internet is infinite. Movies are a static, definable product created by a small number of producers; speech on the Internet is seamless, interactive, and conversational. MPAA ratings also don't come with automatic blocking mechanisms.

### The Problems with User-Based Blocking Software in the Home

With the explosive growth of the Internet, and in the wake of the recent censorship battles, the marketplace has responded with a wide variety of user-based blocking programs. Each company touts the speed and efficiency of its staff members in blocking speech that they have determined is inappropriate for minors. The programs also often block speech based on keywords. (This can result in sites such as www.middlesex.gov or www.SuperBowlXXX.com being blocked because they contain the keywords "sex" and "XXX.").

In *Reno v. ACLU*, the ACLU successfully argued that the CDA violated the First Amendment because it was not the least restrictive means of addressing the government's asserted interest in protecting children from inappropriate material. In supporting this argument, we suggested that a less restrictive alternative was the availability of user-based blocking programs, e.g. Net Nanny, that parents could use in the home if they wished to limit their child's Internet access.

While user-based blocking programs present troubling free speech concerns, we still believe today that they are far preferable to any statute that imposes criminal penalties on online speech. In contrast, many of the new ratings schemes pose far greater free speech concerns than do user-based software programs.

Each user installs the program on her home computer and turns the blocking mechanism on or off at will. The programs do not generally block sites that they haven't rated, which means that they are not 100 percent effective.

Unlike the third-party ratings or self-rating schemes, these products usually do not work in concert with browsers and search engines, so the home user rather than an outside company sets the defaults. (However, it should be noted that this "standalone" feature could theoretically work against free speech principles, since here, too, it would be relatively easy to draft a law mandating the use of the products, under threat of criminal penalties.)

While the use of these products avoids some of the larger control issues with ratings systems, the blocking programs are far from problem-free. A number of products have been shown to block access to a wide variety of information that many would consider appropriate for minors. For example, some block access to safer sex information, although the Supreme Court has held that teenagers have the right to obtain access to such information even without their parent's consent. Other products block access to information of interest to the gay and lesbian community. Some products even block speech simply because it criticizes their product.

Some products allow home users to add or subtract particular sites from a list of blocked sites. For example, a parent can decide to allow access to "playboy.com" by removing it from the blocked sites list, and can deny access to "powerrangers.com" by adding it to the list. However most products consider their lists of blocked speech to be proprietary information which they will not disclose.

Despite these problems, the use of blocking programs has been enthusiastically and uncritically endorsed by government and industry leaders alike. At the recent White House summit, Vice President Gore, along with industry and non-profit groups, announced the creation of www.netparents.org, a site that provides direct links to a variety of blocking programs.

The ACLU urges the producers of all of these products to put real power in users' hands and provide full disclosure of their list of blocked speech and the criteria for blocking.

In addition, the ACLU urges the industry to develop products that provide maximum user control. For example, all users should be able to adjust the products to account for the varying maturity level of minors, and to adjust the list of blocked sites to reflect their own values.

It should go without saying that under no set of circumstances can governments constitutionally require anyone – whether individual users or Internet Service Providers – to run user-based blocking programs when accessing or providing access to the Internet.

### Why Blocking Software Should Not Be Used by Public Libraries

The "never-ending, worldwide conversation" of the Internet, as one lower court judge called it, is a conversation in which all citizens should be entitled to participate – whether they access the Internet from the library or from the home. Just as government cannot require home users or Internet Service Providers (ISPs) to use blocking programs or self-rating programs, libraries should not require patrons to use blocking software when accessing the Internet at the library. The ACLU, like the American Library Association (ALA), opposes use of blocking software in public libraries.

Libraries have traditionally promoted free speech values by providing free books and information resources to people regardless of their age or income. Today, more than 20 percent of libraries in the United States are offering free access to the Internet, and that number is growing daily. Libraries are critical to realizing the dream of universal access to the Internet, a dream that would be drastically altered if they were forced to become Internet censors.

In a recent announcement stating its policy, the ALA said:

> Libraries are places of inclusion rather than exclusion. Current blocking/filtering software prevents not only access to what some may consider "objectionable" material, but also blocks information protected by the First Amendment. The result is that legal and useful material will inevitably be blocked.

Librarians have never been in the business of determining what their patrons should read or see, and the fact that the material is now found on Internet is no different. By installing inaccurate and unreliable blocking programs on library Internet terminals, public libraries – which are almost always governmental entities – would inevitably censor speech that patrons are constitutionally entitled to access.

It has been suggested that a library's decision to install blocking software is like other legitimate selection decisions that libraries routinely make when they add particular books to their collections. But in fact, blocking programs take selection decisions totally out of the hands of the librarian and place them in the hands of a company with no experience in library science. As the ALA noted, "(F)ilters can impose the producer's viewpoint on the community."

Because, as noted above, most filtering programs don't provide a list of the sites they block, libraries won't even know what resources are blocked. In addition, Internet speakers won't know which libraries have blocked access to their speech and won't be able to protest.

Installing blocking software in libraries to prevent adults as well as minors from accessing legally protected material raises severe First Amendment questions. Indeed, that principle – that governments can't block adult access to speech in the name of protecting children – was one of the key reasons for the Supreme Court's decision in *Reno v. ACLU.*

If adults are allowed full access, but minors are forced to use blocking programs, constitutional problems remain. Minors, especially older minors, have a constitutional right to access many of the resources that have been shown to be blocked by user-based blocking programs.

One of the virtues of the Internet is that it allows an isolated gay teenager in Des Moines, Iowa to talk to other teenagers around the globe who are also struggling with issues relating to their sexuality. It allows teens to find out how to avoid AIDS and other sexually transmitted diseases even if they are too embarrassed to ask an adult in person or even too embarrassed to check out a book.

When the ACLU made this argument in *Reno v. ACLU*, it was considered controversial, even among our allies. But the Supreme Court agreed that minors have rights too. Library blocking proposals that allow minors full access to the Internet only with parental permission are unacceptable.

Libraries can and should take other actions that are more protective of online free speech principles. First, libraries can publicize and provide links to particular sites that have been recommended for children. Second, to avoid unwanted viewing by passersby (and to protect the confidentiality of users), libraries can install Internet access terminals in ways that minimize public view. Third, libraries can impose "content-neutral" time limits on Internet use.

## Conclusion

The ACLU has always favored providing Internet users, especially parents, with more information. We welcomed, for example, the American Library Association's announcement at the White House summit of The Librarian's Guide to Cyberspace for Parents and Kids, a "comprehensive brochure and Web site combining Internet terminology, safety tips, site selection advice and more than 50 of the most educational and entertaining sites available for children on the Internet."

In *Reno v. ACLU*, we noted that Federal and state governments are already vigorously enforcing existing obscenity, child pornography, and child solicitation laws on the Internet. In addition, Internet users must affirmatively seek out speech on the Internet; no one is caught by surprise.

In fact, many speakers on the Net provide preliminary information about the nature of their speech. The ACLU's site on America Online, for example, has a message on its home page announcing that the site is a "free speech zone." Many sites offering commercial transactions on the Net contain warnings concerning the security of Net information. Sites containing sexually explicit material often begin with a statement describing the adult nature of the material. Chat rooms and newsgroups have names that describe the subject being discussed. Even individual e-mail messages contain a subject line.

The preliminary information available on the Internet has several important components that distinguish it from all the ratings systems discussed above: (1) it is created and provided by the speaker; (2) it helps the user decide whether to read any further; (3) speakers who choose not to provide such information are not penalized; (4) it does not result in the automatic blocking of speech by an entity other than the speaker or reader before the speech has ever been viewed. Thus, the very nature of the Internet reveals why more speech is always a better solution than censorship for dealing with speech that someone may find objectionable.

It is not too late for the Internet community to slowly and carefully examine these proposals and to reject those that will transform the Internet from a true marketplace of ideas into just another mainstream, lifeless medium with content no more exciting or diverse than that of television.

Civil libertarians, human rights organizations, librarians and Internet users, speakers and providers all joined together to defeat the CDA. We achieved a stunning victory, establishing a legal framework that affords the Internet the highest constitutional protection. We put a quick end to a fire that was all but visible and threatening. The fire next time may be more difficult to detect – and extinguish.

### Appendix: Internet Ratings Systems – How Do They Work?

**The Technology: PICS, Browsers, Search Engines, and Ratings**

The rating and blocking proposals discussed below all rely on a few key components of current Internet technology. While none of this technology will by itself censors speech, some of it may well enable censorship to occur.

**PICS:** The Platform for Internet Content Selection (PICS) is a rating standard that establishes a consistent way to rate and block online content. PICS was created by a large consortium of Internet industry leaders, and became operational last year. In theory, PICS does not incorporate or endorse any particular rating system – the technology is an empty vessel into which different rating systems can be poured. In reality, only three Third-party rating systems have been developed for PICS SafeSurf, Net Shepherd, and the de facto industry standard RSACi.

**Browsers:** Browsers are the software tool that Internet users need in order to access information on the World Wide Web. Two products, Microsoft's Internet Explorer and Netscape, currently control 90% of the browser market. Microsoft's Internet Explorer is now compatible with PICS. That is, the Internet Explorer can now be configured to block speech that has been rated with PICS-compatible ratings. Netscape has announced that it will soon offer the same capability. When the blocking feature on the browser is activated, speech with negative ratings is blocked. In addition, because a vast majority of Internet sites remain unrated, the blocking feature can be configured to block all unrated sites.

**Search Engines:** Search engines are software programs that allow Internet users to conduct searches for content on a particular subject, using a string of words or phrases. The search result typically provides a list of links to sites on the relevant topic. Four of the major search engines have announced a plan to cooperate in the move towards Internet ratings. For example, they may decide not to list sites that have negative ratings or that are unrated.

**Ratings Systems:** There are a few PICS-compatible ratings systems already in use. Two self-rating systems include RSACi and Safe Surf. RSACi, developed by the same group that rates video games, attempts to rate certain kinds of speech, like sex and violence, according to objective criteria describing the content. For example, it rates levels of violence from "harmless conflict; some damage to objects" to "creatures injured or killed." Levels of sexual content are rated from "passionate kissing" to "clothed sexual touching" to "explicit sexual activity; sex crimes." The context in which the material is presented is not considered under the RSACi system; for example, it doesn't distinguish educational materials from other materials.

Safe Surf applies a complicated ratings system on a variety of types of speech, from profanity to gambling. The ratings are more contextual, but they are also more subjective and value-laden. For example, Safe Surf rates sexual content from "artistic" to "erotic" to "explicit and crude pornographic."

Net Shepherd, a third-party rating system that has rated 300,000 sites, rates only for "maturity" and "quality."

## Credits

The principal authors of this white paper are Ann Beeson and Chris Hansen of the ACLU Legal Department and ACLU Associate Director Barry Steinhardt. Additional editorial contributions were provided by Marjorie Heins of the Legal Department, and Emily Whitfield of the Public Education Department. This report was prepared by the ACLU Public Education Department: Loren Siegel, Director; Rozella Floranz Kennedy, Editorial Manager; Ronald Cianfaglione, Designer.

# Will PICS Torch Free Speech on the Internet?

Electronic Frontiers Australia

---

Irene Graham

Rating and labelling of Internet content has been widely hailed as the ideal means of empowering parents to control their children's access to Internet content, without restricting adults' freedom of speech and freedom to read. Whether this is true or not, has become one of the most hotly argued topics in the Internet censorship debate.

In mid 1995, with the black cloud of the US Communications Decency Act (CDA) hanging over the Internet, the World Wide Web Consortium (W3C) began developing an Internet content labelling and selection platform. Their stated goal was to empower people worldwide to control access to online content and thereby reduce the risk of global censorship of the Internet. They announced the result of their endeavours, the Platform for Internet Content Selection (PICS), in September 1995.[1]

PICS, promoted as "Internet Access Controls Without Censorship" with emphasis on a multiplicity of rating systems, voluntary self- rating by content providers and blocking software on home computers, was enthusiastically welcomed by the Internet community.

Few people paused to consider that technological tools which empower parents to control the access of their children, equally empower totalitarian and paternalistic governments to control the access of their adult populace. Few

---

people realised that PICS compatible systems could be installed on upstream network equipment, well beyond the control of end-users.

PICS was, in fact, developed to further empower any person or entity with the power to control other peoples' access to Internet content. This includes parents, schools, universities, employers, Internet service providers and governments.

Since the first two PICS-compatible rating systems became available two years ago, few community groups, commercial organisations or individuals have evidenced interest in developing rating systems. However, governments have shown great interest in PICS, particularly the Australian Government.

### Governments Hijack PICS

Less than twelve months after PICS was announced, the first indications that governments would be unable to resist the beckoning of PICS facilitated censorship systems were seen.

In early June 1996, Mr. Peter Webb, then Chairman of the Australian Broadcasting Authority (ABA), stated: "An obligation to utilise PICS-type systems, and I don't wish to imply that the ABA is endorsing the PICS system to the exclusion of any other similar or superior system, might have to be enforced."[2]

A month later, the ABA released their report on the "Investigation into the Content of On-line Services."[3] The ABA recommended, among other things, the development of a single on-line classification/rating scheme compatible with the PICS standards, for use by Australian content providers and consumers. The writers remarked that: "The support which the on-line community has expressed for the PICS system indicates that it is likely that the PICS protocol or system (or a similar protocol) will be widely and readily adopted by the Australian on-line industry and on-line users."

Unreserved support for PICS systems, then, was hardly surprising. PICS was announced just five months before submissions to the ABA inquiry closed. The first PICS compatible rating and blocking systems were not launched until after the closing date. For most, perhaps all, respondents to the ABA inquiry, PICS was merely a concept; examples of the tools it enables were not available for public scrutiny.

In September 1996, Demon Internet, the largest Internet Service Provider in the UK, announced they would require all their users to rate their web pages using the RSACi rating system[4] by the end of the year. Three weeks later the "R3 Safety-Net" proposal,[5] endorsed by Internet industry associations and the UK Government, was announced. Under this scheme, Internet Service Providers (ISPs) would require all their customers to label their web pages using the RSACi rating system[6] and ISPs would remove web pages hosted on their servers which were "persistently and deliberately mis-rated."

The R3 Safety Net scheme appears to have been dropped following wide opposition to mandatory labelling and criticism of the RSACi rating system. However, in October 1997 the Internet Watch Foundation (formerly the Safety Net Foundation) announced that a large group of industry and government representatives had formed to develop a worldwide rating system.[7] The group includes the Australian Broadcasting Authority and the Recreational Software Advisory Council (RSAC) in the USA.

The prospect of mandatory self-rating and labelling heralded the beginning of a shift in attitude towards PICS. Internet users began considering a wide range of associated issues. Clearly, self-rating cannot be compelled without the application of penalties, potentially criminal penalties, for failure to rate and mis-rating. The purpose of mandating rating, and the ease of rating information correctly, therefore became relevant.

### Labelling Does Not Protect Children

While many people believe that material unsuitable for children must be labelled to prevent access, this is in fact false, because PICS systems work the other way around. PICS compatible blocking programs allow access to unlabelled material, unless the user or administrator of the blocking program has set the controls to block access to unlabelled material.

If every document originating in every country in the world which could be deemed unsuitable for children is labelled, then allowing children to access unlabelled material would be practical. However, this is not foreseeable. Not only is it unlikely that every government will mandate labelling; criminals are unlikely to comply with such laws.

Therefore, to protect children from unsuitable material, the blocking program must be set to deny access to all unlabelled material. Otherwise, children are likely to access unsuitable content. Mandating that, for example, Playboy label photos displaying nudity is therefore pointless. Properly configured blocking programs will block access to unlabelled content anyway.

In other words, the sole purpose of labelling, with regard to children's access, is to make material available to children who are using blocking programs, not to block it. Labelling information which is suitable for children, and which publishers wish to make available to those using blocking programs, clearly has greater merit.

### Mandatory Labelling is a Censorship Tool

Mandatory labelling has the potential to result in censorship by stealth.

Many providers of large quantities of information, including voluntary organisations, community groups and individuals, do not have sufficient staff or time to rate all content. These publishers would be compelled to choose between publishing less information than otherwise, or rating all content at a highly restricted level, knowing that content so labelled will be invisible to many people using blocking programs.

Content providers would also be likely to use more restrictive ratings than necessary because Internet rating systems are inherently subjective. For example, the RSACi system requires content providers to guess what a "reasonable" person would think, eg. "clothing on a male or female which a reasonable person would consider to be sexually suggestive and alluring."

Of course, content providers subject to penalties for mis-rating are likely to avail themselves of web hosting services in countries which do not mandate labelling. Similarly, those opposed to pejoratively rating their own work, using someone else's values, may also take their business off-shore.

### To Rate or Not to Rate

Whether or not governments mandate labelling, widespread usage of rating and blocking systems is likely to banish a vast range of valuable information to the fringes of cyberspace.

Rating systems claimed to be objective, such as the RSACi system, make no allowance for information of artistic, literary, scientific or educational merit. These systems require that information be rated using criteria applicable to blatant pornography and gratuitous violence. For example, a photo of

Michelangelo's David, pictorial instructions on conducting breast examinations and information about safe sex, must be rated using the same criteria as applicable to photos in Hustler magazine.

Rating news reports presents similar problems. As Joshua Quittner, of The Netly News, comments: "How would you 'rate' news sites, after all? News often deals with violent situations, and occasionally with sexual themes and even adult language. How do you rate that? Do you rate every story? On deadline? Or just rate your entire site as off-limits, since sometimes you'll be covering treacherous terrain?"[8]

This conundrum led a group of news organisations in the USA, the Internet Content Coalition, to consider an "N" rating for use by "bona fide" news sites. News sites would rate all content with the "N" label thus enabling parents to choose whether to allow their children access to news. There was just one problem. Who would be given the power to decide who was a "bona fide" news site? Subsequently, in August 1997, representatives from about twenty-five news organisations, including the New York Times, Time Incorporated, the Wall Street Journal Interactive Edition, and the Associated Press, voted not only to drop the plan to create a news label, but went on record opposing Internet ratings for news sites.[9]

While flat refusal to self-rate may be viable for well-known sites, it may not be practical for those whose sites are generally found by using search engines.

### Industry Self-regulation Causes Alarm

Shortly after the US Supreme Court struck down the CDA in June 1997, the US President convened a White House summit on Internet censorship to encourage "self-regulation" of the Internet.

At this meeting, four of the major search engines announced a plan to exclude unrated sites from search results. The president of Lycos was reported to have "thrown down the gauntlet" to the other three. Safesurf, marketers of a PICS compatible blocking program and creators of a PICS rating system, proposed an "Online Cooperative Publishing Act." Under this Act, any parent who felt their child was harmed by "negligent" publishing could sue publishers who fail to rate or mis-rate material. Parents would not be required to prove actual harm, only that the material could reasonably be required to have had a warning label or a more restrictive label.

Civil liberties organisations in several countries including the USA, UK and France have subsequently issued reports cautioning against ill-considered enthusiasm for PICS facilitated systems. In a paper titled "Fahrenheit 451.2: Is Cyberspace Burning?," the American Civil Liberties Union (ACLU) stated that they and other civil liberties organisations were "genuinely alarmed by the tenor of the White House summit and the unabashed enthusiasm for technological fixes that will make it easier to block or render invisible controversial speech." The ACLU warned:

> What may be the result? The Internet will become bland and homogenized. The major commercial sites will still be readily available they will have the resources and inclination to self-rate, and third-party rating services will be inclined to give them acceptable ratings. People who disseminate quirky and idiosyncratic speech, create individual home pages, or post to controversial news groups, will be among the first Internet users blocked by filters and made invisible by the search engines. Controversial speech will still exist, but will only be visible to those with the tools and know-how to penetrate the dense smokescreen of industry "self-regulation."[10]

Undaunted by growing opposition to PICS, in November 1997 the W3C proposed an addition to the PICS standards called PICSRules.[11] PICSRules is a language for writing filtering rules that allow or block access to web sites. The developers envisage that individuals and organisations will develop filtering preference profiles. Internet users will then be able to select pre-configured PICS settings and install them with one click of the mouse button. In addition, PICSRules will help search engines tailor their output. Links to sites which do not meet profile criteria will be invisible to users of the profile. However, given the complexity of the PICSRules language and the few rating systems developed by individuals and organisations, it seems more likely that preference profiles will be developed by governments and installed on upstream computing equipment well beyond the control of Internet users.

During the month in which the PICSRules specification was open for public comment, members of the Global Internet Liberty Campaign (GILC) asked W3C to reject the proposals of the PICSRules Working Group, stating: "we oppose the proposed adoption of PICSRules 1.1 on the grounds that they will provide a tool for widespread global censorship, which will conflict with W3C's mission to 'realize the full potential of the Web . . . as an efficient human-human communications medium.'"[12]

Despite the concerns raised, the W3C approved PICSRules.

W3C representatives defend PICS and PICSRules on the ground that they are merely technical standards. They express the view that it is the role of others to ensure that PICS technologies are not used to control societies. PICS critics contend that PICS is more than a mere technical standard; it is a standard developed with the express purpose of making the architecture of the Internet censor friendly. As such, PICS technologies raise fundamental issues about free speech which should be debated in public. W3C, an organisation of industry and government representatives, readily acknowledge that they have not adopted the position that unrestricted access to information is a fundamental human right that transcends national sovereignty.

For many years, the Net community has proclaimed that the Net treats censorship as damage and routes around it. Until a means of routing around PICS becomes widely available, people concerned about threats to free speech would be well advised to shine the hot light of public scrutiny on W3C and governments interested in PICS. PICS, like the now dead CDA that kindled it, threatens to torch a large segment of the Internet community.

## Notes

1. PICS created - W3C media release http://www.w3.org/PICS/950911_Announce/pics-pr.html.
2. Speech by Peter Webb, Asian Mass Communications Research and Information Centre Conference, Singapore, 1-3 June 1996.
3. ABA Report http://www.aba.gov.au/what/online/olsfin.htm.
4. Demon Internet UK announcement http://www.mit.edu/activities/safe/safe/www/safe/labeling/demon/demon-censor.html.
5. R3 Safety Net Proposal http://dtiinfo1.dti.gov.uk/safety-net/r3.htm.
6. RSACi http://www.rsac.org.
7. Worldwide Internet Content Labelling Development, http://www.iwf.org.uk/press/archives/p011097.html.
8. Dis-Content Coalition, Joshua Quittner, The Netly News, 13 December 1996 http://cgi.pathfinder.com/time/digital/daily/0,2822,11612,00.html.
9. RSAC shelves news rating, Tim Clark and Courtney Macavinta, News.com, 10 Sep 97 http://www.news.com/News/Item/0,4,14139,00.html X-Rated Ratings?, J.D. Lasica, American Journalism Review, October 1997 http://www.newslink.org/ajrjdl21.html.

10. Fahrenheit 451.2: Is Cyberspace Burning? How Rating and Blocking Proposals, May Torch Free Speech on the Internet, ACLU, August 1997 http://www.aclu.org/issues/cyber/burning.html

11. PICSRules Media Release, November 1997 http://www.w3.org/Press/Internet_Summit.

12. GILC submission on PICSRules, December 1997 http://www.gilc.org/speech/ratings/gilc-pics-submission.html.

# Who Watches the Watchmen:
# Internet Content Rating Systems,
# and Privatised Censorship

**Cyber-Rights & Cyber-Liberties (UK)**

---

## Introduction

After much recent publicity concerning the availability of materials on the Internet that are offensive to many people (racist and Nazi propaganda, pornography, and information on disrupting train travel), Internet content rating systems are developing with broad support by the government agencies and by the industry but without much public debate over their utility or about their long-term implications. Civil liberties proponents in many countries who have examined content-control proposals have found them to be much more intrusive and restrictive than the supporters of rating systems and filtering software claim. The proposed systems often exceed their makers' claims in the types of content restricted, the number and type of people prevented from reaching content, the technical changes required to public electronic networks, and the burdens on providers of content or Internet service providers.

Recently the UK Internet Watch Foundation ("IWF") convened an advisory board comprising representatives of content providers, children's charities, regulators from other media, Internet Service Providers and civil liberties groups, to propose a UK-focused system for rating Internet content. (See House of Commons, 26 June 1997, Written Answers, Internet).

Cyber-Rights & Cyber-Liberties (UK), a non-profit civil liberties organisation which promotes free speech and privacy related issues on the Internet, has recently discovered that no "civil liberties" organisations are in fact involved in

---

the development of rating systems at the UK level. It has been wrongly stated many times by the media, by members of the Parliament, and in different EU reports. that UK civil liberties organisations are involved with the development of rating systems and that they have been also consulted on these issues.

It is the purpose of this report to explain why the debates on regulation of Internet content should take place openly and with the involvement of the public at large rather than at the hands of a few industry based private bodies.

### A Short History of Content Regulation and Content Blocking Technology

Until the 1990s there were no restrictions on Internet content. Governments did not concern themselves because Internet access was available mainly to a relatively small (though international) community of academics and engineers at universities, government research institutions, and commercial research institutions.

Despite the largely serious and academic nature of most material, a sub-culture also flourished of odd sexually-oriented, politically-oriented, and other materials often considered "wacko" (insane). The presence of such materials was tolerated by all users and even considered a sign of the health of the medium. In particular, few people were bothered by the presence of pornography in a community made up over 90% of male users.

When the Internet became more widespread and governments began to take notice, the first stage in Internet content control began, consisting of heavy-handed and repressive forays in censorship. The US Communications Decency Act 1996 was a part of this trend, as are more recent but similar proposals by the Australian government.

The first wave of direct censorship ran its course, turned back by concerns over its effects on free expression (the CDA was declared to infringe on constitutionally protected speech, see *Reno v. ACLU*, 117 S. Ct. 2329 (1997)) as well as its technological inappropriateness for the medium and its ineffectiveness in a global environment.

The second stage in content control thus began with the introduction of rating and filtering products that claim to permit users to block unwanted material from their personal systems. The most sophisticated and widely recognised of these systems is the Platform for Internet Content Selection ("PICS"), introduced by the World Wide Web Consortium. European governments were especially interested in this hoped-for solution. They backed away quickly from incidents in the first stage of direct suppression and put forward PICS and rating systems as a proposed standard, both through national governments and the European Union as a self-regulatory solution to Internet content.

There are many problems, however, in rating and filtering systems as will be explained in this report. They are crude and tend to block too many sites. Most focus on the World Wide Web, offering no way to block objectionable content on other distribution mechanisms of the Internet such as newsgroups and ftp sites. Each system is extremely subjective and affected by cultural assumptions, so international exchanges of systems will not satisfy users. Finally, the systems were designed for individual users and do not scale well to use by entire countries and third parties.

Thus, we are beginning to see a third stage emerge in content control: that of international co-operation to remove content from the Internet. For some clearly delineated materials, such as sexually explicit material in which children are actors, such co-operation may be helpful. However, as a general trend this stage is fraught with danger. The public is not likely to support the suppression of material that is legal in their own country but illegal in another.

### EURIM Report and Proposed Legislation

EURIM, a UK body made up of members of parliament, industry representatives and special interest groups, set up a working party to examine illegal content earlier this year. EURIM published a report entitled, "Internet Content Regulation," in July 1997 which found that existing regulations are inadequate to cover the new medium of the Internet.

"There is a need to clarify and refine our existing laws on illegal material. The application of such laws to the Net . . . is not particularly clear . . . but even when the law is clear, we must ensure that those whose job it is to uphold it, our police forces, are given the equipment and specialist training they need," said Baroness Dean, EURIM council representative.

The EURIM Report recommends the strengthening of the Internet Watch Foundation (IWF), or the setting up of a statutory body to monitor the Internet industry. The report states that "the IWF is not independent from the ISPs and lacks the credibility and influence which formal recognition and legal status could give." Tory MP Ian Bruce, vice-chairman of EURIM and a member of the Parliamentary IT Committee, said he aimed for the watchdog to have "legislative teeth" – to cope with cases where Internet service providers refuse to act voluntarily against an offending source. Bruce also suggested it might be necessary to set up an "OFNET", along the lines of OFTEL, to take over the IWF's regulatory work. (See Computing, "MPs act to curb Net abuse," 10 September 1997).

Cyber-Rights & Cyber-Liberties (UK) does not agree that the existing laws need to be clarified to cover the new medium. UK defamation laws were recently updated with the new Defamation Act 1996 and it clarifies the liability of ISPs. The Sexual Offences (Conspiracy & Incitement) Act 1996 refers to the use of the Internet and the child pornography laws is more than adequate to deal with the availability and dissemination of this kind of material on the Internet. There have been many prosecutions following "Operation Starburst" in the UK.

## I. No Pressing Need in Fact

A new bill was presented in the UK Parliament by Mrs. Ann Winterton on Internet (Dissemination of Child Pornography) in June 1997 and this would create new rules that are more restrictive and oppressive on the Internet than in other media. Restrictive legislation of this kind should be resisted as fears and impressions of illegal trafficking on the Internet are exaggerated. Between December 1996 and June 1997, about 1000 illegal items were reported to the Internet Watch Foundation, but only 9 reports involving 75 of them originated from the UK. Therefore, there is no need for heavy-handed legislation involving the dissemination of child pornography on the Internet as most of the illegal content available on the Internet does not originate from the UK. There is also no need for expensive monitoring of the Internet at a national level as the few problems created by the Internet remain global ones.

A recent European Commission working paper agreed and stated that "there is no legal vacuum as regards the protection of minors and human dignity, not even in online and Internet services. According to the principle of territorial jurisdiction, the law applies on the national territory of the State and hence also applies to online services." (see Commission Staff Working paper, "Protection of Minors and Human Dignity in Audio-visual and Information Services: Consultation on the Green Paper," SEC (97) 1203, Brussels, June 1997).

## II. National Legislation is the Wrong Response

However, we do recognise that the Internet is a global medium which does not respect boundaries, and that individual nation-states are losing their capacity for governance. Therefore, heavy handed new legislation at a national level will in any event be inadequate and ineffective. All nations have an important part to play in the fight against internationally defined illegal material, such as forms of child pornography. Although the UK police have been successful with "Operation Starburst" in identifying an international paedophile ring, substantial collaboration at an international level may be needed to fight child pornography between various national police forces. This can be achieved, as suggested by the European Commission, initially at the EU level. Therefore, it is not in the best interest of the UK Parliament to legislate on these matters just because there is a public outcry and moral panic.

### III. Confusion between Illegal and Harmful Content

The regulation of potentially "harmful content" such as pornography on the Internet and regulation of invariably illegal content such as child pornography are different in nature and should not be confused. Child pornography is banned in a wide range of countries because its creation involves child abuse. Other types of offensive content, by contrast, are "victimless crimes" and have no proven ill-effects on other people. For example, a link between the consumption of pornography and sexual abuse has never been established (see e.g. Dennis Howitt and Guy Cumberbatch, Pornography: Impacts and Influences, Research and Planning Unit London: HMSO, 1990). This distinction explains why there is a wide variation among countries (and local communities within those countries) about what is tolerable in pornography involving adults.

### IV. Adults Should not be Treated Like Children

Any regulatory action intended to protect a certain group of people, such as children, should not take the form of an unconditional prohibition of using the Internet to distribute content that is freely available to adults in other media. Therefore, attempts to pass online censorship legislation such as the US Communications Decency Act (part of the 1996 Telecommunications Act) should be avoided and child pornography laws should not be used as false examples of supposed legitimate restriction of freedom of expression. The US Supreme Court recently stated in *Reno v. ACLU*, 117 S. Ct. 2329 (1997) that the Internet is not as "invasive" as radio or television and confirmed the finding of the lower court that "communications over the Internet do not 'invade' an individual"'s home or appear on one's computer screen unbidden. Users seldom encounter content by accident." Partly on the basis of this user-driven aspect of the Internet, the court unanimously struck down the Communications Decency Act, which tried to restrict the distribution of "indecent" material.

This report will now proceed to examine the technical means of restricting content which have been widely proposed as a self-regulatory solution instead of "top-down" regulatory restrictions.

### Self-regulatory Solutions for the Internet

There appears not to be a single solution for the regulation of illegal and harmful content on the Internet because, for example, the exact definition of offences such as child pornography varies from one country to another.

These are pressing issues of public, political, commercial and legal interest. The treatment of material considered harmful may be different in different societies, and what is considered to be harmful depends on cultural differences. It is therefore imperative that international initiatives take into account different ethical standards in different countries in order to explore appropriate rules to protect people against offensive material. For example, the European Court of Human Rights in Handyside (see Handyside case (1976) 19 Y.B.E.C. 506) stated that the steps necessary in a democratic society for the protection of morals will depend on the type of morality to which a country is committed. A Recent European Commission Communication Paper (1996) stated that "each country may reach its own conclusion in defining the borderline between what is permissible and not permissible". A conflict always exists between the desire to allow free expression and the feeling that morality must be enforced. Each society must decide where to draw the line. However, a good rule of thumb is that free expression is more important to a healthy and free society, and should not be seriously harmed by attempts to enforce to moral standards.

In this context it might be useful to quote from one of the more recent judgements of the European Court of Human Rights in *Castells v. Spain* (judgement of 23 April 1992, Series A no. 236, p.22, § 42):

> . . . freedom of expression constitutes one of the essential foundations of a democratic society, one of the basic conditions for its progress. Subject to paragraph 2 of Article 10 [of the European Convention on Human Rights], it is applicable not only to "information" or "ideas" that are favourably received or regarded as inoffensive or as a matter of indifference but also to those that offend, shock or disturb. Such are the demands of that pluralism, tolerance or broadmindedness without which there is no democratic society.

"Harm" is a criterion which will depend upon cultural differences. There have been attempts, for example, by the German government to restrict the availability of hate speech on the Internet, specifically the web sites related to the denial of the Holocaust. Many of these same materials are legal in other countries, even though most of the population finds them offensive. The preservation of the principle of free expression should be more important than the pursuit and prosecution of every potentially dangerous speaker.

Self-regulation is an appropriate tool to address the criteria of harmful content. Dealing with illegal material is a matter for the courts and the law enforcement agencies. (see House of Lords, Select Committee on Science and Technology "Information Society: Agenda for Action in the UK," Session 1995-96, 5th Report, London: HMSO, 23 July 1996, para 4.163).

"Self-regulation in this field has a number of advantages. Rules devised by the media are more likely to be internalised and accepted. In addition, it may avoid heavy-handed legal intervention which carries with it the spectre of government censorship." (See Walker, Clive "Fundamental Rights, Fair Trials and the New Audio-Visual Sector" [1996] MLR 59, 4, 517-539.)

A self-regulatory model for harmful content on the Internet may include the following levels and in this model "self" means as in "individual" without the state involvement:

- User or Parental Responsibility

- Parental Software

On the other hand we offer the following models for fighting such illegal content as forms of child pornography on the Internet and this is a more collective solution different from the above model:

- User Responsibility to report it

- Hotlines for reporting

- Code of Conduct by ISPs

- National Legislation - distribution

- International Level - Co-operation

There is no need for rating systems to be used for illegal content and the next sections explain why there is no need for rating systems to be used for harmful content on the Internet.

## Rating Systems

There have been recent calls in Europe for the regulation of the Internet and these are relevant to the UK developments. Recently European Commission approved a Communication on Illegal and Harmful Content on the Internet (1996) and a Green Paper (1996) on the protection of minors and human dignity in the context of new electronic services in October 1996. The European Commission documents follow the resolution adopted by the Telecommunications Council of Ministers in September 1996, on preventing the dissemination of illegal content on the Internet, especially child pornography. While the Communication gives policy options for immediate action to fight against harmful and illegal content on the Internet, the Green Paper sets out to examine the challenges that society faces in ensuring that these issues of overriding public interest are adequately taken into account in the rapidly evolving world of audiovisual and information services.

The European Commission Communication Paper suggested that:

> the answer to the challenge will be a combination of self-control of the service providers, new technical solutions such as rating systems and filtering software, awareness actions for parents and teachers, information on risks and possibilities to limit these risks and of international co-operation.

All these initiatives at the European level were adopted in a Resolution at the Telecommunications Council of November 1996. The European Parliament also adopted a resolution following these initiatives. The UK Government welcomed the Communication with its emphasis on self-regulation by industry, as entirely consistent with the UK"s approach:

> The UK strongly agrees with the Commission that since a legal framework for regulation of the Internet already exists in Member States, new laws or regulations are unnecessary. (Select Committee on European Legislation, 1996, para 14.8)

Cyber-Rights & Cyber-Liberties (UK) argues that a radical self-regulatory solution for the hybrid Internet content should not include any kind of rating systems and self-regulatory solutions should include minimum government and industry involvement.

Platform for Internet Content Selections ("PICS") is a rating system for the Internet and is similar to the V-chip technology for filtering out violence or pornography on television systems. PICS is widely supported by various governments and industry based organisations such as the Internet Watch Foundation in the UK. PICS works by embedding electronic labels in the text or image documents to vet their content before the computer displays them or passes them on to another computer. The vetting system could include political, religious, advertising or commercial topics. These can be added by the publisher of the material, by the company providing access to the Internet, or by an independent vetting body.

Currently (as of November 1997), there are three PICS related rating systems that are being widely used or promoted:

> **RSACi**: The most common scheme for screening material was developed by the United States based Recreational Software Advisory Council on the Internet ("RSACi"), originally a scheme for rating computer games. It rates material according to the degree of sex, violence, nudity, and bad language depicted. It is usually this PICS/RSACi screening combination that people have in mind when they refer to PICS. As of September 1997, RSACi claims to have over 43,000 sites rated.

> **SafeSurf**: Developed by the SafeSurf corporation, this system's categories include "Age Range", "Profanity", "Heterosexual Themes", "Homosexual Themes", "Nudity", "Violence," "Sex, Violence, and Profanity", "Intolerance", "Glorifying Drug Use", "Other Adult Themes", and "Gambling", with 9 distinctions for each category.

SafeSurf and RSACi both rely on self-rating of Internet sites by web publishers. While apparently being voluntary and fair, this kind of system is likely to end up being a serious burden on content providers. First, the only way to deal with incorrect ratings is to prosecute content providers. That is very dangerous and an infringement on free speech. Secondly, ISPs and search engines will simply block any unrated sites, so that content providers will feel it necessary to rate their sites even if they oppose the system.

> **NetShepherd**: Based in Calgary, Net Shepherd rates sites based on maturity levels (General, Child, Pre-teen, Teen, Adult, and Objectionable), and quality levels (1-5 stars). Unlike SafeSurf and RSAC, NetShepherd conducts third-party ratings of web sites. NetShepherd claim to have rated over 300,000 sites. NetShepherd has also announced partnerships with firms such as Altavista and Catholic Telecom, Inc.

The EURIM Report encourages the development of internationally accepted rating systems so that some sort of "harmful content" may be controlled at the point of access. The Internet Watch Foundation ("IWF"), was seen as a possible way forward on this subject by the EURIM report and the IWF has been working on the introduction of these rating systems together with its European partners (including ECO, the German Electronic Commerce Forum and Childnet International, the UK-based charity) under the Internet Content Rating for Europe ("INCORE") project.

This initiative aims to: (1) create a forum of interested groups to investigate content rating (identifying illegal and classifying legal material. A key element of this will be consumer research as to users' expectations regarding the Internet and, more specifically, the kind of material they would consider to be appropriate to apply ratings to); (2) draw together self-regulatory bodies as hot-line organisations; and (3) consider European input into world-wide standards.

Child pornography is often used as an excuse to regulate the Internet but there is no need to rate illegal content such as child pornography since it is forbidden for any conceivable audience and this kind of illegal content should be regulated by the enforcement of existing UK laws. On the other hand, the Internet contains other kind of content which would be legal but otherwise defined as harmful for instance to children.

According to the Internet Watch Foundation, there is "a whole category of dangerous subjects" that require ratings and these are information related to drugs, sex, violence, information about dangerous sports like bungee-jumping, and hate speech material (see Wired News, "Europe Readies Net Content Ratings," 7 July, 1997). It is surprising to see bomb-making material being omitted from this list, but we can expect it to be added to the list as happened recently in the US. Senator Dianne Feinstein, in the United States introduced legislation specifically making it illegal to distribute bomb-making information on the Internet. This legislation was found unconstitutional in the US and it should be noted that this kind of information, including the Anarchist"s Cookbook are available through well known bookshops such as Waterstones and Dillons within the UK.

We also warn that self-rating systems must not be used as a pretext for "zoning" the Internet, as two dissenting justices suggested in the U.S. Supreme Court, *Reno v. ACLU*, 1 17 S. Ct. 2329 (1997). The dissenting argument, while agreeing that the CDA was unconstitutional, left open the possibility that material could in the future be banned from the open Internet and allowed only in special sites where access would be controlled by identification and screening of users. This proposal is onerous for several reasons: it threatens to restrict socially valuable information that the government does not wish people to see, and requires users to reveal their identities when viewing sensitive materials such as information on sexually transmitted diseases or information for victims of AIDS. This kind of violation would have serious implications for privacy of online users and also would have a chilling effect on use of the Internet.

Recently in the USA, the American Civil Liberties Union was alarmed because of the failure to examine the longer term implications for the Internet of rating and blocking schemes. The ACLU published a white paper in August 1997 entitled "Fahrenheit 451.2: Is Cyberspace Burning? How Rating and Blocking Proposals May Torch Free Speech on the Internet" (contained in this volume). The ACLU paper warned that government-coerced, industry efforts to rate content on the Internet could torch free speech online.

"In the physical world, people censor the printed word by burning books," said Barry Steinhardt, Associate Director of the ACLU and one of the paper's authors. "But in the virtual world, you can just as easily censor controversial speech by banishing it to the farthest corners of cyberspace with blocking and rating schemes." According to the ACLU, third-party ratings systems pose free speech problems and with few third-party rating products currently available, the potential for arbitrary censorship increases. The white paper was distributed with an open letter from Steinhardt to members of the Internet community. "It is not too late for the Internet community to slowly and carefully examine these proposals and to reject those that will transform the Internet from a true marketplace of ideas into just another mainstream, lifeless medium."

The ACLU white paper gave six reasons why self-rating schemes are wrong for the Internet and Cyber-Rights & Cyber-Liberties (UK) endorses these statements:

1) Self-rating schemes will cause controversial speech to be censored.

2) Self-rating is burdensome, unwieldy, and costly.

3) Conversation cannot be rated.

4) Self-rating will create "Fortress America" on the Internet.

5) Self-ratings will only encourage, not prevent, government regulation.

6) Self-ratings schemes will turn the Internet into a homogenised medium dominated by commercial speakers.

It seems likely that there will be many rating authorities, and different communities will consider the same web pages to be in different PICS/RSACi categories. Some rating authorities may judge a certain site as an offensive even though it has a socially valuable purpose, such as web sites dealing with sexual abuse and AIDS. This would mean that there will be no space for free speech arguments and dissent because the ratings will be done by private bodies and the government will not be involved "directly."

The governments do not need to either impose rating systems and rating bodies with different cultural backgrounds, nor get involved in their development.

### Parents Should be Responsible for Protecting Children

The prime responsibility for assuring an appropriate moral environment for children must rest elsewhere. Parents and teachers should be responsible for protecting children from accessing pornographic content which may be harmful to their development. Standards that are overly broad or loose will result if the job is handed over to rating bodies with different cultural backgrounds, the software industry, or even the producers of pornography. This is not a helpless demand for personal responsibility, since the computer industry is also supplying the means of protection.

Most filtering software available is designed for the home market. These are intended to respond to the preferences of parents making decisions for their own children. There are currently 15 blocking and filtering products and these are mainly US based (see http://www.netparents.org/software/) and do not represent the cultural differences in a global environment such as the Internet.

It has been reported many times that, this kind of software is over-inclusive and limits access to or censors inconvenient web sites, or filters potentially educational materials regarding AIDS and drug abuse prevention. Therefore, "censorware" enters homes despite the hype over "parental control" as an alternative to government censorship. The companies creating this kind of software also provide no appeal system to content providers who are "banned," thereby "subverting the self-regulating exchange of information that has been a hallmark of the Internet community." (see CPSR letter dated 18 December 1996 sent to Solid Oak, the makers of CyberSitter at http://www.cpsr.org/cpsr/nii/cyber-rights/)

Therefore, such software should not be used in public and university libraries because libraries are responsible for serving a broad and diverse community with different preferences and views. American Library Association in a resolution adopted in June 1997, stated that "blocking Internet sites is antithetical to library missions because it requires the library to limit information access."

We recommend that any filtering system should be market driven by the local industries, without government interference and that the local industries creating these kind of parental tools should be open and accountable to the online users.

### The Role of Self-Regulatory Bodies such as the Internet Watch Foundation

Internet Watch Foundation, supported by the UK Government, was announced in September 1996 and it follows up a similar initiative in Holland (see below) although there are differences between the two hotline systems. While the Dutch hotline is established by the Dutch Foundation for Internet Providers ("NLIP"), Dutch Internet users, the National Criminal Intelligence Service ("CRI"), National Bureau against Racial Discrimination and a psychologist, the UK Internet Watch Foundation ("IWF") is predominantly industry based.

---

**The Dutch Model**

The Dutch hotline has been operating quite successfully since June 1996, resulting in a substantial reduction of the amount of child pornography pictures distributed from Holland and resulting in the actual prosecution of authors, in close co-operation with the police. Furthermore, a procedure has been developed to deal with child pornography originating from other countries than the Netherlands. In case such complaint is sent to the hot-line, the foreign author and service provider are notified. If this action does not lead to the actual removal of the content, the Dutch police, after being informed by a representative of the hot-line, notifies their colleagues in the country of origination.

---

The Metropolitan Police in London has a free confidential telephone hot-line (0800-789321) to combat terrorism, and a similar step should have been taken to combat child pornography and child sexual abuse whether related to the Internet or not. This would have had a general purpose. The idea of removing materials containing child pornography from the Internet at UK level seems not to be a solution in a multi-national environment. The IWF is playing with fire as their possible future involvement with other kinds of content which may be offensive but totally legal, may set up a dangerous unprecedented act of privatised censorship where there is no space for dissent.

IWF has an e-mail, telephone and fax hot-line for users to be able to report materials related to child pornography and other obscene materials. IWF, informs all British ISPs once they locate the "undesirable content." The ISPs will have no excuse in law of being unaware of the offending material and the UK police will probably take action against those ISPs who do not remove the relevant content requested from IWF.

In contrast to the Dutch Model, the IWF proposals state that the UK ISPs should bear responsibility for their services and they need to implement reasonable, practicable and proportionate measures to hinder the use of the Internet for illegal purposes. But it is wrong to assume that ISPs should be responsible for content provided by the third parties on the Internet.

There are also technical problems with the utility of the IWF initiatives where on-line users will report the unwanted materials. Users will probably report material unacceptable according to their taste and moral views, but it should be remembered that it is for the Courts and judges to decide whether something is obscene or illegal. It should also be noted that with reporting systems the interpretation of images will always be subjective. IWF also promotes and recommends the use of rating systems such as PICS (see above) but industry based organisations backed up by governments do not need to either impose rating systems and rating bodies with different cultural backgrounds, nor get involved in their development. The application and utility of the IWF will have to be assessed and maybe reviewed.

### Internet Service Providers' Liability

ISPs differ in nature in different countries, but the main aim remains the provision of Internet related services to the online users. Technically it is not possible to access the Internet without the services of an ISP and therefore the role of the ISPs is crucial to access the Internet. The crucial role they play in providing access to the Internet made them visible targets for the control of "content regulation" on the Internet.

A recent European Commission Communication to the European Parliament, The Council, The Economic and Social Committee and the Committee of the Regions on Illegal and Harmful Content on the Internet, (1996) stated that "Internet access providers and host service providers play a key role in giving users access to Internet content. It should not however be forgotten that the prime responsibility for content lies with authors and content providers."

Blocking access at the level of access providers has been criticised by the EU communication paper on the ground that these actions go far beyond the limited category of illegal content and "such a restrictive regime is inconceivable for Europe as it would severely interfere with the freedom of the individual and its political traditions." Therefore "the law may need to be changed or clarified to assist access providers and host service providers, whose primary business is to provide a service to customers."

The EU developments are very important and would affect both the UK and other Member States. "Therefore, the position of the ISPs should be clarified, and they should not be targeted by the individual governments and law enforcement bodies where the ISPs have no control of the Internet content."

Two technical factors prevent a service provider, such as the CompuServe branch prosecuted twice in Germany over the past two years, from blocking the free flow of information on the Internet. First, an Internet service provider cannot easily stop the incoming flow of material and the thousands of unsolicited commercial e-mails that go through the systems of the ISPs is a good example of this. No one can monitor the enormous quantity of network traffic, which may consist of hundreds of thousands of emails, newsgroup messages, files, and Web pages that pass through in dozens of text and binary formats, some of them readable only by particular proprietary tools. As the European Commission noted recently, "it is as yet unclear how far it is technically possible to block access to content once it is identified as illegal. This is a problem which also affects the degree of liability of the access providers."

A second technical problem is that a provider cannot selectively disable transmission to particular users. Electronic networks typically do not allow for the identification of particular users or their national region. Thus, CompuServe correctly claimed that it cannot provide material in one country while blocking it in another; such a distinction would require an enormous new infrastructure on top of the current network.

Some networking technologies, such as newsgroups, may allow individual operators to select some groups or items and block others. But many technologies, such as the widely used World Wide Web, currently do not support such selectivity.

The recent "Bonn Declaration" underlined the importance of clearly defining the relevant legal rules on responsibility for content of the various actors in the chain between creation and use. The Declaration recognised the need to make a clear distinction between the responsibility of those who produce and place content in circulation and that of intermediaries such as the Internet Service Providers. (see <http://www2.echo.lu/bonn/ final.html>.)

The current situation at the UK does not represent a self-regulatory solution as suggested by the UK Government. It is moving towards a form of censorship, a privatised and industry based one where there will be no space for dissent as it will be done by the use of private organisations, rating systems and at the entry level by putting pressure on the UK Internet Service Providers. One can only recall the events which took place in the summer of 1996 and how the ISPs were pressured by the Metropolitan police to remove around 130 newsgroups from their servers.

## Policing the Internet and the Role of the UK Police

Internet related crimes are not a priority for the UK police forces while there is an insatiable demand for the bobby on the beat and reduction of the street crimes such as car thefts are a priority. Considering the international aspect of the Internet, it would not be only up to the UK police, or any other police force in its own to try to patrol the Internet.

The action taken by the UK Metropolitan police in August 1996 to censor usenet discussion groups was ill-considered and did not reduce the availability of pornographic content on the Internet. The list of newsgroups provided by the UK police included much material that is not illegal, such as legitimate discussion groups for homosexuals, and discussion groups which do not contain any pictures, but contain text, sexual fantasies and stories. These would almost certainly not infringe UK obscenity laws. The action of the Metropolitan police also amounts to censorship of material without any public debate. Any action with regard to regulation of the Internet should take place following informed debate and policy-making by Parliament and not by the police (or the industry itself). Sensible action by the UK government is needed to resolve the problem rather than censoring or banning distasteful material on the Internet and it is wrong to treat the ISPs as "usual suspects" for the provision of illegal content on the Internet.

## Conclusion

With rating systems and the moral panic behind the Internet content, the Internet could be transformed into a "family friendly" medium, just like the BBC. But it should be remembered that the Internet is not as intrusive as the TV and users seldom encounter illegal content such as child pornography. Like other historical forms of censorship, current attempts to define and ban objectionable content are vague and muddy, reaching out far beyond their reasonable targets to hurt the promise of open communication systems.

Government-imposed censorship, over-regulation, or service provider liability will do nothing to keep people from obtaining material the government does not like, as most of it will be on servers in another country (as happened recently with the availability of the JET Report in 37 different web sites on the Internet outside the UK). Such restrictions would, however, make Britain, like any other jurisdiction that goes too far, a very hostile place for network development or any other high-tech industry and investment.

If there is anyone who needs to be educated on Internet matters, it is the government officials, the police and MPs together with the media in the first place but not online users, parents and children. We do not need moral crusaders under the guise of industry based organisations to decide what is acceptable and not acceptable.

Child pornography is another matter, and its availability and distribution should be regulated whether on the Internet and elsewhere. But the main concern should remain the prevention of child abuse – the involvement of children in the making of pornography or its use to groom them to become involved in abusive acts, rather than discussion and fantasy. It was reported recently by the Home Department that the National Criminal Intelligence Service ("NCIS") Paedophile Section has spent £53,027 (1995-96) and £61,672 (1996-97) for gathering information on all forms of paedophile activity. More money should be spent to gather information about paedophiles and online paedophilia activity rather than spending the available resources on developing rating systems.

When censorship is implemented by government threat in the background, but run by private parties, legal action is nearly impossible, accountability difficult, and the system is not open and becomes undemocratic. These are sensitive issues and therefore, before introducing these systems there should be an open public debate possibly together with a consultation paper from the DTI. It should be noted that the IWF is predominantly industry based and therefore it does not necessarily represent the public at large and the UK society.

### Credits

Cyber-Rights & Cyber-Liberties (UK) Report, "Watching the Watchmen: Internet Content Rating Systems, Hotlines and Privatised Censorship" was written by Yaman Akdeniz. Professor Clive Walker, Centre for Criminal Justice Studies, University of Leeds, Ms. Louise Ellison, Faculty of Law, University of Manchester and Mr. Andrew Oram, Computer Professionals for Social Responsibility (USA) contributed to this report.

# Faulty Filters: How Content Filters Block Access to Kid-Friendly Information on the Internet

**Electronic Privacy Information Center**

## Executive Summary

In order to determine the impact of software filters on the open exchange of information on the Internet, the Electronic Privacy Information Center conducted 100 searches using a traditional search engine and then conducted the same 100 searches using a new search engine that is advertised as the "world's first family-friendly Internet search site." We tried to locate information about 25 schools; 25 charitable and political organizations; 25 educational, artistic, and cultural institutions; and 25 concepts that might be of interest to young people. Our search terms included such phrases as the "American Red Cross," the "San Diego Zoo," and the "Smithsonian Institution," as well as such concepts as "Christianity," the "Bill of Rights" and "eating disorders." In every case in our sample, we found that the family-friendly search engine prevented us from obtaining access to almost 90 percent of the materials on the Internet containing the relevant search terms. We further found that in many cases, the search service denied access to 99 percent of material that would otherwise be available without the filters. We concluded that the filtering mechanism prevented children from obtaining a great deal of useful and appropriate information that is currently available on the Internet.

## Introduction

The subject of whether to promote techniques to limit access to information available on the Internet grows out of the litigation against the Communications Decency Act. In that case, the Supreme Court ruled that the First Amendment protected the right to publish information on the Internet. The Court also found that "the interest in encouraging freedom of expression in a democratic society outweighs any theoretical but unproven benefit of censorship."

Shortly after the Supreme Court issued its decision, the White House convened a meeting to discuss the need to develop content filters for the Internet. The Administration unveiled a "Strategy for a Family Friendly Internet." According to the White House proposal, a key component would be the promotion of labeling and screening systems designed to shield children from inappropriate Internet content.

President Clinton said that he thought it was necessary to develop search engines specifically designed to screen out objectionable material. He said that it "must be our objective" to ensure that the labeling of Internet content "will become standard practice." Vice President Gore said, "Our challenge is to make these blocking technologies and the accompanying rating systems as common as the computers themselves."

In a statement released during the White House meeting, five Internet companies – CNET, Excite, Infoseek, Lycos and Yahoo! – expressed their support of the "White House proposal for the Internet industry to adopt a self-regulated rating system for content on the Web."

Following the White House summit, several companies announced that they would develop products and services for content filtering. On October 6, 1997, Net Shepherd and AltaVista launched Family Search. They described the product as "the world's first family-friendly Internet search site." Family Search is the first product to incorporate two of the goals identified at the July White House meeting – content rating and filtered search engines.

### The "Family Search" Service

Net Shepherd Family Search is a web-based search engine located on the Internet at http://family.netshepherd.com. According to the "Frequently Asked Questions" (FAQ) file available at the site, Family Search "is designed to make the Internet a friendlier, more productive place for families. This is achieved though filtering out web sites judged by an independent panel of demographically appropriate Internet users, to be inappropriate and/or objectionable to average user families."

The Family Search service operates as follows: A user submits a search request, such as "American Red Cross." That request is then directed to the AltaVista search engine. The AltaVista results are then filtered through Net Shepherd's ratings database, and the filtered results are presented to the user. For this reason, conducting a search using the AltaVista search engine, and then conducting the same search using the Net Shepherd search engine, shows exactly how much information is removed by the Net Shepherd filter.

Net Shepherd claims that it has completed the most comprehensive rating of material on the World Wide Web. According to the company (as reported in the FAQ), in March of 1997 it had rated "97% of the English language sites on the Web."

For this survey, it is particularly important to emphasize two claims made by Net Shepherd about its family-friendly search engine. First, Net Shepherd states that the filtering criterion is whether a web site is "inappropriate and/or objectionable to average user families." Second, Net Shepherd states that its review of material available on the Web is comprehensive – "97% of the English language sites."

## Survey Methodology

We set out to determine the actual effect of the filtering process – to quantify the amount of information that was actually blocked by a filtered search engine. Family Search's use of AltaVista results enabled us to conduct a straightforward comparison of a filtered and an unfiltered search. We first entered our search criteria into the AltaVista search engine [http://altavista.digital.com] and recorded the number of documents produced in reponse to our request. This number appeared at the top of search results returned by AltaVista.

We then duplicated our search request with Family Search and recorded the number of documents located through that search engine. Unlike AltaVista, Family Search does not report the number of matching documents. We had to read each page of the search results and manually count the number of documents retrieved.

All of our searches that contained more than one word in the search were submitted in quotation marks.

Family Search allows the user to designate a desired "quality" level for its search results. In conducting our searches, we used the default of "no preference." This is the most comprehensive setting and allowed us to retrieve all of the documents that Family Search would provide.

All of our searches were conducted between November 17 and November 26, 1997. We conducted 100 searches for key phrases using the unfiltered and the filtered search engines. We divided the 100 searches into four groups:

- Elementary, middle and high schools
- Charitable and political organizations
- Educational, artistic and cultural institutions
- Miscellaneous concepts and entities

We were particularly interested in the topics that would interest young people. For this reason we selected search phrases for organizations and ideas that we thought would be or should be of interest to children ages 18 and below. We are aware that not all families would agree that all of the phrases we selected would be appropriate for their children, but by and large we thought the 100 phrases we selected would likely be the types of searches that children who are using the Internet for non-objectionable purposes would conduct and that their parents would probably encourage.

Our findings are contained in the attached table. The results are summarized below:

### Survey of Elementary, Middle and High Schools

With the growth of the Internet, many schools are today taking advantage of new communications technology. Not only are students able to access information around the world from a computer terminal in their classroom, they are also able to set up web sites. Many of these sites contain practical information – how to contact teachers, homework assignments, and cancellation policies. Many sites also include school projects. Although the content of the sites is as different as are the schools, one thing seems clear – the web sites in this category are web sites created for young people and often by young people. Thus when we tried locating these sites through the family-friendly search engine, we were surprised by the outcome.

The Arbor Heights Elementary School in Seattle, Washington maintains a highly regarded web site located at http://www.halcyon.com/arborhts/ arborhts.html. More than 70,000 people have visited the web site in the last two years. The school also publishes a magazine specifically for kids aged 7 through 12 called "Cool Writers Magazine" that is available at the web site.

If you go to the AltaVista search engine and search for "Arbor Heights Elementary," you will get back 824 hits. But if you use the Net Shepherd family-friendly search engine, only three documents are returned. In other words, Net Shepherd blocks access to more than 99 percent of the material that would otherwise be available on AltaVista containing the search phrase "Arbor Heights Elementary."

We found similar results with other searches. More than 96 percent of the material referring to "Providence School" is blocked by Family Search. Over 98 percent of the material referring to "Ralph Bunche School" is also blocked.

This seemed extraordinary to us. The blocking criteria deployed by Net Shepherd is, according to the company, whether a site is "inappropriate and/or objectionable to average user families." We looked at several of the pages that were returned with the unfiltered search engine but not with the filtered search engine. We could not find anything that an average user family would consider to be inappropriate or objectionable.

### Survey of Charitable and Political Organizations

We selected 25 organizations representing national charities and groups across the political spectrum. Many of these organizations were established to provide services and assistance to children and parents. All have made important use of the Internet to provide timely and useful information on-line at little or no cost to families across the country.

The American Red Cross site (http://www.crossnet.org/), for example, provides an extraordinary collection of information about public health and medical resources. The American Red Cross has a special interest in families. It designated November "Child Safety and Protection Month." If you go to this web page [http://www.crossnet.org/healthtips/firstaid.html] you will find a special section devoted to "Health and Safety Tips: How to Protect Your Family with First Aid Training."

These resources and other similar materials are available if you conduct an AltaVista search for "American Red Cross." Almost 40,000 document were returned with the search. But a search with Family Search for the same phrase produced only 77 hits. The search engine filter had blocked access to 99.8

percent of the documents concerning the "American Red Cross" that would otherwise be available on the Internet.

Similar results were found when we conducted searches for the "Child Welfare League of America," "UNICEF" and "United Way."

Political organizations are also subject to extensive filtering. More than 4,000 documents about the NAACP can be found by means of AltaVista, but Family Search seems to believe that only 15 documents on the Internet concerning the NAACP are appropriate for young people.

## Survey of Educational, Artistic and Cultural Institutions

Many organizations use the Internet today to provide all types of valuable information for young people. We conducted searches for many well known kids' activities, such as "Disneyland," "National Zoo," and the "Boy Scouts of America."

The National Aquarium in Baltimore is one of top attractions for young people in the mid-Atlantic region. The Aquarium has created an extensive web site [http://www.aqua.org/], filled with a lot of neat stuff. If you go to Think Tank, you can try to answer a daily question about aquatic life. In the Education section of the web site, titled "Wonder Leads to Understanding," you will learn more about special programs at the National Aquarium for young people. The Aquarium's resources are widely found across the Internet. An AltaVista search produced 2,134 responses. But the family-friendly search engine produced only 63 responses.

Intrigued by the tremendous discrepancy, we decided to visit every one of the first 200 web pages returned by Alta Vista to see how it could be that, on average, 97 percent of the material would be considered objectionable to the average user family. We did find several speeches and papers that mentioned the National Aquarium as well as several events that were held at the National Aquarium. We also learned that the United States does not have the only National Aquarium. Others can be found in Australia and the Phillipines. We learned that a few people take family pictures when they go to the National Aquarium and that people who work at the Aquarium mention it on their resumes. But we couldn't find any objectionable or inappropriate material.

For searches of information on the Internet on many of the most popular educational institutions in the United States for kids, Family Search routinely blocked 99 percent of the documents. "Yellowstone National Park" produced a blocking rate of 99.8 percent. The blocking rate for the "San Diego Zoo" was 99.6 percent.

One of the most peculiar results in the entire survey concerned our search for the "National Basketball Association." A straightforward search on AltaVista produced 18,018 hits. But when we tried Family Search, only two documents were provided. We have no idea what is in the remaining 18,016 documents that Family Search considers to be objectionable for the average family using the Internet.

### Survey of Miscellaneous Concepts and Entities

For this last category, we considered the topics that students might be interested in learning more about as part of a school research paper or similar project. We tried to select concepts and entities from a range of areas appropriate for young people – science, history, geography, government, religion, as well as famous people.

Consider, for example, a young student who is writing a research paper on "Thomas Edison," one of the greatest inventors of all time. If the student undertakes a search with AltaVista, 11,522 documents are returned. But if the student uses the Family Search site, only nine documents are produced. Similar results will be found with such search phrases as "Betsy Ross," "Islam," "Emily Dickinson," and "United States Supreme Court."

We recognize that young people also have concerns about sensitive topics such as eating disorders, puberty, and teen pregnancy. Parents' views on how best to handle such issues varies considerably from family to family. Not surprisingly, most of the documents available on the Internet about these topics are extensively blocked by Family Search. But what was surprising to us is that the blocking of these sensitive matters was not any greater than with such topics as "photosynthesis" (99.5 percent), "astronomy" (99.9 percent) or "Wolfgang Amadeus Mozart" (99.9 percent). In other words, it is just as difficult to get information about the "Constitution of the United States" – actually, somewhat more so – as it is to get information about "puberty" using a family-friendly search engine.

Even Dr. Suess fares poorly with this family-friendly search engine. Only eight of the 2,638 references on the Internet relating to Dr. Suess are made available by Family Search. And one of the eight documents that was produced by the search engine turned out to be a parody of a Dr. Suess story using details from the murder of Nicole Brown Simpson.

## Limitations of Survey

We recognized in the course of the survey a number of limitations on our survey method. First, the figures that we provide regarding how much material the search engine blocks actually represent a percentage of the information blocked that would otherwise be available by means of the AltaVista search engine. There is material available on the Internet that is not located by AltaVista, but could be found by other locator services such as Yahoo! or Hotbot. If this factor were taken into account, the percentage of materials blocked by Family Search, expressed as a percentage of all the material available on the Internet containing the relevant search phrases, would necessarily increase.

We also recognize that there is some ambiguity in search terms and that context is often necessary to establish meaning. We tried where possible to select search terms that would reduce the risk of ambiguity.

W did not attempt to review all of the filtering products currently available. For the reasons described above, and particularly the emphasis that filter proponents have placed on search engines that can perform this task, we believed it was appropriate to limit our study to the one search engine specifically designed to block access to "inappropriate material."

## Conclusion

Our research showed that a family-friendly search engine, of the kind recommended by proponents of Internet rating schemes at the White House summit in July 1997, typically blocked acccess to 95-99 percent of the material available on the Internet that might be of interest to young people. We also found that as information on popular topics became more widely available on the Internet, the search engine was likely to block an even higher percentage. We further found that the search engine did not seem to restrict sensitive topics for young people any more than it restricted matters of general interest. Even with the very severe blocking criteria employed, we noted that some material which parents might consider to be objectionable was still provided by the family-friendly service.

Our review led us to conclude that proponents of filters and rating systems should think more carefully about whether this is a sensible approach. In the end, "family-friendly" filtering does not seem very friendly.

## Recommendations

While it is true that there is material available on the Internet that some will find legitimately objectionable, it is also clear that in some cases the proposed solutions may be worse than the actual problem. Filtering programs that deny children access to a wide range of useful and appropriate materials ultimately diminish the educational value of the Internet.

> The White House should reconsider its support for the Internet filtering effort, and particularly for the idea of filter-based search engines. This approach is flawed and these programs make it more difficult for young people to find useful and appropriate information.

> Vendors of filtering and tagging products need to be much more forthcoming about the actual effect of their programs and services. It is deceptive and fraudulent to say that a program blocks "objectionable content" when it also blocks a great deal of information that is useful and valuable for young people.

> Alternatives to software filters and tagging should be explored. The European Union has recently proposed a range of options including codes of conduct, hotlines, and warnings.

> Parents should learn more about the benefits of the Internet for their children and families. In the ongoing debate about the availability of objectionable materials, one key point has been lost – the Internet is a wonderful resource for young people.

> Parents should continue to take a strong interest in their children's use of the Internet. Helping children tell right from wrong is not something that should be left to computer software or search engines.

We hope that additional research will be done on the impact other filtering programs may have on the ability of young people to obtain useful information on the Internet. Without such studies, it is not possible to say whether it is sensible to promote these programs.

## Resources

**Internet Free Expression Alliance** [http://www.ifea.net/] – IFEA was established to protect the free flow of information on the Internet. It includes more than two dozen member organizations. Information is available from the IFEA web site about rating and filtering systems, including the views of the American Civil Liberties Union, the American Library Association, the Computer Professionals for Social Responsibility, the Electronic Frontier Foundation, the Electronic Privacy Information Center, the National Campaign for Freedom of Expression, the National Coalition Against Censorship, and others.

## About EPIC

The Electronic Privacy Information Center is a public interest research organization, based in Washington, DC.

Electronic Privacy Information Center 666 Pennsylvania Ave., SE Suite 301 Washington, DC 20003 +1 202 544 9240 (tel) +1 202 547 5482 (fax) http://www.epic.org/

Appendix – Tables of Search Results

## Table 1: Elementary, Middle and High Schools

| Search Terms | Hits: AltaVista | Hits: Family Search | Percent Filtered |
|---|---|---|---|
| Arbor Heights Elementary | 824 | 3 | 99.6%* |
| Avocado Elementary School | 181 | 26 | 85.6% |
| Biboohra State School | 35 | 2 | 94.2% |
| Camp Creek Elementary School | 83 | 9 | 89.1% |
| Clearview Elementary School | 94 | 10 | 89.3% |
| Evergreen Elementary School | 210 | 12 | 94.2% |
| Frenchtown School | 69 | 1 | 98.5% |
| Grace Church School | 67 | 6 | 91.0% |
| Hillside Elementary | 1737 | 20 | 98.8% |
| Keolu Elementary School | 48 | 4 | 91.6% |
| Marshall Elementary School | 465 | 15 | 96.7% |
| New Hope Elementary School | 71 | 5 | 92.9% |
| Oak Hill Academy | 492 | 16 | 96.7% |
| Providence Day School | 241 | 9 | 96.2% |
| Ralph Bunche School | 981 | 14 | 98.5% |
| Riverdale School | 446 | 25 | 94.3% |
| Shady Hill School | 191 | 16 | 91.6% |
| St. Therese School | 160 | 7 | 95.6% |
| University Park Elementary | 575 | 11 | 98.0% |
| Woodward Avenue Elementary School | 92 | 2 | 97.8% |
| Vista Middle School | 647 | 13 | 97.9% |
| Trinity Christian School | 377 | 17 | 95.4% |
| Claremont High School | 773 | 8 | 98.9% |
| Los Alamos High School | 609 | 15 | 97.5% |
| Westview Centennial Secondary School | 89 | 2 | 97.7% |

Table 2: Charitable and/or Political Organizations

| Search Terms | Hits: AltaVista | Hits: Family Search | Percent Filtered |
|---|---|---|---|
| American Association of Retired Persons | 8498 | 25 | 99.7% |
| American Cancer Society | 38762 | 6 | 99.9% |
| American Family Association | 3335 | 12 | 99.6% |
| American Red Cross | 39434 | 77 | 99.8% |
| Catholic Relief Services | 1777 | 18 | 98.9% |
| Child Welfare League of America | 2170 | 19 | 99.9% |
| Christian Coalition | 16170 | 19 | 99.8% |
| Concerned Women for America | 2182 | 23 | 98.9% |
| Congress of National Black Churches | 282 | 27 | 90.4% |
| Cystic Fibrosis Foundation | 2830 | 15 | 99.4% |
| Family Friendly Libraries | 181 | 20 | 88.9% |
| Family Research Council | 4286 | 32 | 99.2% |
| Focus on the Family | 6172 | 23 | 99.6% |
| Hostelling International American Youth Hostels | 374 | 10 | 99.7% |
| Klaas Foundation | 933 | 64 | 93.1% |
| Leukemia Society of America | 2723 | 13 | 99.5% |
| National Association for the Advancement of Colored People | 4076 | 15 | 99.6% |
| National Association of Homes and Services for Children | 135 | 7 | 94.8% |
| National Consumers League | 1692 | 10 | 99.4% |
| National Organization for Women | 8270 | 35 | 99.5% |
| National Rifle Association | 11828 | 19 | 99.8% |
| UNICEF | 1423 | 17 | 98.8% |
| United Cerebral Palsy Association | 941 | 21 | 97.7% |
| United Jewish Appeal | 3024 | 1 | 99.9% |
| United Way | 54300 | 23 | 99.9% |

**Table 3: Educational, Artistic and/or Cultural Institutions**

| Search Terms | Hits: AltaVista | Hits: Family Search | Percent Filtered |
|---|---|---|---|
| Art Institute of Chicago | 9785 | 10 | 99.9% |
| Boy Scouts of America | 22297 | 35 | 99.8% |
| Carnegie Library | 5755 | 32 | 99.4% |
| Cleveland Orchestra | 2689 | 18 | 99.3% |
| Dance Theater of Harlem | 317 | 27 | 91.4% |
| Disneyland | 11129 | 31 | 99.7% |
| Folger Shakespeare Library | 1421 | 18 | 98.7% |
| Future Farmers of America | 2205 | 22 | 99.0% |
| Future Homemakers of America | 1280 | 12 | 99.0% |
| Girl Scouts of America | 1606 | 30 | 98.1% |
| Grand Old Opry | 371 | 31 | 91.6% |
| Independence Hall | 3281 | 22 | 99.3% |
| Julliard School of Music | 500 | 11 | 97.8% |
| Kennedy Center | 13068 | 71 | 99.4% |
| Metropolitan Museum of Art | 19930 | 50 | 99.7% |
| Museum of Modern Art | 23566 | 31 | 99.8% |
| National Aquarium | 2134 | 63 | 97.0% |
| National Basketball Association | 18018 | 2 | 99.9% |
| National Gallery of Art | 8655 | 73 | 99.1% |
| National Zoo | 4142 | 6 | 99.8% |
| Public Broadcasting System | 3603 | 26 | 99.2% |
| Radio City Music Hall | 5594 | 20 | 99.6% |
| San Diego Zoo | 5895 | 21 | 99.6% |
| Smithsonian Institution | 51033 | 37 | 99.9% |
| Yellowstone National Park | 14933 | 26 | 99.8% |

**Table 4: Miscellaneous Concepts or Entities (potential research topics)**

| Search Terms | Hits: AltaVista | Hits: Family Search | Percent Filtered |
|---|---|---|---|
| Astronomy | 121306 | 22 | 99.9% |
| Betsy Ross | 3055 | 23 | 99.2% |
| Bill of Rights | 46195 | 44 | 99.9% |
| Catholicism | 4590 | 12 | 99.7% |
| Christianity | 37574 | 13 | 99.9% |
| Christopher Columbus | 13498 | 5 | 99.9% |
| Constitution of the United States | 17877 | 31 | 99.8% |
| Democratic Party | 56333 | 22 | 99.9% |
| Dr. Seuss | 2638 | 8 | 99.6% |
| Eating Disorders | 11602 | 23 | 99.8% |
| Emily Dickinson | 10050 | 8 | 99.9% |
| First Amendment | 58529 | 94 | 99.8% |
| Frederick Douglass | 7286 | 24 | 99.6% |
| House of Representatives | 158972 | 38 | 99.9% |
| Islam | 27572 | 10 | 99.9% |
| Judaism | 11985 | 7 | 99.9% |
| Photosynthesis | 4963 | 23 | 99.5% |
| Puberty | 2276 | 25 | 98.9% |
| Republican Party | 28218 | 21 | 99.9% |
| Romeo and Juliet | 24428 | 47 | 99.8% |
| Teen pregnancy | 13113 | 46 | 99.6% |
| Thomas Edison | 11522 | 9 | 99.9% |
| U.S. Senate | 18810 | 41 | 99.7% |
| United States Supreme Court | 19917 | 20 | 99.9% |
| Wolfgang Amadeus Mozart | 7074 | 7 | 99.9% |

* All percentages have been rounded down to the nearest tenth of a percent.

# Censored Internet Access in Utah Public Schools and Libraries

**The Censorware Project**

---

## Abstract

The Utah Education Network (www.uen.org) is an agency of the Utah state government charged with providing telecommunications services, including internet access, to public schools and libraries in Utah. UEN uses a commercial software package to censor the internet access of all of the 40 school districts and at least eight of the 70 library districts in Utah.

An examination of the results of this censoring during the period September 10-October 10, 1998, found that many users were banned from accessing sites useful for educational and research purposes. Banned accesses made up less than 1% of overall accesses, most of which were banner ads presumed (by the software) to be sexually explicit. Very few people used the internet to access sexually explicit material, and students were the least likely to do so. It thus appears that the stated problem of minors accessing sexually explicit material (inadvertently or deliberately) is considerably less than some organizations would have the public and the Congress believe.

UEN censors many things that are not in any way illegitimate for Utah adults or students to view. Among the documents which UEN prevented citizens from viewing:

- The Declaration of Independence
- The United States Constitution

---

Written by Michael Sims with Bennett Haselton, Jamie McCarthy, James S. Tyre, Jonathan Wallace, David Smith and Gabriel Wachob (Version 1.1, March 1999). The complete text of this report, including detailed charts and appendices, is available at The Censorware Project's website: http://censorware.org/reports/utah/.

---

- The Bible
- The Book of Mormon
- The Koran
- The Adventures of Sherlock Holmes
- A Connecticut Yankee in King Arthur's Court
- George Washington's Farewell Address
- The Mayflower Compact
- All of Shakespeare's plays
- The Canterbury Tales
- Wuthering Heights
- "Marijuana: Facts for Teens" (a U.S. Government brochure)

as well as many others, including safe-sex sites, sites discussing AIDS prevention, magazines available at any newsstand (Glamour, Seventeen), etc.

Statistics on the banning are presented, with a discussion of the results.

## Introduction

In April 1998, the Salt Lake Tribune, a Utah newspaper, ran a story entitled "Web Sex Sites: Public School Logs Show Denied Hits." The story was picked up by the Associated Press and eventually ran in a number of newspapers nationwide. The story indicated, among other things, that the Utah Education Network, which provides internet access for essentially all Utah public schools and many libraries, kept log files of the internet accesses made through their service and employed a software censoring product, Smartfilter, to censor internet access at schools and libraries. (Smartfilter is a product of Secure Computing Corporation, http://www.securecomputing.com/ ).The Censorware Project and David Smith decided to request these log files under Utah's Government Records Access and Management Act (known as GRAMA, this is Utah's "Freedom of Information" act).

Internet access in schools and libraries is a hot topic. And there is a great lack of hard data about it. We hope this report (and the accompanying data, which is also available) will begin to fill that void.

Obtaining the files was easier decided upon than accomplished. UEN refused to provide these public records, and under GRAMA, we appealed to the Utah State Records Committee. UEN's cited reasons included an invasion of privacy of the users of the system, although many administrators have access to these computer log files and UEN specifically bans websites which users could use to protect their privacy on-line. In June 1998, after a hearing on the issue, the State Records Committee ordered UEN to provide the files. To eliminate any question of invading the privacy of the users, all of the originating internet addresses were redacted. The log files as presented represent an anonymous picture of the aggregate usage of UEN's network.

In July 1998, UEN decided not to appeal the decision of the State Records Committee and offered a set of the log files. UEN had flouted Utah state law by destroying the log files from April - May 1998, which we had requested, and instead offered the current files from July, when school was not in session and the log files were therefore much less useful. We complained to the State Records Committee, which took a step it had never before taken: they recommended the matter to the Salt Lake County District Attorney, Neal Gunnarson, for investigation and possible prosecution.

Mr. Gunnarson, who achieved fame in 1997 by getting caught destroying copies of a Utah newspaper which he took exception to, failed to investigate or take any action against UEN. The complaint was promptly buried and forgotten, proving that no matter what the law says, and no matter how blatant the violation, if the will to enforce it is not present, the law is worthless.

Since the original log files had been destroyed, we decided to get a set of files from September 1998, when school would be in session. We obtained them, with much better cooperation from UEN this time, and after some delays, produced the following report.

**Methodology, Background and Sample Population**

Log files created by UEN's eleven proxy servers running the Smartfilter software were collected and analyzed. A "proxy server" is a computer through which requests for documents on the internet pass. The software running on the proxy server examines each request as it is made and decides whether to accept it (and fetch the requested document) or reject it. The decision is made by consulting an encrypted list of internet addresses which were determined, by Secure Computing Corporation, to fall into one of 27 categories. When the access is accepted or rejected, the proxy servers note the result in an electronic log file.

The log files covered the period 10 September through 10 October 1998, inclusive, which represented 20 days when school was in session and 11 non-school days. The files contained the following information:

IP address of accessing computer [REDACTED by UEN]
Date/time of access
Method of access
URL accessed
HTTP specification
HTTP status code
Number of bytes returned
Smartfilter category classification

The log files ended up being 838 Mb compressed; approximately 6.5 Gigabytes uncompressed, and included about 53 million lines of data, with each line representing one access or attempted access of a resource on the World Wide Web. Email, chat (except for web-based chat), and other methods of using the internet are not covered by these log files and are not known to be intercepted by Smartfilter.

The log files were not pristine. Files from the various proxy servers were combined into a single file for transmission to us. When received, they contained inconsistencies, especially in the places where one file ended and the next began. A very small number of URLs were discarded due to these errors in the files. This is not expected to bias the results in any measurable fashion.

The files were scanned by a custom-written computer program (perl), which collected statistics about the files and separated the URLs by which category(ies) they were banned under. Smartfilter classifies documents on the web into 27 categories, any or all of which can be activated by the entity controlling the software (UEN). UEN has five of the 27 categories activated: "Sex," "Gambling," "Criminal Skills," "Hate Speech," and "Drugs." A URL can be classified in multiple categories. If a user tries to access a URL which is classified in any of the five categories which UEN has activated, they will generally receive a message saying that access has been denied.

Certain statistics regarding the files were also collected with image files excluded, to the extent possible. For these statistics, URLs ending in "gif" or "jpg" or "jpeg" were excluded, as well as all URLs from domains known to be dedicated to serving banner ads. This process is slightly overinclusive – if a user visited the banner ad domain directly, to look up advertising rates for example, these accesses would be discarded. It is also moderately underinclusive – there are sites which serve image files in various non-standard methods,which would not be caught nor discarded by this procedure.

UEN has no access to Smartfilter's list of banned sites. They will know a given site is banned only by attempting to access it and being blocked from doing so. UEN does not make additions to the list of banned sites and makes very few removals (see discussion). For all practical purposes, the makers of Smartfilter (Secure Computing Corporation of San Jose, California) make the final decisions as to what Utah students, adults and library patrons can view over the internet.

Costs to UEN for maintaining the censoring proxy servers are significant. A newspaper article indicated the cost for the software alone is approximately $20,000 per year. UEN's budget for fiscal year 1999 indicates they were allocated $12,000 for proxy software and $124,048 for proxy hardware. There are also substantial costs associated with the personnel to maintain and administer these servers.

After the files were scanned and separated into categories, the URLs which had been banned in each category were reviewed. For the four smaller categories, this review was simply scanning over the list looking for URLs which seemed "out of place." For the "Sex" category, another script (computer program) was employed to aid in the review. URLs which appeared to represent valuable resources wrongly or irrationally banned were called up (see discussion). The review process likely missed many such URLs. The review process should have been efficient enough to discover the majority (>50%; perhaps >75%) of the wrongful bans present in the log files. Note that this applies only to the list of wrongly or irrationally banned sites at the end of the report; the statistics and graphs presented were compiled by a simple computer program and are presumed to be 100% accurate. Achieving 100% accuracy in reviewing the banned sites would require humans to examine the document at every URL banned, which is prohibitively difficult.

The user population which created these log files is diverse. During school days, the users are predominantly public school students. The vast majority of Utah public schools are wired for internet access (although sometimes this means having one computer with a modem); a majority of the wired schools have computing facilities available to students. In general, it appears that many Utah high schools are well-connected and have multiple computers available to students, while many elementary schools may have only a single computer with a dial-up connection to the internet, which may be available only for class demonstrations and the like and not for student use. It is assumed that the bulk of student internet accesses are from students aged 13-18. From information provided by UEN and our own research, it is believed that all public elementary and secondary schools in Utah have all of their internet access provided through UEN's Smartfilter-equipped proxy servers.

According to the Census Bureau, Utah has some 500,000 residents between the ages of 5 and 17. Not all of them attend public schools; there are approximately 30 private schools plus the possibility of home schooling. Considering this factor and the factors listed previously, we believe a reasonable estimate for the number of public school students who had the opportunity to use the internet during the sampled time period to be in the neighborhood of 100,000-150,000. We have no estimate for the number of library patrons and dial-up educators whose accesses contribute to the non-school day logs.

During non-school days, the users are predominantly library patrons, with a smattering of dial-up users (these people would also be present during the school days, of course, and make up a sort of "background" presence to the scholastic users). UEN provides dial-up access at all hours of the day and night to an unknown number of teachers statewide. Thus, accesses which occur at times when neither libraries or schools are open are from these dial-up services. Of the 70 public library systems in Utah, at least eight use UEN's proxy servers, and probably several more. A few public libraries in Utah use other censoring software products. Many public libraries do not censor internet access. Urban areas may be less likely to have censored internet access than rural areas. Nationally, the average age of internet users is 30-35, so this population can probably be assumed to be significantly older than the student population.

Internet usage during school days is approximately 20 times that of non-school days.

## Discussion

The results show that only a small percentage of the URLs accessed were banned by Smartfilter. Overall, approximately 0.39% of all accesses were stopped by the program. Additionally, there were substantial differences in the access patterns between the times when school was in session and when it was not. (The distinction between school and non-school days is crucial. See Methodology for more information.)

Overall, about one out of every 260 requests was banned. For school days, the figure was lower: about one out of every 280 requests. For days when school was not in session, the figure was twice as high: about one out of every 120 requests was censored. One can view this in two ways: high school students are much less likely to access banned material, or adults are more likely to.

## Tables 1 and 2. Overall Statistics

| Time Period | Total Accesses | Total Banned Accesses | Sex | Drugs | Hate Speech | Criminal Skills | Gambling |
|---|---|---|---|---|---|---|---|
| All days | 53,103,387 | 205,737 | 193,272 | 1,588 | 791 | 4,934 | 5,772 |
| All School Days | 50,461,490 | 182,600 | 171,509 | 1,557 | 762 | 4,440 | 5,129 |
| All Non-School Days | 2,641,897 | 23,137 | 21,763 | 31 | 29 | 494 | 643 |

| Time Period | Total Accesses (%) | Total Banned Accesses (%) | Sex (%) | Drugs (%) | Hate Speech (%) | Criminal Skills (%) | Gambling (%) |
|---|---|---|---|---|---|---|---|
| All days | 100 | 0.387 | 0.364 | 0.0030 | 0.0015 | 0.0093 | 0.011 |
| All School Days | 100 | 0.362 | 0.340 | 0.0031 | 0.0015 | 0.0088 | 0.010 |
| All Non-School Days | 100 | 0.876 | 0.824 | 0.0012 | 0.0011 | 0.019 | 0.024 |

During the examination, it became apparent that many of the accesses which were being banned, primarily in the "Sex" category, were banner ads. Some websites include banner ads which are sent from other sites, internet advertising companies which send out hundreds of thousands of banner ads daily. Smartfilter was banning many of these banner ad sites under its "Sex" category, possibly because some of them displayed banner ads on sexually-explicit websites or displayed sexually-explicit banner ads. This seemed to considerably inflate the number of banned accesses under the "Sex" category, because someone could be visiting, say, Yahoo.com, and if Yahoo was using one of the banned banner ad sites, each page visited on Yahoo would lead to another entry in the logfiles as the banner ad was rejected. Thus it is entirely possible to generate banned accesses in these log files when the user never intended to visit any sort of sexually-explicit site (see also the discussion of wrongly banned sites).

In order to examine this situation, we resolved to examine the log files without counting images. It is important to understand the procedure that occurs when one accesses a web page:

**Situation A**. Load a page. The HTML file (the text on the page) is loaded first. It may reference anywhere from zero to hundreds of images in its code. When the HTML page is loaded, the individual images are then loaded. The total number of accesses is equal to one for the HTML page plus one for each image loaded.

**Situation B**. Load a page. The page is banned by Smartfilter and rejected. No images are loaded. The total number of accesses is one.

Thus, eliminating images from consideration effectively normalizes the distribution: accessing one page, whether it is banned or not, counts as one access. We felt this might be a more useful tally (although of course the straight access count is valid as well).

We undertook to exclude all images from the logfiles and recompile the statistics on a no-images basis. (See the Methodology for more information.) The results were roughly as expected. Eliminating the images eliminated very many of the overall hits, more than two-thirds. The percentage of bans was therefore increased across the board, although the number of banned hits dropped as well with the elimination of the images. The "Sex" category showed the greatest drop: almost half of the "Sex" accesses were eliminated, showing that very many of the original "Sex" bans were not caused by people looking for pornography but were banner ads, probably completely innocent, that were served from banned domains.

**Tables 3 and 4. Statistics Excluding Images and Known Banner-Ad Sites**

| Time Period | Total Accesses | Total Banned Accesses | Sex | Drugs | Hate Speech | Criminal Skills | Gambling |
|---|---|---|---|---|---|---|---|
| All days | 15,434,442 | 95,059 | 86,957 | 1,298 | 526 | 3,753 | 3,649 |
| All School Days | 14,462,434 | 83,503 | 76,267 | 1,273 | 498 | 3,383 | 3,111 |
| All Non-School Days | 972,008 | 11,556 | 10,690 | 25 | 28 | 370 | 538 |

| Time Period | Total Accesses (%) | Total Banned Accesses (%) | Sex (%) | Drugs (%) | Hate Speech (%) | Criminal Skills (%) | Gambling (%) |
|---|---|---|---|---|---|---|---|
| All days | 100's | 0.616 | 0.563 | 0.0084 | 0.0034 | 0.024 | 0.024 |
| All School Days | 100 | 0.577 | 0.527 | 0.0088 | 0.0034 | 0.023 | 0.022 |
| All Non-School Days | 100 | 1.189 | 1.100 | 0.0026 | 0.0029 | 0.038 | 0.055 |

Examination of the log files also showed that late-night (i.e., adult) accesses were much more likely to be banned. Graphs of these data (available at http://www.censorware.org/reports/utah/charts.shtml) relate the time of day and whether it was a school or non-school day to the number of accesses and number of bans recorded at that time. The charts also include a category called "universal," which is shorthand for sites which are banned under *all* of Smartfilter's categories. These universal bans are on sites which might allow someone to get around the banning, such as www.anonymizer.com.

Figures 1-4 show total statistics. Both charts showing total accesses (Fig. 1,3) show a very pronounced "bell" shape, having many more accesses occurring during the middle of the day. The curves for banned accesses (Fig. 2,4) show somewhat flatter shapes, as more of the bans occur in the evenings and late nights. Figures 5-8 show the same statistics with images removed. These graphs are much flatter, especially the graphs of banned sites. The fact that removing banned images flattens the graphs shows that more of the "unintentional," banner-ad bans occurred during the day while accesses at night were less likely to be of this variety. Generally, school accesses which generated "Sex" bans were more likely to be "innocent" than accesses attributable to library or dial-up usage.

## Wrongful Bans

Wrongful bans are another important part of the equation. The Appendix to this paper includes a listing of sites which some Utah resident attempted to access and which were censored, during September 10-October 10. It is important to note that these represent real people being banned from real sites - the document at the banned URL is described underneath the URL. Each URL listed was banned at least once during the sample period. Many URLs were attempted to be accessed many times, but are listed only once in the listing. In many cases, to avoid boring the reader, we have listed only one URL from a site even though many URLs from that site were attempted to be accessed and banned.

Wrongful bans are listed in the Appendix. Some interesting evidence turns up upon scrutiny of them. Secure Computing states:

> As a rule, sites are not added to the Control List without first
> being viewed and approved by our staff.

There is a great deal of evidence that this is untrue. Offspring.com is banned under the Criminal Skills category for lyrics which use phrases like "crack the codes," "tap" and "surveillance" – but it's a rock group, not a site discussing "Criminal Skills." A website about a computer game named "Grand Theft Auto" is banned for its "Criminal Skills." A scholarly paper about Nazi Germany is banned, as well as sites which *oppose* hate speech and racism. National Families in Action and the Life Education Network, two groups which oppose drug abuse, are banned. A music group called "Bud Good and the Goodbuds" is banned under Drugs, for obvious reasons. An appeals court decision in a drug case is banned under Drugs. The Iowa State Division of Narcotics Enforcement is banned. A government brochure put out by the National Institute of Health is banned under Drugs. It is entitled "Marijuana: Facts for Teens." A page at Florida State University is banned under Gambling:

> http://mailer.fsu.edu/~wwager/index_public.html

Look carefully at that URL. Do you see the phrase "wwager" in it? The author of the page is named Walter Wager. That is why this page was banned under Gambling – because a computer, not a human, read that page and decided that since it involved "wager"ing, it should be categorized under Gambling. Similarly, a computer can read a page which uses the word "Narcotics," and, not realizing that it's the Iowa State Police, adds it to the list.

These are the sorts of mistakes computers make. Companies that make censoring software employ computers to search through the world wide web looking for materials which meet their criteria. A computer sees a page which uses the phrase "grand theft auto," and decides immediately that this must involve Criminal Skills, and adds the page immediately to the list of banned sites. No human would decide that the page for a computer game involved Criminal Skills, but a computer easily could. Nor would a page written by Walter Wager be classified under Gambling by a human - but a computer might.

Secure Computing states that every site on their list was examined by a human before being added to the blacklist. (UEN, in a report to their superiors during the implementation of the Smartfilter system, stated that "[Smartfilter] uses *educators* to evaluate if the site is appropriate or not," emphasis added, although this is not and has never been true.) In fact, the most likely case is that humans may be employed to supervise and monitor the computers, and make some decisions about banning some sites, but that the computer program itself also adds sites to the blacklist on its own initiative. This is a cost-effective way to deal with the 500,000,000 or so web pages available over the internet, and since few customers will discover the errors that it creates, companies which make censoring software will be tempted to delegate more and more responsibility to computer programs. The Censorware Project has examined many different censorware products and to date, all of them have exhibited characteristics which indicated that the companies involved were lying about employing humans and humans alone to add sites to the list. Companies are unwilling to take the public relations hit that would come from admitting that computers perform the selection of "bad" sites, but they are also unwilling to take the financial hit from hiring the hundreds or thousands of humans it would take to have a chance at keeping up with the internet's rate of change and growth.

The other interesting factor disclosed by the wrongful bans is the ban on candyland.com. This site resolves to the corporate homepage of Hasbro, the toymaker (who owns the rights to the board game Candy Land). Originally owned by a porn site, this domain was sued by Hasbro in 1996 and forced to stop using it in, if our information is correct, February 1996. They took all content off the site and for a while it was simply empty. It formally turned over to Hasbro in March 1997. Therefore, Smartfilter has not reviewed this site since at least March 1997, and more probably since 1996, because any recent review would have found no content or Hasbro instead of porn. This provides a good indication as to how frequently sites are re-reviewed for changed content - most likely, they are never re-reviewed. Candyland.com will stay banned as a porn site indefinitely (or until Secure Computing reads this report), although it has had no pornography for more than two years, because the constant growth of the internet requires censorware companies to spend their time searching for new sites, not reviewing old sites already on their blacklist. Over time, this will also lead to substantial errors as domains and individual users turn over, change content, etc.

### Overridden Bans

UEN has the capability to override bans of certain sites. If a site comes to UEN's attention which should not be banned, yet is, UEN can enter this site into the software and allow it to be accessed. UEN puts several barriers in the way of actually implementing this, though; appeals regarding banned sites must run through the scholastic chain of command, through the school principal and district supervisor. Obviously few teachers or other persons encountering a wrongly banned site would pursue this, and this is shown by the extremely few number of sites which UEN has bothered to override from the default blacklist presented to them by Secure Computing. The following sites showed up as overridden in the log files:

**http://209.75.21.6/**
This is a company which serves banner ads.

**http://www.mormon.com/**
All things Mormon. Currently banned under Sex, but overridden. [Not entirely, see further discussion.]

**http://fafsaws1.fafsa.ed.gov/**
The Free Application for Federal Student Aid, a form which is required to be filed for all applicants for college financial aid.

**http://netaddress.usa.net/**
Free web-based email service. Currently banned under Chat (thus, not banned under UEN's settings, but obviously was at some time.)

**http://www.cyberteens.com/**

Stories and whatnot, by and for teenagers. Like mormon.com, this site has both banned and unbanned accesses.

**http://www.infoseek.com/**
All ads at Infoseek (http://www.infoseek.com/ads/) are banned under the Sex category. This was apparently causing some problems, or perhaps all of Infoseek was banned, so this override was placed.

Mormon.com and cyberteens.com are the most interesting. Both of these sites have instances in the log files where they are banned, and instances where they are permitted to be accessed due to an override placed by UEN. It is our suspicion that UEN attempted to override the bans on these sites, but did not do so for all of the eleven proxy servers – thus, in some areas of Utah, students attempting to access mormon.com will be banned from doing so and in some areas they will be allowed. Neither mormon.com nor cyberteens.com has any material inappropriate for teenagers.

**Previous Evaluations**

It is difficult to compare these statistics to past performance, in Utah or elsewhere, as this is the first comprehensive evaluation of censoring software performance in real-life conditions. (Documentation relating to the lawsuit filed in Loudoun County, Virginia, provides the second-best source of such information; available online at http://censorware.org/legal/loudoun/). A document written in November 1996, just after UEN began using Smartfilter, indicates that "less than 0.7%" of all accesses were banned at that time. During the intervening two years to September 1998, gross accesses have increased by 1300% and the percentage of accesses banned has decreased somewhat to approximately 0.4% (see previous tables). Another document from March 1998 indicates that at that time, 0.60% of all accesses were banned. Although UEN states that they undertake to evaluate the effectiveness and performance of the censoring software they use, they were unable to provide any documentation of ever having done so beyond compiling gross statistics on the number and percentage of accesses banned, which their software does automatically.

It is perhaps worth noting that when UEN began providing internet access to Utah schools, the original plan was to allow each school district to create their own list of sites which they did not wish to be accessible over the internet, and for UEN to enforce these lists for each district. If they had implemented that plan, it is likely that documents such as the U.S. Constitution and Declaration of Independence would not today be banned in Utah.

## Conclusion

When the Declaration of Independence is banned from the citizens of Saudi Arabia, so that they won't get ideas, we call it culturally backward. And when it's banned from our own public libraries by our own government, then what do we call it?

Readers who skim the Appendix will note that the entire Internet Wiretap server (wiretap.area.com or wiretap.spies.com) is banned under the Criminal Skills category. The archive contains hundreds of megabytes of books out of copyright, governmental and civics material, religious material, etc. What got it banned might have been the statement on its opening page, which a computer routine probably considered to be indicative of bomb-making:

Wiretap's Inspiration
The First Amendment

"Congress shall make no law respecting an establishment of religion, or prohibiting the free exercise thereof; or abridging the freedom of speech, or of the press; or the right of the people peaceably to assemble, and to petition the Government for a redress of grievances."

Disturbed by free speech?

"Printer's ink has been running a race against gunpowder these many, many years. Ink is handicapped, in a way, because you can blow up a man with gunpowder in half a second, while it may take twenty years to blow him up with a book. But the gunpowder destroys itself along with its victim, while a book can keep on exploding for centuries."

Christopher Morley, "The Haunted Bookshop"

It is a sad day when a quotation about free speech can get hundreds of books banned without any public oversight or review. UEN, in its quest to eliminate so-called undesirable content, has instead eliminated the one thing that makes the United States different and better than other countries around the world: the ability for citizens to speak and read freely, without the government watching over your shoulder.

## Acknowledgements

Special thanks to –

Seth Finkelstein, who provided valuable technical assistance in obtaining and dealing with the log files; Joel Campbell, Freedom of Information Chairman of the Utah Chapter of the Society of Professional Journalists; The Utah State Records Committee, especially Chairman Max Evans; Chip Ward, on the Utah Library Association's Intellectual Freedom Committee; Ethel Jacob, Head Graphing Consultant for this report; and of course to UEN, without whom none of this would have been possible (or necessary).

# Computer Professionals for Social Responsibility Filtering FAQ

**Version 1.2  April, 2001**

**Written by Harry Hochheiser, CPSR Board Member, hhochheiser@cpsr.org**

## Introduction

Seen by some as a powerful tool for protecting children from online pornography and by others as "censorware," Internet content filters have generated much controversy, debate, and confusion.

This document attempts to describe the concerns and issues raised by the various types of filtering software. It is hoped that these questions and answers will help parents, libraries, schools, and others understand the software that they may be considering (or using).

Additions, clarifications, and corrections regarding the content of this document will be most graciously accepted: please send email to hhochheiser@cpsr.org.

## What's New?

Version 1.2 is the first revision of this document since October 1998. Most of the content is unchanged, but the following changes have been made:

- Links in "Where can I Find More Information" have been updated, removed, and revised as necessary.
- The discussion of available PICS ratings schemes has been updated.
- The discussion of PICS ratings systems has been updated to include the Internet Content Rating Association (ICRA).

Translations of this document are available:
Spanish: http://www.arnal.es/free/info/faq-filtros.htm

## 1) Basics

1.1) What is a content filter?

A content filter is one or more pieces of software that work together to prevent users from viewing material found on the Internet. This process has two components.

Rating: Value judgments are used to categorize web sites based on their content. These ratings could use simple allowed/disallowed distinctions like those found in programs like CyberSitter or NetNanny, or they can have many values, as seen in ratings systems based on Platform for Internet Content Selection (PICS, see question 3.0).

Filtering: With each request for information, the filtering software examines the resource that the user has requested. If the resource is on the "not allowed" list, or if it does not have the proper PICS rating, the filtering software tells the user that access has been denied and the browser does not display the contents of the web site.

The first content filters were stand-alone systems consisting of mechanisms for determining which sites should be blocked, along with software to do the filtering, all provided by a single vendor.

The other type of content filter is protocol-based. These systems consist of software that uses established standards for communicating ratings information across the Internet. Unlike stand-alone systems, protocol-based systems do not contain any information regarding which sites (or types of sites) should be blocked. Protocol-based systems simply know how to find this information on the Internet, and how to interpret it.

1.2) Why do many people want filtering?

The Internet contains a wide range of materials, some of which may be offensive or even illegal in many countries. Unlike traditional media, the Internet does not have any obvious tools for segregating material based on content. While pornographic magazines can be placed behind the counter of a store, and strip-tease joints restricted to certain parts of town, the Internet provides everything through the same medium.

Filters and ratings systems are seen as tools that would provide the cyberspace equivalent of the physical separations that are used to limit access to "adult" materials. In rating a site as objectionable, and refusing to display it on the user's computer screen, filters and ratings systems can be used to prevent children from seeing material that their parents find objectionable. In preventing access, the software acts as an automated version of the convenience-store clerk who refuses to sell adult magazines to high-school students.

Filters are also used by businesses to prevent employees from accessing Internet resources that are either not work related or otherwise deemed inappropriate.

1.3) Can filtering programs be turned off?

It is assumed that parents or other authoritative users who install filtering programs would control the passwords that allow the programs to be disabled. This means that parents can enable the filter for their children but disable it for themselves. As with all other areas of computer security, these programs are vulnerable to attack by clever computer users who may be able to guess the password or to disable the program by other means.

1.4) I don't want to filter, but I do want to know what my child is viewing. Is that possible?

Some products include a feature that will capture the list of all Internet sites that have been visited from your computer. This allows a parent to see what sites their child has viewed, albeit after the fact. Similar software allows employers to monitor the Internet use of their employees. Users of these systems will not know that their Internet use is being watched unless they are explicitly told.

Whether used in homes or workplaces, these tools raise serious privacy concerns.

1.5) What is the scope of Internet content filtering? Do filters cover the WWW? Newsgroups? IRC? Email?

While some stand-alone systems claim to filter other parts of the Internet, most content filters are focused on the World-Wide-Web. Given the varied technical nature of the protocols involved, it's likely that filtering tools will do well with some of these, and poorly with others. For example, filtering software can easily block access to newsgroups with names like "alt.sex". However, current technology cannot identify the presence of explicit photos in a file that's being transferred via FTP. PICS-based systems currently only filter web sites.

## 2) Stand-alone Systems

2.1) What is a stand-alone system?

A stand-alone filtering system is a complete filtering solution provided by a single vendor. These filters block sites based on criteria provided by the software vendor, thus "locking in" users. If a customer does not like the vendor's selection of sites that are to be blocked, she must switch to a different software product.

2.2) Who decides what gets blocked and what doesn't?

This is the biggest practical difference between stand-alone systems and protocol-based systems. Stand-alone systems limit users to decisions made by the software vendor, although some let the parents or installers and and remove sites. Protocol-based systems provide users with a choice between alternative ratings systems, which publishers and third parties can use to develop ratings for content. See question 3.2 for more information.

2.3) How do stand-alone programs determine what should be blocked?

Currently available filtering tools use some combination of two approaches to evaluate content: lists of unacceptable (or acceptable) sites, and keyword searches.

List-based blocking works by explicitly enumerating sites that should either be blocked or allowed. These lists are generally provided by filter vendors, who search for sites that meet criteria for being classified as either "objectionable" or "family-friendly".
Filtering software vendors vary greatly in the amount of information and control they make available to users. Most vendors do not allow users to see the actual list of blocked sites, as it is considered to be a kind of trade secret. However, some vendors provide detailed descriptions of the criteria used to determine which sites should be blocked. Some vendors might allow users to add sites to the list, either in their own software or by sending sites to the vendor for review.

Stand-alone filtering tools also vary in the extent to which they can be configured by users. Some software packages allow users to make selections from a list of the categories they would like blocked. For example, a parent may wish to block explicit sex but not discussions of homosexuality as a life-style. Others might allow users to choose from a range of choices in any given topic area. For example, instead of simply blocking all nudity, these tools might allow users to chose to allow partial nudity while blocking full nudity.

Keyword-based blocking uses text searches to categorize sites. If a site contains objectionable words or phrases, it will be blocked.

2.4) What's wrong with list-based filtering?

There are several problems with filtering based on lists of sites to be blocked.

First, these lists are incomplete. Due to the decentralized nature of the Internet, it's practically impossible to definitively search all Internet sites for "objectionable" material. Even with a paid staff searching for sites to block, software vendors cannot hope to identify all sites that meet their blocking criteria. Furthermore, since new web sites are constantly appearing, even regular updates from the software vendor will not block out all adult web sites. Each updated list will be obsolete as soon as it is released, as any as any site that appears after the update will not be on the list, and will not be blocked. The volatility of individual sites is yet another potential cause of trouble. Adult material might be added to (or removed from) a site soon after the site is added to (or removed from) a list of blocked sites.

Blocking lists also raise problems by withholding information from users, who may or may not have access to information describing the criteria used to block web sites. While some vendors provide descriptions of their blocking criteria, this information is often vague or incomplete. Several vendors have extended blocking beyond merely "objectionable" materials. In some instances, political sites and sites that criticize blocking software have been blocked.

This obscurity is compounded by practices used to protect these lists of blocked sites. Vendors often consider these lists to be proprietary intellectual property, which they protect through mathematical encryption, which renders the lists incomprehensible to end users. As a result, users are unable to examine which sites are blocked and why. This arbitrary behavior demeans the user's role as an active, thoughtful participant in their use of the Internet.

2.5) What's wrong with filtering based on keyword searches?

Keyword searching is a crude and inflexible approach that is likely to block sites that should not be blocked while letting "adult" sites pass through unblocked. These problems are tied to two shortcomings of this approach:

Keyword searches cannot use contextual information. While searches can identify the presence of certain words in a text, they cannot evaluate the context in which those words are used. For example, a search might find the word "breast" on a web page, but it cannot determine whether that word was used in a chicken recipe, an erotic story, or in some other manner. In one notable incident, America Online's keyword searches blocked a breast cancer support group.

Keyword searches cannot interpret graphics. It is not currently possible to "search" the contents of a picture. Therefore, a page containing sexually explicit pictures will be blocked only if the text on that page contains one or more words from the list of words to be blocked.

### 3) The Platform for Internet Content Selection (PICS)

3.1) What is PICS?

The Platform for Internet Content Selection (PICS) was developed by the W3 Consortium - the guiding force behind the World-Wide-Web - as a protocol for the exchange of rating information. Paul Resnick - University of Michigan professor and the creator of PICS - described PICS in a Scientific American (March 1997) article:

The Massachusetts Institute of Technology's World Wide Web Consortium has developed a set of technical standards called PICS (Platform for Internet Content Selection) so that people can electronically distribute descriptions of digital works in a simple, computer-readable form. Computers can process these labels in the background, automatically shielding users from undesirable material or directing their attention to sites of particular interest. The original impetus for PICS was to allow parents and teachers to screen materials they felt were inappropriate for children using the Net. Rather than censoring what is distributed, as the Communications Decency Act and other legislative initiatives have tried to do, PICS enables users to control what they receive.

There are two components involved in the practical use of PICS: ratings systems, and software that uses ratings systems to filter content.

3.2) How does PICS-based filtering differ from stand-alone systems?

Stand-alone filtering products generally include lists of sites to be filtered and explicit filtering criteria. Purchasers of these products are tied to the filtering decisions made by the software vendor.

PICS-based software uses an alternative approach based on distributed sharing of ratings information. Instead of using blocking lists or keyword searches, programs that use PICS use standardized "ratings systems" to determine which sites should be blocked. Available from software vendors or from Internet sites, these ratings systems are be used to describe the content of Internet sites (see question 3.7 for a description of how PICS works in practice). Users of PICS-based software are usually given the ability to choose which ratings system they would like to use.

As an open standard, PICS can be used for a wide range of applications. In addition to providing a means for blocking content deemed unsuitable for children, PICS might also be used for describing content in terms of its educational content, potential for violations of privacy, or any other criteria that involve rating of Internet sites.

In some senses, programs that use PICS are much more flexible than stand-alone filtering software. Users of PICS software are not tied to the judgments of the software vendor, and the descriptions of the criteria used by the ratings systems are publicly available. However, users are currently limited to choosing between a small number of ratings systems, each of which has its own biases and viewpoints. Users that disagree with the popular ratings systems may be unable to use PICS in a manner that fits their needs and viewpoints.

3.3) What is a ratings system?

A ratings system is a series of categories and gradations within those categories that can be used to classify content. The categories that are used are chosen by the developer of the ratings system, and may include topics such as such as "sexual content," "race," or "privacy." Each of these categories would be described along different levels of content, such as "Romance; no sex ", "Explicit sexual activity", or somewhere in between. Prominent ratings systems currently in use include ICRA and SafeSurf. A rating is a description of some particular Internet content, using the terms and vocabulary of some ratings system.

3.4) How are ratings systems developed?

The PICS developers and the W3 Consortium built PICS to be an open standard, so anyone can create a ratings system. Individuals and groups can develop ratings systems by defining categories and describing ratings within those categories. Once a ratings system is developed, it must be publicized to users and publishers.

3.5) Who rates sites?

The PICS standard describes two approaches to the rating of sites:

Self-Rating: Web site publishers can evaluate their own content and put PICS rating information directly into their web pages. Currently, this evaluation can be done through Web pages provided by developers of the major ratings services.

Third-Party Ratings: Interested third parties can use PICS ratings systems to evaluate web sites and publish their own ratings for these sites. Educational groups, religious groups, or individuals can rate sites and publish these ratings on the Internet for users to access.

3.6) What PICS-based ratings systems can I use?

From a technical perspective, you can use any PICS-based ratings system. However, your practical options are somewhat more limited. While you might configure your browser to use "Joe's Internet Ratings", it's unlikely that many sites have ratings for Joe's system, so it wouldn't be of very much use.

Your browser software may influence choice of ratings service. If you use Microsoft's Internet Explorer, you only have one choice (RSACi) built in to the initial distribution. To use other ratings services, IE users must download files from the 'Net and install them on their PCs.

The three most prominent PICS services are: RSACi: Sponsored by the Recreational Software Advisory Council (known for ratings on video games), RSACi is probably the most widely used PICS ratings system in use today. RSACi's ratings categories include violence, nudity, sex, and language, with 5 ratings within each category. At one point, RSACi claimed to have over 43,000 sites rated. IRCA In December 2000, the Internet Content Rating Assocation's (ICRA) rating scheme was launched as as a succssor to RSACi. ICRA has a ratings scheme that is more detailed and nuanced than that of RSACi. However, the extent of ICRA's adoption is not yet clear. SafeSurf: Developed by the SafeSurf corporation, this system's categories include "Age Range," "Profanity," "Heterosexual Themes," "Homosexual Themes," "Nudity," "Violence," "Sex,

Violence, and Profanity, " "Intolerance," "Glorifying Drug Use," "Other Adult Themes," and "Gambling," with 9 distinctions for each category.

IRCA, RSACi, and SafeSurf all rely on self-rating of Internet sites by web publishers.

3.7) How do I use PICS?

To use PICS, users start by configuring their browsers or PICS software to use a ratings system (such as ICRA or SafeSurf). Once the ratings system is chosen, users must examine each of the categories in order to choose a preferred level of information for that category. In practical terms, this means deciding how much they are willing to allow. For example, one ratings system's choices for nudity include "none," "revealing attire," "partial nudity," "frontal nudity," and "explicit."

Once these choices have been made, the browser software uses them to filter sites. When an Internet site is requested, the browser compares the site's rating with the user's selection. If the site has ratings for the chosen system and those ratings fit within the parameters chosen by the user, it is displayed as usual. If the appropriate ratings fall outside of those parameters (perhaps the site has "frontal nudity," while the user was only willing to accept "partial nudity"), access to the site is prohibited, and the user is shown a message indicating that the site is blocked.

Since most web sites are not currently rated, most software provides users with the option of blocking out sites that do not contain PICS ratings.

In order to prevent mischievous children from changing ratings or disabling PICS altogether, most browsers can be configured to require a password before disabling PICS.

3.8) Should I rate my site?

The answer to this question will depend upon who's being asked.

ICRA, SafeSurf, and other proponents of ratings would obviously like everyone to rate their sites, while civil libertarians and opponents of ratings argue against any ratings.

Publishers of family-oriented sites or those who are trying to reach audiences concerned with Internet content might consider rating. Similarly, purveyors of adult material might rate their sites in order to be "good citizens".

3.9) What should a publisher consider before self-rating?

Web site publishers must decide which (if any) ratings systems to use. Since each ratings system requires a separate valuation process, and separate modifications to web pages, it may not be practical for web-site publishers to use all of the popularly available ratings.

In evaluating ratings systems, publishers may want to examine the categories used by each system and the distinctions used by those categories. Different systems will classify ratings systems in different ways, some of which may misrepresent the content of web sites. For example, sites discussing safe sex might not want to be placed in the same category with pornographic sites.

Web site publishers might also consider the popularity of the ratings services. There are only a few major ratings services. Publishers are free to user other ratings, but these may not be useful to the Internet users who rely upon the popular systems. This presents a dilemma for some publishers, who can either accept the ratings of the popular systems, even if those ratings misrepresent their material, or refuse to rate their sites, knowing that this might cause their sites to be unavailable to some users.

Versions of Microsoft's Internet Explorer have provided an extreme example of this problem. Although IE allows user to use any PICS ratings system, RSACi is the only system that is built in to the selection list (as recently as IE 5.5). Since Internet Explorer is the most widely-used PICS-capable browser, it seems likely that many PICS users will rely upon RSACi. For publishers interested in reaching a wide audience, this market force may determine their choice of ratings system.

Finally, philosophical concerns may cause some people to decide not to rate. Web-site publishers who are not comfortable with the general content of available ratings systems, or who object to the concept of ratings, may choose not to rate their own sites.

MSNBC's troubles with ratings provide an ironic illustration of this possibility. Displeased with the RSACi ratings that would be necessary, MSNBC management removed all rating information from the site. MSNBC and other news organizations briefly discussed the possibility of creating a new ratings system specifically for news reporting.

While this proposal was eventually rejected, it illustrates some of the problems with content ratings. Well-funded publishers like MSNBC might be able to effectively create ratings systems that meet their needs, but smaller publishers who want to rate their sites may be forced to accept unsatisfactory ratings.

3.10) What concerns are raised by third-party ratings?

Since third-party ratings aren't validated by any technical means, third-party ratings can be easily misused. Just as stand-alone filtering software can block sites for political or business reasons (even if those sites do not contain adult content), third party raters might apply inaccurate labels to web sites in order to make sure that they would be blocked by PICS-compliant software.

To make matters worse, third party rating does not require the consent or even notification of a web-site publisher. Since third party ratings are distributed by third party "label bureaus," a web-site publisher may not know if her pages have been rated, or what the ratings said.

Third-party ratings also present significant technical challenges that may discourage their development. Unlike self-ratings, third party PICS ratings do not reside on publisher's web pages. Instead, they must be distributed to users using one of two methods:

File Transfer: Users could download ratings from the web sites provided by third-party services. For ratings services that cover any significant portion of the Internet, this could easily amount to megabytes of data, which could be cumbersome to download using slow modems. Furthermore, these lists would quickly become obsolete, and would therefore require regular updates. Label Bureaus: Third-party raters (or others) might establish servers that would provide ratings information. In this model, users of a rating service would retrieve a rating from the rating service, and this rating would be used to determine whether or not the site should be blocked. For a widely-used ratings system, this would require computing power and Internet bandwidth capable of handling constant streams of requests for ratings. This might be cost-prohibitive for many potential ratings services.

3.11) What about sites that aren't rated? What if someone puts the wrong rating on a site?

PICS ratings can be truly useful for parents only if a significant percentage of the Internet's web sites are accurately rated. At one point, RSACi and NetShepherd had claimed to have rated 40,000 and 500,000 sites, respectively. Cumulatively, these numbers represent a tiny fraction of the total number of web sites available. However, the effective total may be even smaller: as of April 2001, NetShepherd does not seem to exist as an active filtering company. Some software, such as Microsoft's Internet Explorer, provides users with the option of blocking out any site that does not have a rating. This choice may be appropriate for some, but it severely restricts the available options. By blocking out most of the Web (including possibly some sites designed for younger users), this approach presents children with a severely restricted view of the world.

The accuracy of PICS ratings is obviously a concern. For example, unscrupulous purveyors of adult material might attempt to use an inaccurate rating in an attempt to slip through PICS filters. In RSACi's terms of use, the RSAC reserves the right to audit sites in order to guarantee accuracy of ratings. SafeSurf takes this one step further. The proposed Online Cooperative Publishing Act calls for legal penalties for sites that label inaccurately, or refuse to rate. In June 1997, Sen. Patty Murray (D-Washington) proposed the Child-safe Internet Act of 1997, which called for similar penalties. While these legislative suggestions might be effective in promoting the use of ratings, they raise serious concerns in terms of first-amendment rights and possibilities for overly aggressive enforcement. Question 4.1 discusses these possibilities in more depth. There are currently no quality controls on third-party ratings.

These issues of quality and accountability would become even trickier if numerous schemes were to come into use. If there were dozens of PICS ratings schemes to choose from, publishers would not know which to choose, and users might not know which to trust.

3.12) What if I don't like the ratings systems that are available? Can individuals and organizations start new ratings systems?

Currently, there are two choices for individuals and organizations that are uncomfortable with the existing ratings systems.

The first - and currently the only viable alternative - is to avoid use of PICS for self-rating, and in Internet browsers.

The second approach would be to develop a new ratings vocabulary, as an alternative to ICRA, SafeSurf, or other currently available ratings systems. This involves several steps:

The first step is generation of a ratings system, including categories that would be discussed and distinctions within those categories. This would require a discussion of the values that will be represented in the ratings system, and how these values should be expressed.

Once the system has been developed, sites must be rated. This can be done in one of two ways:

The developers of the ratings system could convince web-site publishers to self-rate. This would require significant resources, as raising awareness of the new ratings system through advertising, press contacts, and other means can be quite expensive. Of course, this new ratings system would raise "chicken-and-the-egg" concerns. Why should publishers use this system for self-rating unless they know that it's being used? And, conversely, why should users choose a ratings system that doesn't have very many sites rated? The new ratings system can create third-party ratings for the Web. This would also require significant human resources to generate these ratings. If we assume that workers could generate these ratings at a rate of 1/minute, or 480 over the course of an 8-hour day, it would take 8 people working 40-hour weeks roughly an entire year to rate one million web sites. Of course, the Internet already has more than one million sites, and it will have grown significantly before those 8 people finish their year of ratings work. Furthermore, workers rating web sites at this rate would probably make more than a few mistakes in their choice of ratings. As described in question 3.10, distribution of third-party ratings also presents significant technical challenges and expenses.

Once the ratings have been generated for the web sites, the new ratings system must be publicized to potential users. As described above, this could be expensive and difficult.

Given the significant resources that will be needed to effectively deploy a new ratings system, it seems unlikely that there will be a large number of PICS alternatives available in the near future.

3.13) What's wrong with PICS and Internet ratings in general?

In theory, there are many useful applications of rating information.

Book reviews and movie ratings are only two examples of the many ways in which we use information filters. Used in conjunction with other information sources - including advertising and word-of-mouth - these ratings provide a basis for making informed decisions regarding information.

Unfortunately, PICS does not currently provide users with the contextual information and range of choices necessary for informed decision making. When deciding which movies to see, we have access to reviews, advertisements and trailers which provide information regarding the content. These details help us choose intelligently based on our values and preferences. On the other hand, PICS-based systems do not provide any contextual detail: users are simply told that access to a site is denied because the site's rating exceeds a certain value on the rating scale.

Furthermore, the limited range of currently available PICS ratings system does not provide users with a meaningful choice between alternatives. Parents who are not comfortable with any of the current ratings systems may not find PICS to be a viable alternative.

Continuing with our analogies to other media, consider book reviews in a world where only two or three publications reviewed books. This might work very well for people who agree with the opinions of these reviewers (and, of course, for the reviewers themselves!), but it would work very poorly for those who have differing viewpoints.

Some might argue that the "success" of a single set of movie ratings offers a model for PICS. However, ratings are generally applied only to movies made for entertainment by major producers. Documentaries and educational films are generally not rated, but similar web sites could be rated under PICS.

Movie ratings also provide a cautionary lesson that should be considered with respect to the Internet. Unrated movies, or movies with certain ratings, often have a difficult time reaching audiences, as they may not be shown in certain theaters or carried by large video chains. This has led to self-censorship, as directors trim explicit scenes in order to avoid NC-17 ratings. This may be appropriate for commercially-oriented entertainment, but it could be dangerous when applied to safe-sex information on the Internet.

Ratings systems also fail to account for the global nature of the Internet. Legal or practical pressures aimed at convincing Internet publishers to rate their own sites will have little effect, as these businesses or individuals have the option of simply moving their material to a foreign country. Furthermore, the existing ratings systems are of limited value to those in countries that do not share western values.

Concerns about unrated international material or differing cultural values could be addressed through direct censorship. For example, governments might use PICS ratings or proprietary filtering software to implement "national firewalls" which would screen out objectionable material. Alternatively, ratings might be used to "punish" inappropriate speech. If search engines chose to block sites with certain ratings (or unrated sites), or if browsers blocked certain ratings (or lack of ratings) by default, these sites might never be seen.

It is possible that a wide range of PICS ratings system could come into use, providing families with a real opportunity to choose ratings that meet their values. The utility of PICS might also be increased by use of new technologies like "metadata" (data about data, used to describe the content of web pages and other information resources), which might be used to provide contextual information along with PICS ratings. However, these tools may not be available for general use for some time, if at all.

Some people confuse ratings with the topical organization that is used in libraries and Web sites like Yahoo. While no system of organization of information is neutral, topical schemes attempt to describe what a resource is "about". Rating rarely helps us find information resources topically and is usually too narrowly focused on a few criteria to be useful for information retrieval.

### 4) Alternatives

4.1) Can anything work?

The answer to this question will depend largely on the perspective of the asker. If this question is taken to mean: "Are there any solutions that would provide children with the ability to use the Internet without ever seeing material that is explicit or "adult," the answer is probably yes. This would require a combination of three factors:

1.Legislation requiring "accurate" ratings and specifying penalties for those who do not comply. 2.Technical measures to prevent the transmission of unlabeled material, or any material from foreign sites (which would not be subject to US laws). 3.Mandatory use of filtering software, using mandated settings.

The obvious legal, political, and practical problems with this scenario would certainly doom it to failure. While mandated standards have been suggested by some groups, it is quite likely that they would be found unconstitutional and in violation of the Supreme Court's *Reno v. ACLU* decision that overturned key provisions of the Communications Decency Act. Furthermore, the accuracy of content ratings is a matter of judgment that would not easily be legislated. Practically, laws requiring the use of filtering software would be virtually unenforceable. Finally, if efforts aimed at "sanitizing" the Internet somehow managed to survive legal challenges, they would have a chilling effect upon speech on the Internet.

If the question is interpreted as meaning: "Are there any solutions that provide some protection from adult or objectionable material without restricting free speech?" the answer is much less clear. Stand-alone systems clearly don't meet these criteria, as they place users at the whims of software vendors, who may block sites for arbitrary reasons. In theory, PICS might fit this role, but the lack of a meaningful choice between substantially different ratings systems leaves parents and publishers with the choice of using ratings that they may not agree with, or that fail to adequately describe their needs or materials.

Describing speech as "adult" or "appropriate for children" is inherently a tricky and value-laden process. In the U.S., many people have attempted to prevent schools and libraries from using everyday publications like Huckleberry Finn and descriptions of gay/lesbian lifestyles. The fierce debates over these efforts show that no consensus can be reached. Increased use of filtering software would likely be the beginning, rather than the end, of debates regarding what Internet materials are "appropriate" for children, and who gets to make that decision.

4.2) I understand that there are many problems with filters and ratings. What can I do to protect my children?

The first thing that parents should do is to consider the extent of the problem. While some news reports might leave parents with the impression that the Internet is nothing but pornography, this is far from the case. In fact, it's unlikely that children would randomly stumble across pornographic material. Furthermore, many adult sites have explicit warnings or require payment by credit card, which further decrease the chances of children "accidentally" finding pornography.

Secondly, parents should play an active role and interest in their children's use of the Internet. For some children this might mean restricting Internet use to closely supervised sessions. Other children might be able to work with clearly defined rules and guidelines. To discourage unsupervised use of the Internet, parents might consider measures such as placing the family computer in a common space in the home and retaining adult control over any passwords required for Internet access.

Parents should also work to educate children regarding proper use of the Internet. Just as parents teach children not to talk to strangers on the street, parents might discourage children from visiting certain web sites, divulging personal or family information, or participating in inappropriate chats.

Some parents might consider using filtering software, despite all of the potential drawbacks. Parents considering this route should closely examine their options, in order to understand their options and the implications of any choice.

For stand-alone filtering systems, this means investigating the criteria used in developing blocking lists and/or news reports describing the software. If possible, parents might try to find stand-alone systems that allow users to view and edit the lists of blocked sites.

Parents considering the use of PICS systems should investigate the categories used by the various ratings systems, in order to find one that meets their needs. Information about PICS-based systems can be found at the home pages of the respective ratings systems.

In general, the use of a filtering product involves an implicit acceptance of the criteria used to generate the ratings involved. Before making this decision, parents should take care to insure that the values behind the ratings are compatible with their beliefs.

Finally, parents should realize that the Internet is just a reflection of society in general. Much of the "adult" content on the Internet can be found on cable TV, at local video stores, or in movie theaters. Since other media fail to shield children from violence or sexual content, restrictions on the Internet will always be incomplete.

4.3) What roles can ISPs play?

Some have called upon ISPs to play a greater role in helping parents filter the 'Net for their children. There are two ways that ISPs might participate in these efforts:

ISP-Based Filtering: ISPs might do the filtering themselves, preventing their customers from accessing objectionable materials, even if those customers do not have their own filtering software. This requires the use of a proxy server, which would serve as a broker between the ISP's customers and remote web sites. When a customer of a filtering ISP wants to see a web site, his request goes to the proxy server operated by the ISP. The proxy server will then check to see if the site should be blocked. If the site is allowable, the proxy server retrieves the web page and returns it to the customer.

This approach is technically feasible. In fact, it's currently used by many corporations, and some ISPs that offer this service. However, proxying requires significant computational resources that may be beyond the means of smaller ISPs. Even if the ISP can afford the computers and Internet bandwidth needed, this approach is still far from ideal. In order to do the filtering, proxy servers would have to use stand-alone or PICS-based systems, so they would be subject to the limitations of these technologies (see 2.4, 2.5, and 3.13). The shortcomings of existing filtering systems may prove particularly troublesome for ISPs that advertise filtering services, as these firms could be embarrassed or worse if their filters fail to block adult material. Finally, ISPs that filter material may lose customers who are interested in unfiltered access to the Internet.

Providing Filtering Software: Others have suggested that ISPs should be required to provide users with filtering software. While this might be welcome by parents who are thinking about getting on to the 'Net (and by software vendors!) it could present a financial serious burden for smaller ISPs.

4.4) What about Internet access in libraries?

Internet access in public libraries has been a contentious area of discussion. Claiming concern for children using library computers to access the Internet, numerous municipalities have installed, or are considering installing filtering software on publicly-accessible Internet terminals. However, as cyberspace lawyer, publisher, and free-speech activist Jonathan Wallace has pointed out, the use of blocking software in public libraries may be unconstitutional:

Most advocates of the use of blocking software by libraries have forgotten that the public library is a branch of government, and therefore subject to First

Amendment rules which prohibit content-based censorship of speech. These rules apply to the acquisition or the removal of Internet content by a library. Secondly, government rules classifying speech by the acceptability of content (in libraries or elsewhere) are inherently suspect, may not be vague or overbroad, and must conform to existing legal parameters laid out by the Supreme Court. Third, a library may not delegate to a private organization, such as the publisher of blocking software, the discretion to determine what library users may see. Fourth, forcing patrons to ask a librarian to turn off blocking software has a chilling effect under the First Amendment.

## 5) Credits

5.1) Who gets the credit?

This document grew out of discussions held by CPSR's Cyber-Rights working group and other concerned individuals during the summer of 1997, and has been maintained by the author since then. Andy Oram, Craig Johnson, Karen Coyle, Marcy Gordon, Bennett Haselton, Jean-Michel Andre, and Aki Namioka provided invaluable assistance. Please feel free to distribute or copy this document. Comments can be sent to hhochheiser@cpsr.org.

5.2) Who is CPSR?

CPSR is a public-interest alliance of computer scientists and others concerned about the impact of computer technology on society. We work to influence decisions regarding the development and use of computers because those decisions have far-reaching consequences and reflect our basic values and priorities. As technical experts, CPSR members provide the public and policymakers with realistic assessments of the power, promise, and limitations of computer technology. As concerned citizens, we direct public attention to critical choices concerning the applications of computing and how those choices affect society.

# Impact of Self-Regulation and Filtering on Human Rights to Freedom of Expression

**Global Internet Liberty Campaign**

---

**Presented to OECD "Internet Content Self-Regulation Dialogue,"**

**March 25, 1998, Paris.**

## Principles

The Global Internet Liberty Campaign is a group of human rights and civil liberties organisations which advocate the following:

- Prohibiting prior censorship of on-line communication.

- Requiring that laws restricting the content of online speech distinguish between the liability of content providers and the liability of data carriers.

- Insisting that on-line free expression not be restricted by indirect means such as excessively restrictive governmental or private controls over computer hardware or software, telecommunications infrastructure, or other essential components of the Internet.

- Including citizens in the Global Information Infrastructure (Internet) development process from countries that are currently unstable economically, have insufficient infrastructure, or lack sophisticated technology.

- Prohibiting discrimination on the basis of race, colour, sex, language, religion, political or other opinion, national or social origin, property, birth or other status.

- Ensuring that personal information generated on the Internet for one purpose is not used for an unrelated purpose or disclosed without the person's informed consent and enabling individuals to review personal information on the Internet and to correct inaccurate information.

- Allowing on-line users to encrypt their communications and information without restriction.

We, the undersigned members of the Global Internet Liberty Campaign consider that the following issues are important with respect to Content and Conduct on the Internet.

### Human Rights Doctrines Protecting Freedom of Expression are Fully Applicable to the Internet

International human rights law enshrines the rights to freedom of expression and access to information. These core documents explicitly protect freedom of expression "without regard to borders," a phrase especially pertinent to the global Internet:

> "Everyone has the right to freedom of opinion and expression; this right includes freedom to hold opinions without interference and to seek, receive and impart information and ideas through any media, and regardless of frontiers." (Article 19, Universal Declaration of Human Rights).

> "Everyone shall have the right to freedom of expression; this right shall include freedom to seek, receive, and impart information and ideas of all kinds, regardless of frontiers, either orally, in writing or in print, in the form of art, or through any other media of his choice." (Article 19, International Covenant on Civil and Political Rights).

> "Everyone has the right to freedom of expression. This right shall include freedom to hold opinions and to receive and impart information and ideas without interference by public authority and regardless of borders." (Article 10, European Convention for the Protection of Human Rights and Fundamental Freedoms).

## Freedom of Speech is Fundamental on the Internet

The Internet is a unique communication medium and is more than a meer industry. Like no other medium before, it allows individuals to express their ideas and opinions directly to a world audience, while allowing them access to other ideas, opinions and information to which they may not otherwise have access.

While the mass media usually responds to the economic and political interests of those who control it, such controls do not presently exist on the Internet. Here, citizens from the most repressive regimes are able to find information about matters concerning their governments or their human rights records that no local newspaper may dare print, while denouncing the conditions under which they live, for the world to hear. The Internet allows us an intimate look at other countries, other people and other cultures which few before were ever able to attain. This power to give and receive information, so central to any conception of democracy, can be truly achieved on the Internet, as nowhere before.

This unprecedented power, however, can be very threatening to repressive regimes. Traditional methods of censorship – embargoing newspapers, threatening journalists, closing down presses – do not work on the Internet – the censoring techniques that these regimes will engage in, and their rationalisations, are not as well unknown, but they can be just as destructive.

## Free Expression on the Internet Enhances Democracy, Culture, and the Economy

- The vast majority of Internet use is for legitimate purposes;

- The effect of access and use of this global interactive medium has been to promote and defend civil and political rights worldwide;

- The experiences of communities in different countries indicates that few things could be more threatening to authoritarian regimes than access and use of the medium which knows no boundaries and is very hard to control;

- On the Internet, citizens are not mere consumers of content but also creators of content and the content on the Internet is as diverse as human thought. (from the judgment against the US Communications Decency Act); and

- Individuals and communities have been using the new-found freedom online to link, interact and work collectively in this global work space. This fundamental shift in power has created a possibility for every individual to be a publisher.

## Anonymity

Central to free expression and the protection of privacy is the right to express political beliefs without fear of retribution and to control the disclosure of personal identity. Protecting the right of anonymity is therefore an essential goal for the protection of personal freedoms in the online world.

The right of anonymity is recognized in law and accepted by custom. It has been an integral part of the growth and development of the Internet. Some governments are working to extend techniques for anonymity. The Netherlands and the Canadian provence of Ontario are pursuing a study on anonymity. The German government has recently adopted legislation that would encourage the adoption of anonymous payments systems for the Internet.

But other efforts are underway to establish mandatory identification requirements and to limit the use of techniques that protect anonymity. For example, the G-8 recently considered a proposal to require caller identification for Internet users. Some local governments have also tried to adopt legislation that would prohibit access to the Internet without the disclosure of personal identity.

- Governments should not require the identification of Internet users or restrict the ability to express political beliefs on the Internet anonymously.

- Efforts to develop new techniques to protect anonymity and indentity should be encouraged The governments of Canada, Germany, and the Netherland are to be commended for their recent efforts to suppport anonymity.

- ISPs should not establish unnecessary indentification requirements for customers and should, wherever practicable, preserve the right of users to access the Internet anonymously.

## "Self-Regulation," Criminal Law and the Need for Due Process

As with any other sphere of human interaction, criminal activity exists online, as well as offline. The role of an Internet Service Provider is crucial for access to the Internet and because of the crucial role that they play they have been targeted by law enforcement agencies in many countries to act as content censors.

While Internet Service Providers ought to provide law enforcement reasonable assistance in investigating criminal activity, confusing the role of private companies and police authorities risks substantial violation of individual civil liberties.

### "Self-regulation" in the Context of the Internet is a Misnomer

In the normal sense of the phrase "self-regulation" is when a group of people, or companies decide that in their own best interest, they should themselves regulate how they go about their joint interests. In the eyes of those who would see the "Internet Industry" "self-regulate", the "industry" must include all content providers, which includes many who's only connection with the Internet is that they use it. What is being suggested in the name of "self-regulation" is not that ISP's should as a group regulate their own behaviour, but that of their customers.

What is often promoted as Internet "self-regulation" is nothing of the sort. Rather it is "privatised censorship". That's not "private", but "privat-ISED," referring to the fairly common occurrence of having a formerly direct government function turned over to administration by a private agency. It's a more sophisticated means of achieving the same goal. The backing is still state power and government threat, but the actual implementation and mechanics of the suppression of material is delegated to a trade group.

### "Self-regulatory" regimes ought not to place private ISPs in the role of police officers for the Internet

While we applaud the efforts of ISPs that provide responsible assistance to police in the investigation of crime, it is essential that private entities not take on the role of police or prosecutors.

- Due process: "Self-regulatory" regimes in which a group of ISPs combine to remove possibly illegal material in advance of legal judgement by competent public authorities denies individual speakers due process and risks substantial suppression of protected, though possibly controversial, speech. No matter how careful the guidelines employed by such groups are, the act of removing speech from the Internet on the theory that it might be illegal, without a legal finding to that effect, is an inappropriate suppression of speech. Moreover, if such a self-regulatory regime has the general support of the government, it may even constitute state censorship.

- Incentive for "self-regulators" to over-censor: When ISPs come together to self-regulate certain classes of content in exchange for some limit on legal liability for that content, the overwhelming pressure will be to censor more material, rather than less, in an effort by ISPs to be certain that they have removed any material that might be illegal. Where ISPs are dependent on government grants of liability limitations, their "self-regulating" actions must satisfy the perceived demands of law enforcement, even if this results in removal of legal, protected speech.

- A recent EU communication paper stated that ISPs play a key role in giving users access to Internet content. It should not however be forgotten that the prime responsibility for content lies with authors and content providers. Blocking access at the level of access providers has been criticised by the EU communication paper on the ground that these actions go far beyond the limited category of illegal content and such a restrictive regime is inconceivable for Europe as it would severely interfere with the freedom of the individual and its political traditions.

### "Self-regulatory" Regimes have not yet Proven Effective

Initial reports from "self-regulatory" systems cast doubt on their effectiveness and suggest that the only effective way to combat crime such as child pornography is with well trained police. The two most important hotlines in Europe, the Dutch hotline and the UK hotline, have observed that despite the large amount of complaints they receive, this amount is tiny compared to the vast volume available on the Internet. The effects these hotlines have on dissemination of illegal content is also tiny. The Dutch Hotline, in its annual report, warned that it had absolutely no effect on distribution of illegal content in chat-boxes and E-mail, and that its influence on such distribution in newsgroups was very limited. And, according to the Internet Watch Foundation Annual Report, of the 4300 items blocked by private action, "[o]nly the few articles appearing to have originated in the UK are suitable for investigation and action by the UK police." Thus with little measurable law enforcement impact, thousands of presumable legal items were nevertheless removed from the Internet.

### Filtering, Rating and Labeling Systems Pose Risks to the Free Flow of Information and Can Be Used by Governments to Violate Human Rights

**Blocking, filtering, and labelling techniques can restrict freedom of expression and limit access to information.**

Specifically, such techniques can prevent individuals from using the Internet to exchange information on topics that may be controversial or unpopular, enable the development of country profiles to facilitate a global/universal rating system desired by governments, block access to content on entire domains, block access to Internet content available at any domain or page which contains a specific key-word or character string in the URL, and over-ride self-rating labels provided by content creators and providers.

- Government-mandated use of blocking, filtering, and label systems violates basic international human rights protections: No matter what the means, government restriction on speech or access to speech of others violates basic freedom of expression protections.

- Global rating or labeling systems squelch the free flow of information: Efforts to force all Internet speech to be labelled or rated according to a single classification system distorts the fundamental cultural diversity of the Internet and will lead to domination of one set of political or moral viewpoints. Such systems will either be easy to use and not have enough categories for all cultures or it will have so many categories to cater for all cultures that it will be unusable. These systems are antithetical to the Internet and should be rejected.

- Infrastructure distortions to force labeling must be rejected: Extra-legal means of forcing individuals to use filtering, labels or ratings such as ratings requirements in search engines or default settings in browsers restrict the free flow of information online and distort the basic openness of the Internet.

- Transparency must be maintained: Users must be made aware if their Internet access is being filtering, and, if so, based on what filtering system. They must also be able to disable the filtering at any point.

- White lists, rather than black list are preferable: Access to a variety of tools which make positive suggestions (white lists) pointing to certain content, rather than blocking content (black lists), should be encouraged.

- Filtering is inappropriate in public educational institutions and libraries.

- Diversity is essential: To the extent that individuals choses to employ filtering tools, it is vital that they have access to a wide variety of such tools.

## List of Signatories

ALCEI - Electronic Frontiers Italy
American Civil Liberties Union
Bulgarian Institute for Legal Development
Center for Democracy and Technology
CITADEL Electronic Frontier France
CommUnity, The Computer Communicators' Association (UK)
Computer Professionals for Social Responsibility
Cyber-Rights & Cyber-Liberties (UK)
Derechos Human Rights
Digital Citizens Foundation Netherlands (DB-NL)
Electronic Frontier Canada
Electronic Frontier Foundation
Electronic Frontiers Australia
Electronic Privacy Information Center
Equipo Nizkor
Fronteras Electronicas Espanya
Index on Censorship
Imaginons un Réseau Internet Solidaire
NetAction
Privacy International
Quintessenz User Group

# Mission Statement

## Internet Free Expression Alliance

The Internet is a powerful and positive forum for free expression. It is the place where "any person can become a town crier with a voice that resonates farther than it could from any soapbox," as the U.S. Supreme Court recently observed. Internet users, online publishers, library and academic groups and free speech and journalistic organizations share a common interest in opposing the adoption of techniques and standards that could limit the vibrance and openness of the Internet as a communications medium. Indeed, content "filtering" techniques already have been implemented in ways inconsistent with free speech principles, impeding the ability of Internet users to publish and receive constitutionally protected expression.

The Internet Free Expression Alliance will work to:

Ensure the continuation of the Internet as a forum for open, diverse and unimpeded expression and to maintain the vital role the Internet plays in providing an efficient and democratic means of distributing information around the world;

Promote openness and encourage informed public debate and discussion of proposals to rate and/or filter online content;

Identify new threats to free expression and First Amendment values on the Internet, whether legal or technological;

Oppose any governmental effort to promote, coerce or mandate the rating or filtering of online content;

Protect the free speech and expression rights of both the speaker and the audience in the interactive online environment;

Ensure that Internet speakers are able to reach the broadest possible interested audience and that Internet listeners are able to access all material of interest to them;

Closely examine technical proposals to create filtering architectures and oppose approaches that conceal the filtering criteria employed, or irreparably damage the unique character of the Internet; and

Encourage approaches that highlight "recommended" Internet content, rather than those that restrict access to materials labelled as "harmful" or otherwise objectionable, and emphasize that any rating that exists solely to allow specific content to be blocked from view may inhibit the flow of free expression.

## Member Organizations

American Booksellers Foundation for Free Expression
American Civil Liberties Union
American Society of Newspaper Editors
Association of Independent Video and Filmmakers
Boston Coalition for Freedom of Expression
Computer Professionals for Social Responsibility
Electronic Frontier Foundation
Electronic Privacy Information Center
Feminists for Free Expression
First Amendment Project
Gay & Lesbian Alliance Against Defamation
Human Rights Watch
Institute for Global Communications
International Periodical Distributors Association
Journalism Education Association
National Association of Artists Organizations
National Campaign for Freedom of Expression
National Coalition Against Censorship
National Writers Union
NetAction
Online Policy Group
Oregon Coalition for Free Expressio
Peacefire

PEN American Center
People for the American Wa
Publishers Marketing Association
Society of Professional Journalists
The Censorware Project
Washington Independent Writers
Z publishing

# Censorship in a Box: Why Blocking Software is Wrong for Public Libraries

American Civil Liberties Union

## Executive Summary

The Internet is rapidly becoming an essential tool for learning and communication. But the dream of universal Internet access will remain only a dream if politicians force libraries and other institutions to use blocking software whenever patrons log on.

This special report by the American Civil Liberties Union provides an in depth look at why mandatory blocking software is both inappropriate and unconstitutional in libraries. We do not evaluate any particular product, but rather seek to demonstrate how all blocking software censors valuable speech and gives librarians, educators and parents a false sense of security when providing minors with Internet access.

Our report follows up an August 1997 ACLU special report, "Fahrenheit 451.2: Is Cyberspace Burning?" in which we warned that government coerced, industry efforts to rate content on the Internet could torch free speech online. In that report, we offered a set of guidelines for Internet Service Providers and other industry groups contemplating ratings schemes.

Similarly, in Censorship in a Box, we offer a set of guidelines for libraries and schools looking for alternatives to clumsy and ineffective blocking software:

- Acceptable Use Policies. Schools should develop carefully worded policies that provide instructions for parents, teachers, students, librarians and patrons on use of the Internet.

- Time Limits. Instead of blocking, schools and libraries can establish content-neutral time limits as to when and how young people should use the Internet. Schools can also request that Internet access be limited to school-related work.

- "Driver's Ed" for Internet Users. Students should be taught to engage critical thinking skills when using the Internet and to be careful about relying on inaccurate resources online. One way to teach these skills in schools is to condition Internet access for minors on successful completion of a seminar similar to a driver's education course. Such seminars could also emphasize the dangers of disclosing personally identifiable information and communicating about intimate matters with strangers.

- Recommended Reading. Libraries and schools should publicize and provide links to websites that have been recommended for children and teens.

- Privacy Screens. To avoid unwanted viewing of websites by passers-by – and to protect users' privacy when viewing sensitive information – libraries and schools should place privacy screens around Internet access terminals in a way that minimizes public view

Taken together, these approaches work much better than restrictive software that teaches no critical thinking skills and works only when students are using school or library computers.

Like any technology, blocking software can be used for constructive or destructive purposes. In the hands of parents and others who voluntarily use it, it is a tool that can be somewhat useful in blocking access to some inappropriate material online. But in the hands of government, blocking software is nothing more than censorship in a box.

### Introduction

In libraries and schools across the nation, the Internet is rapidly becoming an essential tool for learning and communication. According to the American Library Association, of the nearly 9,000 public libraries in America, 60.4 percent offer Internet access to the public, up from 27.8 percent in 1996. And a recent survey of 1,400 teachers revealed that almost half use the Internet as a teaching tool. But today, unfettered access to the Internet is being threatened by the proliferation of blocking software in libraries.

America's libraries have always been a great equalizer, providing books and other information resources to help people of all ages and backgrounds live, learn, work and govern in a democratic society. Today more than ever, our nation's libraries are vibrant multi-cultural institutions that connect people in the smallest and most remote communities with global information resources.

In 1995, the National Telecommunications and Information Administration of the U.S. Department of Commerce concluded that "public libraries can play a vital role in assuring that advanced information services are universally available to all segments of the American population on an equitable basis. Just as libraries traditionally made available the marvels and imagination of the human mind to all, libraries of the future are planning to allow everyone to participate in the electronic renaissance."

Today, the dream of universal access will remain only a dream if politicians force libraries and other institutions to use blocking software whenever patrons access the Internet. Blocking software prevents users from accessing a wide range of valuable information, including such topics as art, literature, women's health, politics, religion and free speech. Without free and unfettered access to the Internet, this exciting new medium could become, for many Americans, little more than a souped-up, G-rated television network.

This special report by the American Civil Liberties Union provides an in depth look at why mandatory blocking software is both inappropriate and unconstitutional in libraries. We do not offer an opinion about any particular blocking product, but we will demonstrate how all blocking software censors valuable speech and gives librarians, educators and parents a false sense of security when providing minors with Internet access.

Like any technology, blocking software can be used for constructive or destructive purposes. In the hands of parents and others who voluntarily use it, it is a tool that can be somewhat useful in blocking access to some inappropriate material online. But in the hands of government, blocking software is nothing more than censorship in a box.

The ACLU believes that government has a necessary role to play in promoting universal Internet access. But that role should focus on expanding, not restricting, access to online speech.

### Reno v. ACLU: A Momentous Decision

Our vision of an uncensored Internet was clearly shared by the U.S. Supreme Court when it struck down the 1996 Communications Decency Act (CDA), a federal law that outlawed "indecent" communications online.

Ruling unanimously in *Reno v. ACLU*, the Court declared the Internet to be a free speech zone, deserving of at least as much First Amendment protection as that afforded to books, newspapers and magazines. The government, the Court said, can no more restrict a person's access to words or images on the Internet than it could be allowed to snatch a book out of a reader's hands in the library, or cover over a statue of a nude in a museum.

The nine Justices were clearly persuaded by the unique nature of the medium itself, citing with approval the lower federal court's conclusion that the Internet is "the most participatory form of mass speech yet developed," entitled to "the highest protection from governmental intrusion." The Internet, the Court concluded, is like "a vast library including millions of readily available and indexed publications," the content of which "is as diverse as human thought."

### Blocking Software: For Parents, Not the Government

In striking down the CDA on constitutional grounds, the Supreme Court emphasized that if a statute burdens adult speech – as any censorship law must – it "is unacceptable if less restrictive alternatives were available."

Commenting on the availability of user-based blocking software as a possible alternative, the Court concluded that the use of such software was appropriate for *parents*. Blocking software, the Court wrote, is a "reasonably effective method by which parents can prevent their children from accessing material which the *parents* believe is inappropriate." [Emphasis in the original]

The rest of the Court's decision firmly holds that government censorship of the Internet violates the First Amendment, and that holding applies to government use of blocking software just as it applied when the Court struck down the CDA's criminal ban.

In the months since that ruling, the blocking software market has experienced explosive growth, as parents exercise their prerogative to guide their childrens' Internet experience. According to analysts at International Data Corporation, a technology consulting firm, software makers sold an estimated $14 million in blocking software last year, and over the next three years, sales of blocking products are expected to grow to more than $75 million.

An increasing number of city and county library boards have recently forced libraries to install blocking programs, over the objections of the American Library Association and library patrons, and the use of blocking software in libraries is fast becoming the biggest free speech controversy since the legal challenge to the CDA.

## How Does Blocking Software Work?

The best known Internet platform is the World Wide Web, which allows users to search for and retrieve information stored in remote computers. The Web currently contains over 100 million documents, with thousands added each day. Because of the ease with which material can be added and manipulated, the content on existing Web sites is constantly changing. Links from one computer to another and from one document to another across the Internet are what unify the Web into a single body of knowledge, and what makes the Web unique.

To gain access to the information available on the Web, a person uses a Web "browser" – software such as Netscape Navigator or Microsoft's Internet Explorer – to display, print and download documents. Each document on the Web has an address that allows users to find and retrieve it.

A variety of systems allow users of the Web to search for particular information among all of the public sites that are part of the Web. Services such as Yahoo, Magellan, Alta Vista, Webcrawler, Lycos and Infoseek provide tools called "search engines." Once a user has accessed the search service she simply types a word or string of words as a search request and the search engine provides a list of matching sites.

Blocking software is configured to hide or prevent access to certain Internet sites. Most blocking software comes packaged in a box and can be purchased at retail computer stores. It is installed on individual and/or networked computers that have access to the Internet, and works in conjunction with a Web browser to block information and sites on the Internet that would otherwise be available.

## What Kind of Speech is Being Blocked?

Most blocking software prevents access to sites based on criteria provided by the vendor. To conduct site-based blocking, a vendor establishes criteria to identify specified categories of speech on the Internet and configures the blocking software to block sites containing those categories of speech. Some Internet blocking software blocks as few as six categories of information, while others block many more.

Blocked categories may include hate speech, criminal activity, sexually explicit speech, "adult" speech, violent speech, religious speech, and even sports and entertainment.

Using its list of criteria, the software vendor compiles and maintains lists of "unacceptable" sites. Some software vendors employ individuals who browse the Internet for sites to block. Others use automated searching tools to identify which sites to block. These methods may be used in combination. (Examples of blocked sites can be found below and in the Appendix.)

Typical examples of blocked words and letters include "xxx," which blocks out Superbowl XXX sites; "breast," which blocks website and discussion groups about breast cancer; and the consecutive letters "s," "e" and "x," which block sites containing the words "sexton" and "Mars exploration," among many others. Some software blocks categories of expression along blatantly ideological lines, such as information about feminism or gay and lesbian issues. Yet most websites offering opposing views on these issues are not blocked. For example, the same software does not block sites expressing opposition to homosexuality and women working outside the home.

Clearly, the answer to blocking based on ideological viewpoint is not more blocking, any more than the answer to unpopular speech is to prevent everyone from speaking, because then no viewpoint of any kind will be heard. The American Family Association, a conservative religious organization, recently learned this lesson when it found that CyberPatrol, a popular brand of blocking software, had placed AFA on its "Cybernot" list because of the group's opposition to homosexuality.

AFA's site was blocked under the category "intolerance," defined as "pictures or text advocating prejudice or discrimination against any race, color, national origin, religion, disability or handicap, gender or sexual orientation. Any picture or text that elevates one group over another. Also includes intolerance jokes or slurs." Other "Cybernot" categories include "violence/profanity," "nudity," "sexual acts," "satanic/cult," and "drugs/drug culture."

In a May 28th news release excoriating CyberPatrol, AFA said, "CyberPatrol has elected to block the AFA website with their filter because we have simply taken an opposing viewpoint to the political and cultural agenda of the homosexual rights movement." As one AFA spokesman told reporters, "Basically we're being blocked for free speech."

The AFA said they are planning to appeal the blocking decision at a June 9th meeting of CyberPatrol's Cybernot Oversight Committee, but expressed doubt that the decision would be overturned. The conservative Family Research Council also joined in the fight, saying they had "learned that the Gay Lesbian Alliance Against Defamation (GLAAD) is a charter member of Cyber Patrol's oversight committee," and that "it was pressure by GLAAD that turned CyberPatrol around."

Until now, AFA, FRC and similar groups had been strong advocates for filtering software, and AFA has even assisted in the marketing of another product, X-Stop. AFA has said that they still support blocking but believe their group was unfairly singled out.

Indeed, as the AFA and others have learned, there is no avoiding the fact that somebody out there is making judgments about what is offensive and controversial, judgments that may not coincide with their own. The First Amendment exists precisely to protect the most offensive and controversial speech from government suppression. If blocking software is made mandatory in schools and libraries, that "somebody" making the judgments becomes the government.

**To Block or Not to Block: You Decide**

According to a recent story in The Washington Post, a software vendor's "own test of a sample of Web sites found that the software allowed pornographic sites to get through and blocked 57 sites that did not contain anything objectionable."

And in a current lawsuit in Virginia over the use of blocking software in libraries, the ACLU argues that the software blocks "a wide variety of other Web sites that contain valuable and constitutionally protected speech, such as the entire Web site of Glide Memorial United Methodist Church, located in San Francisco, California, and the entire Web site of The San Francisco Chronicle."

Following are real-world examples of the kind of speech that has been found to be inaccessible in libraries where blocking software is installed. Read through them – or look at them online – and then decide for yourself: Do you want the government telling you whether you can access these sites in the library?

**www.afa.net**

The American Family Association is a non-profit group founded in 1977 by the Rev. Donald Wildmon. According to their website, the AFA "stands for traditional family values, focusing primarily on the influence of television and other media – including pornography – on our society."

**www.cmu.edu**

Banned Books On-Line offers the full text of over thirty books that have been the object of censorship or censorship attempts, from James Joyce's Ulysses to Little Red Riding Hood.

**www.quaker.org**

The Religious Society of Friends describes itself as "an Alternative Christianity which emphasizes the personal experience of God in one's life." Their site boasts the slogan, "Proud to Be Censored by X-Stop, a popular brand of blocking software."

**www.safersex.org**

The Safer Sex Page includes brochures about safer sex, HIV transmission, and condoms, as well as resources for health educators and counselors. X-Stop, the software that blocks these pages, does not block the "The Safest Sex Home Page," which promotes abstinence before marriage as the only protection against sexually transmitted diseases.

**www.iatnet.com/aauw**

The American Association of University Women Maryland provides information about its activities to promote equity for women. The Web site discusses AAUW's leadership role in civil rights issues; work and family issues such as pay equity, family and medical leave, and dependent care; sex discrimination; and reproductive rights.

**www.sfgate.com/columnists/morse**

Rob Morse, an award-winning columnist for The San Francisco Examiner, has written more than four hundred columns on a variety of issues ranging from national politics, homelessness, urban violence, computer news, and the Superbowl, to human cloning. Because his section is considered off limits, the entire www.sfgate.com site is blocked to viewers.

**http://www.youth.org/yao/docs/books.html**

Books for Gay and Lesbian Teens/Youth provides information about books of interest to gay and lesbian youth. The site was created by Jeremy Meyers, an 18-year-old senior in high school who lives in New York City. X-Stop, the software that blocks this page, does not block web pages condemning homosexuality.

**www.sfgate.com**

This website is the home of Sergio Arau, a Mexican painter, composer, and musician, who has been called one of Mexico's most diversely talented artists. He has recorded several successful compact disks, including a recent release on Sony Records, and his paintings have been exhibited in numerous museums and galleries, including the Museo Rufino Tamayo in Mexico City.

**www.spectacle.org**

The Ethical Spectacle is a free online magazine that addresses issues at the intersection of ethics, law, and politics in American life. Jonathan Wallace, the creator of the site, is also co-author with Mark Mangan of Sex, Laws, and Cyberspace, which received much critical praise and is widely available in libraries and book stores around the country.

In addition to these examples, a growing body of research compiled by educators, public interest organizations and other interested groups demonstrates the extent to which this software inappropriately blocks valuable, protected speech, and does not effectively block the sites they claim to block. A list of these studies can be found in Appendix I.

### Teaching Responsibility: Solutions that Work . . .

Instead of requiring unconstitutional blocking software, schools and libraries should establish content-neutral rules about when and how young people should use the Internet, and hold educational seminars on responsible use of the Internet.

For instance, schools could request that Internet access be limited to school-related work and develop carefully worded acceptable use policies (AUPs), that provide instructions for parents, teachers, students, librarians and patrons on use of the Internet. (See Appendix III for information about AUPs and other alternatives to blocking software.)

Successful completion of a seminar similar to a driver's education course could be required of minors who seek Internet privileges in the classroom or library. Such seminars could emphasize the dangers of disclosing personally identifiable information such as one's address, communicating with strangers about personal or intimate matters, or relying on inaccurate resources on the Net.

Whether the use of blocking software is mandatory or not, parents should always be informed that blind reliance on blocking programs cannot effectively safeguard children.

Libraries can and should take other actions that are more protective of online free speech principles. For instance, libraries can publicize and provide links to particular sites that have been recommended for children.

Not all solutions are necessarily "high tech." To avoid unwanted viewing by passers-by, for instance, libraries can place privacy screens around Internet access terminals in ways that minimize public view. Libraries can also impose content-neutral time limits on Internet use.

These positive approaches work much better than restrictive software that works only when students are using school or library computers, and teaches no critical thinking skills. After all, sooner or later students graduate to the real world, or use a computer without blocking software. An educational program could teach students how to use the technology to find information quickly and efficiently, and how to exercise their own judgment to assess the quality and reliability of information they receive.

### . . . and Don't Work

In an effort to avoid installing blocking software, some libraries have instituted a "tap on the shoulder" policy that is, in many ways, more intrusive and unconstitutional than a computer program. This authorizes librarians to peer at the patron's computer screen and tap anyone on the shoulder who is viewing "inappropriate" material.

The ACLU recently contacted a library in Newburgh, New York to advise against a proposed policy that would permit librarians to stop patrons from accessing "offensive" and "racially or sexually inappropriate material." In a letter to the Newburgh Board of Education, the ACLU wrote: "The Constitution protects dirty words, racial epithets, and sexually explicit speech, even though that speech may be offensive to some." The letter also noted that the broad language of the policy would allow a librarian to prevent a patron from viewing on the Internet such classic works of fiction as Chaucer's Canterbury Tales and Mark Twain's Adventures of Huckleberry Finn, and such classic works of art as Manet's Olympia and Michelangelo's David.

"This thrusts the librarian into the role of Big Brother and allows for arbitrary and discriminatory enforcement since each librarian will have a different opinion about what is offensive," the ACLU said.

The First Amendment prohibits librarians from directly censoring protected speech in the library, just as it prevents indirect censorship through blocking software.

### Battling Big Brother in the Library

In Loudoun County, Virginia, the ACLU is currently involved in the first court challenge to the use of blocking software in a library. Recently, the judge in that case forcefully rejected a motion to dismiss the lawsuit, saying that the government had "misconstrued the nature of the Internet" and warning that Internet blocking requires the strictest level of constitutional scrutiny. The case is now set to go to trial this fall.

Earlier this year, the ACLU was involved in a local controversy over the mandatory use of Internet blocking programs in California's public libraries. County officials had decided to use a blocking program called "Bess" on every library Internet terminal, despite an admission by Bess's creators that it was impossible to customize the program to filter only material deemed "harmful to minors" by state law.

After months of negotiation, the ACLU warned the county that it would take legal action if officials did not remove Internet blocking software from public library computers. Ultimately, the library conceded that the filters presented an unconstitutional barrier to patrons seeking access to materials including legal opinions, medical information, political commentary, art, literature, information from women's organizations, and even portions of the ACLU Freedom Network website.

Today, under a new policy, the county provides a choice of an unfiltered or a filtered computer to both adult and minor patrons. No parental consent will be required for minors to access unfiltered computers.

The ACLU has also advocated successfully against mandatory blocking software in libraries in San Jose and in Santa Clara County, California. The ACLU continues to monitor the use of blocking software in many libraries across the nation, including communities in Massachusetts, Texas, Illinois, Ohio and Pennsylvania.

### The Fight in Congress: Marshaling the Cyber-Troops Against Censorship

In February of this year, Senator John McCain (R-AZ) introduced the "Internet School Filtering Act," a law that requires all public libraries and schools to use blocking software in order to qualify for "e-rate," a federal funding program to promote universal Internet access. An amendment that would have allowed schools and libraries to qualify by presenting their own plan to regulate Internet access – not necessarily by commercial filter – failed in committee.

Another bill sponsored by Senator Dan Coats (R-IN) was dubbed "Son of CDA," because much of it is identical to the ill-fated Communications Decency Act.

The ACLU and others are lobbying against these bills, which have not yet come up for a vote as of this writing.

### Censorship in the States: A Continuing Battle

Federal lawmakers are not the only politicians jumping on the censorship bandwagon. In the last three years, at least 25 states have considered or passed Internet censorship laws. This year, at least seven states are considering bills that require libraries and/or schools to use blocking software.

These censorship laws have not held up to constitutional scrutiny. Federal district courts in New York, Georgia and Virginia have found Internet censorship laws unconstitutional on First Amendment grounds in challenges brought by the ACLU. In April, the ACLU filed a challenge to an Internet censorship law in New Mexico that is remarkably similar to the failed New York law.

## Conclusion

The advent of new forms of communication technology is always a cause for public anxiety and unease. This was as true for the printing press and the telephone as it was for the radio and the television. But the constitutional ideal is immutable regardless of the medium: a free society is based on the principle that each and every individual has the right to decide what kind of information he or she wants – or does not want – to receive or create. Once you allow the government to censor material you don't like, you cede to it the power to censor something you do like – even your own speech.

Censorship, like poison gas, can be highly effective when the wind is blowing the right way. But the wind has a way of shifting, and sooner or later, it blows back upon the user. Whether it comes in a box or is accessed online, in the hands of the government, blocking software is toxic to a democratic society.

### Questions and Answers about Blocking Software

In the interest of "unblocking" the truth, here are answers to some of the questions the ACLU most often encounters on the issue of blocking software:

Q: Why does it matter whether Internet sites are blocked at the library when people who want to see them can just access them at home?

A: According to a recent Nielsen Survey, 45 percent of Internet users go to public libraries for Internet access. For users seeking controversial or personal information, the library is often their only opportunity for privacy. A Mormon teenager in Utah seeking information about other religions may not want a parent in the home, or a teacher at school, looking over her shoulder as she surfs the web.

Q: What about library policies that allow patrons to request that certain sites be unblocked?

A: The stigma of requesting access to a blocked site deters many people from making that request. Library patrons may be deterred from filling out a form seeking access, because the sites they wish to visit contain sensitive information. For instance, a woman seeking to access the Planned Parenthood website to find out about birth control may feel embarrassed about justifying the request to a librarian.

Q: But as long as a library patron can ask for a site to be unblocked, no one's speech is really being censored, right?

A: Wrong. Web providers who want their speech to reach library patrons have no way to request that their site be unblocked in thousands of libraries around the country. They fear patrons will be stigmatized for requesting that the site be unblocked, or simply won't bother to make the request. If public libraries around the country continue to use blocking software, speakers will be forced to self-censor in order to avoid being blocked in libraries.

Q: Isn't it true that librarians can use blocking software in the same way they select books for circulation?

A: The unique nature of the Internet means that librarians do not have to consider the limitations of shelf space in providing access to online material. In a recent ruling concerning the use of blocking software in Virginia libraries, a federal judge agreed with the analogy of the Internet as "a collection of encyclopedias from which defendants [the government] have laboriously redacted [or crossed out] portions deemed unfit for library patrons."

Q: Doesn't blocking software help a librarian control what children see online?

A: The ability to choose which software is installed does not empower a school board or librarian to determine what is "inappropriate for minors." Instead, that determination is made by a software vendor who regards the lists of blocked sites as secret, proprietary information.

Q: Why shouldn't librarians be involved in preventing minors from accessing inappropriate material on the Internet?

A: It is the domain of parents, not librarians, to oversee their children's library use. This approach preserves the integrity of the library as a storehouse of ideas available to all regardless of age or income. As stated by the American Library Association's Office of Intellectual Freedom: "Parents and only parents have the right and responsibility to restrict their own children's access – and only their own children's access – to library resources, including the Internet. Librarians do not serve *in loco parentis*."

Q: What do librarians themselves think about blocking software?

A: The overwhelming majority of librarians are opposed to the mandatory use of blocking software. However some, under pressure from individuals or local officials, have installed blocking software. The ALA has a Library Bill of Rights, which maintains that filters should not be used "to block access to constitutionally protected speech."

Q: Isn't blocking software an inexpensive way for libraries to monitor Internet use?

A: While parents may be able to purchase a blocking program for around $40, the cost for library systems is much greater. One library has estimated the initial installation of blocking software at $8,000 plus an additional $3,000 a year to maintain. As the court noted in ongoing case in Virginia case, "it costs a library more to restrict the content of its collection by means of blocking software than it does for the library to offer unrestricted access to all Internet publications."

Q: Are libraries required to use blocking software in order to avoid criminal liability for providing minors access to speech that may not be protected by the Constitution?

A: No. The First Amendment prohibits imposing criminal or civil liability on librarians merely for providing minors with access to the Internet. The knowledge that some websites on the Internet may contain "harmful" matter is not sufficient grounds for prosecution. In fact, an attempt to avoid any liability by installing blocking software or otherwise limiting minors' access to the Internet would, itself, violate the First Amendment.

Q: Would libraries that do not use blocking software be liable for sexual harassment in the library?

A: No. Workplace sexual harassment laws apply only to employees, not to patrons. The remote possibility that a library employee might inadvertently view an objectionable site does not constitute sexual harassment under current law.

Q: Can't blocking programs be fixed so they block only illegal speech that is not protected by the Constitution?

A: There is simply no way for a computer software program to make distinctions between protected and unprotected speech. This is not a design flaw that may be "fixed" at some future point but a simple human truth. (For more on this subject, see Appendix II.)

Q: What if blocking software is only made mandatory for kids?

A: Even if only minors are forced to use blocking programs, constitutional problems remain. The Supreme Court has agreed that minors have rights too, and the fact that a 15-year-old rather than an 18 year-old seeks access online to valuable information on subjects such as religion or gay and lesbian resources does not mean that the First Amendment no longer applies. In any case, it is impossible for a computer program to distinguish what is appropriate for different age levels, or the age of the patron using the computer.

Q: Is using blocking software at schools any different than using it in public libraries?

A: Unlike libraries, schools do act in place of parents, and play a role in teaching civic values. Students do have First Amendment rights, however, and blocking software is inappropriate, especially for junior and high school students.

In addition, because the software often blocks valuable information while allowing access to objectionable material, parents are given a false sense of security about what their children are viewing. A less restrictive – and more effective – alternative is the establishment of content-neutral "Acceptable Use Policies" (AUPs). (See Appendix III).

Q: Despite all these problems, isn't blocking software worth it if it keeps some pornography from reaching kids?

A: Even though sexually explicit sites only make up a very small percentage of content on the Internet, it is impossible for any one program to block out every conceivable web page with "inappropriate" material.

When blocking software is made mandatory, adults as well as minors are prevented from communicating online, even in schools. According to a recent news story in the Los Angeles Times, a restrictive blocking program at a California school district meant coaches couldn't access the University of Notre Dame's website, and math instructors were cut off from information about Wall Street because of a block on references to money and finance.

Q: Does this mean that parents can't use blocking software in the home?

A: No. The ACLU believes that parents have a right to use – or not use – whatever blocking software they choose.

# Additional Resources

(All Internet citations are valid as of March 30, 2001)

*Access Denied: The Impact of Internet Filtering Software*
*on the Lesbian and Gay Community*
Gay & Lesbian Alliance Against Defamation
http://www.glaad.org/org/publications/access/index.html

This report analyzes the legal, political and social implications of enforced invisibility on the Web. The report also includes a thorough review of the currently available software, ratings systems and search engines, as well as recommendations for industry leaders on how to make the Internet both friendly and fair.

*Blacklisted by Cyber Patrol: From Ada to Yoyo*
The Censorware Project
http://censorware.net/reports/cyberpatrol/ada-yoyo.html

This report examines some of the thousands of sites that Cyber Patrol blocks in their entirety, against two criteria: first, that blocking should be accurate, and second, that blocking should not be overbroad. It finds that Cyber Patrol blocks a great many sites which do not deserve to be, and that furthermore, looking at past reports of the product's accuracy, fixing these errors is a low priority.

*Blocking Software FAQ*
Peacefire
http://www.peacefire.org/info/blocking-software-faq.html

Questions and answers about blocking software and its impact on free expression.

*Censorship in a Box: Why Blocking Software*
*is Wrong for Public Libraries*
American Civil Liberties Union

http://www.aclu.org/issues/cyber/box.html

This special report by the American Civil Liberties Union provides an in-depth look at why mandatory blocking software is both inappropriate and unconstitutional in public libraries.


*Censorware Project*
http://www.censorware.net/

A group dedicated to exposing the phenomenon of censorware: "software which is designed to prevent another person from sending or receiving information, usually on the web."


*Clairview Internet Sheriff: An Independent Review*
Electronic Frontiers Australia
http://www.efa.org.au/Publish/report_isheriff.html

In June 1999, the Australian Government enacted Internet censorship legislation requiring Internet Service Providers (ISPs) to block adults' access to particular content on the Internet. This report evaluates one of the country's filtered ISPs in terms of its stated objectives.


*Computer Professionals Question Internet Filtering Agreement*
Computer Professionals for Social Responsibility
http://www.cpsr.org/dox/issues/filters.html

Brief reaction to industry proposals presented at a White House Summit promoting the use of content rating labels. These labels would be used by browsers and other software to block sites with objectionable content.


*Content Rating and Filtering*
Electronic Frontiers Australia
http://www.efa.org.au/Issues/Censor/cens2.html

A comprehensive listing of resources on filtering and rating issues from an Australian perspective.

*Deja Voodoo: The "X-Stop Files" Revisited.*
The Censorware Project
http://censorware.net/reports/xstop/

A study of the "X-Stop" filtering system, which was installed on all computers in the public libraries in Loudoun County, Virginia, before the practice was declared unconstitutional by a federal court.

*Encouraging Value Over Filters: A Concise Guide to the "Internet Content Problem" for Parents, Teachers and Netizens Worldwide.*
http://members.tripod.com/~rtiess/networth/

A review of alternative approaches to objectionable content that do no require the use of content filters.

*Faulty Filters: How Content Filters Block Access to Kid-Friendly Information on the Internet*
Electronic Privacy Information Center
http://www2.epic.org/reports/filter-report.html

A report on the impact of software filters on the open exchange of information on the Internet, based on a comparison between 100 searches using a traditional search engine and the same 100 searches using a new search engine that is advertised as the "world's first family-friendly Internet search site."

*Filtering FAQ*
Computer Professionals for Social Responsibility
http://quark.cpsr.org/~harryh/faq.html

This document attempts to describe the concerns and issues raised by the various types of filtering software. It is hoped that these questions and answers will help parents, libraries, schools, and others understand the software that they may be considering (or using).

*Internet Censorship Report: The Challenges for Free Expression Online*
Canadian Committee to Protect Journalists

http://www.ccpj.ca/publications/internet/index.html

Reviews the potential impact of software filters on the free exchange of information and ideas over the Internet.

*The Internet Filter Assessment Project*
http://www.bluehighways.com/tifap/

The Internet Filter Assessment Project ran from April to September, 1997. It was a librarian-led project managed by librarian and author Karen G. Schneider. The purpose of this project was to take a hard look at Internet content filters from a librarian's point of view.

*Joint Statement for the Record on "Kids and the Internet:*
*The Promise and the Perils"*
Submitted to the National Commission on Library and Information Science by members of the Internet Free Expression Alliance
http://www.ifea.net/joint_nclis_statement.html

This joint submission argues against the use of filtering and rating systems in public libraries and urges the development of educational programs to teach children "critical thinking skills when using the Internet."

*Loudoun County, Virginia Library Filtering Lawsuit*
People for the American Way
http://www.pfaw.org/courts/index.shtml#intcensorship

Background information on the litigation that resulted in a judicial decision declaring the use of Internet filters in public libraries unconstitutional. Includes the text of the court decision and selected legal documents.

*Nation Trending Toward Do-it-Yourself Censorship*
Tony Mauro (published by The Freedom Forum First Amendment Center)
http://www.fac.org/fanews/fan9709/cover.htm

Report on the privatization of censorship following the CDA decision.

*The Net Labeling Delusion – Saviour or Devil?*
Irene Graham
http://libertus.net/liberty/label.html

This site offers an alternative resource for information about PICS and PICS facilitated systems. Here you will find reasons for the view that PICS is the devil, rather than our saviour.

*Passing Porn, Banning the Bible: N2H2's Bess in Public Schools.*
The Censorware Project.
http://censorware.net/reports/bess/

A study of the "Bess" Internet blocking software from N2H2 Inc. finds that the product blocks many innocuous sites, including a version of the Bible compiled by Thomas Jefferson, a site on Darwin and evolution, an issue of Redbook Magazine, and sites dealing with issues as diverse as Serbia, baseball, psychiatry and celibacy.

Peacefire: Youth Alliance Against Internet Censorship
http://www.peacefire.org

Peacefire.org was created in August 1996 to represent the interests of people under 18 in the debate over freedom of speech on the Internet. The Web site and mailing lists are maintained by Bennett Haselton, a mathematics student in Nashville. Peacefire has about 3,300 members on its mailing list as of January 1999; you can join Peacefire and get on the mailing list at no cost. Peacefire also has about 12 staff members that run the organization, and almost all the staff members are teenagers, although some of the older ones are starting to turn 20.

*A Practical Guide for Internet Filters*
Karen G. Schneider
http://www.bluehighways.com/filters/

Includes product reviews of leading filter products, how filters work, a key features to look for, and configuring filters for most appropriate use in a library environment. Case studies of libraries using filters – and not using filters – will help you decide what your response is for your library, today, and arm you with best current practices to support your decision. One chapter describes The Internet Filter Assessment Project.

*Ratings Today, Censorship Tomorrow*
J. D. Lasica (published by Salon Magazine)
http://www.salonmagazine.com/july97/21st/ratings970731.html

"The Net industry is rushing to embrace ratings systems for the Web. The technology will help parents keep their kids away from porn. It can also help anyone censor anything."

*The Rights of Children in the Digital Age*
Jon Katz (published in Wired Magazine)
http://www.wired.com/wired/archive/4.07/kids.html

"The idea that children are moving beyond our absolute control may be the bitterest pill for many to swallow in the digital era. The need to protect children is reflexive, visceral, instinctive. All the harder, then, to change."

*Statement on Internet Filtering*
American Library Association, 1997
http://www.ala.org/alaorg/oif/filt_stm.html

"The use in libraries of software filters which block Constitutionally protected speech is inconsistent with the United States Constitution and federal law and may lead to legal exposure for the library and its governing authorities."

*Tyranny in the Infrastructure*
Lawrence Lessig (printed in Wired magazine)
http://www.wired.com/wired/archive/5.07/cyber_rights.html

Law professor Lawrence Lessig reviews the Platform for Internet Content Selection (PICS) filtering proposal and concludes that "PICS is the devil."

*X-Rated Ratings?*
J.D. Lasica (published by American Journalism Review)

http://ajr.newslink.org/ajrjdl21.html

The Clinton administration and the Internet industry have championed voluntary ratings for Web sites to create a "family-friendly" environment in cyberspace. Their campaign nearly led online news organizations to create a licensing system for Web journalism.